1 MONTH OF
FREE
READING

at
www.ForgottenBooks.com

By purchasing this book you are eligible for one month membership to ForgottenBooks.com, giving you unlimited access to our entire collection of over 1,000,000 titles via our web site and mobile apps.

To claim your free month visit:

www.forgottenbooks.com/free1374151

ISBN 978-1-397-33140-3
PIBN 11374151

This book is a reproduction of an important historical work. Forgotten Books uses
state-of-the-art technology to digitally reconstruct the work, preserving the original format
whilst repairing imperfections present in the aged copy. In rare cases, an imperfection in
the original, such as a blemish or missing page, may be replicated in our edition. We do,
however, repair the vast majority of imperfections successfully; any imperfections that
remain are intentionally left to preserve the state of such historical works.

THIRTIETH ANNUAL REPORT

OF THE

Provincial Board of Health

OF

Ontario, Canada

FOR THE YEAR

1911

PRINTED BY ORDER OF
THE LEGISLATIVE ASSEMBLY OF ONTARIO

TORONTO:
Printed and Published by L. K. CAMERON, Printer to the King's Most Excellent Majesty
1912

Printed by
WILLIAM BRIGGS,
29-31 Richmond Street West,
TORONTO.

To His Honour Sir John Morison Gibson, K.C., LL.D., K.C.B., etc.,

Lieutenant-Governor of the Province of Ontario.

May it Please Your Honour,—I herewith beg to present for your consideration the Thirtieth Annual Report of the Provincial Board of Health for the year 1911.

Respectfully submitted,

W. J. Hanna,

Provincial Secretary.

To The Honourable W. J. Hanna, K.C., M.P.P.,

Provincial Secretary of Ontario.

Sir,—I have the honour to submit for your approval the Thirtieth Annual Report of the Provincial Board of Health, made in conformity with and under the provisions of the Public Health Act, for the year 1911.

I have the honour to be,

Sir,

Your obedient servant,

John W. S. McCullough,

Chief Officer of Health.

PROVINCIAL BOARD OF HEALTH OF ONTARIO
1911.

ADAM H. WRIGHT, M.D., *Chairman* .... Toronto
DAVID B. BENTLEY, M.D. .... Sarnia
GEORGE C. CLINTON, M.D. .... Belleville
WILLIAM H. HOWEY, M.D. .... Sudbury
PAUL J. MOLONEY, M.D. .... Cornwall
JAMES ROBERTS, M.D., M.H.O. .... Hamilton

Secretary and Chief Officer of Health,

JOHN W. S. McCULLOUGH, M.D.

Provincial Inspector,

R. W. BELL, M.D.

Provincial Bacteriologist,

J. A. AMYOT, M.D.

Branch Laboratory—Kingston,

W. T. CONNELL, M.D.

Provincial Chemist,

H. M. LANCASTER, B.A.Sc.

Sanitary Inspector,

GEORGE E. YOUNG.

CONTENTS.

Resumé of the Transactions of the Board

For the Year Ending December 31st, 1911

BY THE SECRETARY

This is the 30th Annual Report of the Provincial Board of Health for Ontario, being for the year ending December 31st, 1911. During the year the Board held four regular meetings.

The following plans and descriptions of water works and sewage disposal systems were passed by the Board during the year:

Water Works—Cochrane, (with Sewerage system), Harriston, Tavistock, Welland, Windsor, (new Intake Pipe).

Sewerage and Sewage Disposal—Carleton Place, (Sewerage and Water), Cobalt (Extension), Midland, Napanee, North Toronto (amended plans), Oakville, Peterborough (Sedimentation Tank), Sandwich, Simcoe, Sudbury, Thorold, Maple Leaf Milling Co., Port Colborne, (Sewage Disposal amended plans), Y.M.C.A. Camp, Lake Couchiching, (Sewage Disposal).

The plans for sewerage system for Niagara Town were not approved.

Early in the year there was an outbreak of smallpox at Porcupine. The cases were taken charge of by an officer of the Board, tents, provisions and medical supplies being transported there. Those who came in contact with the infected cases were vaccinated. These timely means sufficed to check the outbreak. The result of vaccination in this instance is but one of the numerous ones seen by our officers each year, and is to us the strongest evidence of the value of this measure. In no other way could we check these outbreaks so rapidly and so effectively. Our Inspector found extremely bad sanitary conditions in this community. By active work, however, the place was cleaned up and, although the water supplies were any but the best, we were able to prevent an outbreak of typhoid fever, so much feared in these mining camps. Following the disastrous fire of July 1911, our Inspector again spent some time in the camp and through his efforts some drainage work was accomplished and the water supplies improved. The camps have since then become organized and it is hoped will give proper attention to sanitary matters.

The various reports of our Sanitary Inspector in respect to lumber and other camps, as well as to the sanitary conditions of New Ontario generally, are included herein.

The reports of the Medical Inspector, Dr. R. W. Bell, are included in this volume.

Early in the year there was a considerable outbreak of typhoid fever in the City of Ottawa, and the writer was asked by the Health Officer to make a report upon the cause. As the enclosed report indicates, the cause seemed to be from the water supply and a subsequent exhaustive investigation made by Dr. Chas. A. Hodgetts, of the Commission of Conservation, and the Board's Inspector, amply corroborated this opinion. The water used by the city is taken from the Ottawa River, and with the use of hypochlorite treatment the typhoid was rapidly got under control.

With a view of securing a pure and adequate supply of water, the Council of the City of Ottawa appointed a Commission to investigate the whole question of water supply and sewage disposal. This Commission comprised Mr. Allen Hazen an eminent sanitary engineer of New York, Dr. Chas. A. Hodgetts, Medical Adviser to the Commission of Conservation, Chas. H. Keefer, C.E., of Ottawa and the writer. The members of the Commission spent considerable time in studying the Ottawa and Gatineau Rivers, and that district in Quebec forming the watershed of the Blanche River. The waters were carefully examined and a final report, which appears in this volume made. The question of sewage disposal was not fully conssidered and so far the report in this respect is not fully completed.

The various amendments to the Public Health Act made in the session of 1911 were incorporated in the report of last year. During the early portion of this year just as this report goes to press, the Legislature has under consideration a new and revised Health Act, as well as a revised Vaccination Act, both of which will doubtless become law before this report is issued. It is hoped that the provisions of these Acts will commend them to those interested in the progress of Public Health.

In the early portion of the year there were few cases of rabies reported to the Board. In the fall season the number increased. Altogether there were 23 treated during the year.

In October the Laboratory staff moved into our new quarters at No. 5 Queen's Park, where better facilities are afforded for this important branch of our Board of Health. The reports of this Laboratory, as well as those of the Branch Laboratory at Kingston, are included in this volume.

Steps are being taken to increase our laboratory facilities by having the work of the south-western portion of the Province done at the Hygienic Institute, London. When this Laboratory is ready it should prove a great convenience to the physicians of that part of the Province.

The work of the Experimental Station of our Laboratory in Clifford Street is progressing favourably, and it is confidently expected that we shall at an early date be able to publish some interesting data, the results of our labours there. One practical result has been achieved, viz., the supplying of all the Government offices in the city since July of this year with pure sand-filtered water. This has not only wiped out a considerable item of expenditure, but has also ensured that the staff of these offices should have a water supply which is absolutely pure.

The travelling Tuberculosis Exhibit was continued in the early months of the year, visits being paid to the following places: Claremont, Myrtle, Peterboro, Norwood, Havelock, Bobcaygeon, Lindsay, Orillia, Midland, Barrie. Stayner, Collingwood, Thornbury, Meaford. Bradford, Newmarket and Aurora.

As a result of an appropriation of $1,000 passed by the Legislature, a beginning was made in establishing a Public Health Exhibit, and for the first time such an exhibit was held in connection with the Educational Exhibit at the Canadian National Exhibition in Toronto. This exhibit created a great deal of interest. In connection therewith there was held in the Women's Pavilion a Moving Picture Exhibit and lectures upon various health subjects each day of the fair. The thanks of the Board are due to the ladies and gentlemen who contributed to these lectures and to the exhibit itself.

Individual exhibitions form too large a number to mention here, but our thanks are especially due to:

(1) The American Association for the Conservation of Vision,

(2) The American Association for the Prevention of Infant Mortality,

(3) The Department of Health, Chicago.

To Dr. St. Clair Drake, who was in charge of the Chicago exhibit, the greatest amount of credit is due for his efforts in making the exhibit a success.

Near the end of the year an outbreak of Typhoid Fever occurred in the town of Sarnia, where amongst a population of 10,000 people 136 cases occurred in the months of November and December. Altogether there were 151 cases in the town during the year with 14 deaths. A full report of an investigation held by the Chief Officer of Health appears in a special report and shows the cause to have been due, like the outbreak in Ottawa early in the year, to impure water supplies.

These epidemics of fever emphasize most strongly the necessity of greater care of the public water supplies of cities and towns. Why should municipalities not be as liable in case of illness and loss of life due to negligence in this respect as they at present are if they fail to keep streets and bridges in a proper state of repair?

The writer notes with the greatest satisfaction the increased interest being taken by the public in prevention of disease, evidenced by the introduction of medical inspection of schools, lectures on housing, town planning, the prevention of slums and regulation of apartment houses. It may be called a healthy sign when "the man in the street" shows his appreciation of these matters. Does it not mark the beginning of the day when Public Health will become, in fact as well as in theory, the greatest of all public questions. Optimism is a good quality. Let us have a full measure of it in regard to Public Health matters.

REPORT UPON TYPHOID FEVER OUTBREAK IN OTTAWA.

TORONTO, February 7th, 1911.

SIR,—Consequent upon the request of the Medical Health Officer of your city I made an examination of the water supply and sanitary conditions of the city on February 4th inst., for the purpose of ascertaining the cause of the present epidemic of Typhoid Fever. In this I was assisted by Dr. Law, M.H.O., Engineer Ker and Mr. J. O. Meadows, Sanitary Engineer for the Province of Quebec. In addition, I interviewed Mayor Hopewell, Controller Champagne, Alderman Forward and several medical men as well as other parties who seemed to have some knowledge of the situation.

The distribution of the disease all over the city and in the recently annexed portion known as Hintonburgh, both of which have a common water supply, its comparative infrequency in the adjoining village of Mechanicsville, which has a local water supply, as well as the positive reports as to infection of the city's water made by the Provincial Laboratory, all point to the drinking water as being the carrier of the disease.

The supply is carried from the main channel of the Ottawa River by an intake pipe. During low water I am informed by the Engineer that it has been the custom in case of fire to open a valve at pier No. 1 with the object of increasing the pressure. This valve was opened for longer or shorter periods 19 times during the

26 days from December 9th until January 4th last. It was during this period that a large proportion of the infection apparently occurred. The situation of Nepean Bay where the valve is placed, it being the immediate waterfront of the city, would naturally make its waters unfit for domestic use. Besides there is another circumstance which indicates that it is dangerous as a source of infection. A portion of Hintonburgh is drained by a tiny stream called Cave Creek. The district along this creek is thickly populated. The water closets belonging to the various houses are either adjacent to or set over the stream which in its course meanders behind, alongside and in some cases in front of these houses. It is consequently an open sewer. The sanitary condition is one which would hardly be tolerated in any hamlet in the Province of Ontario, much less in the capital city of the Dominion of Canada. *Some at least of the effluent from this open sewer enters Nepean Bay and most of necessity foul its waters.*

Further up the river there is, I understand, no typhoid fever in either Province. Altogether I am convinced that the source of infection is a local one and the chief cause of it is the opening of the valve at pier No. 1.

I beg respectfully to suggest :—

(1) That the valve at pier No. 1 be permanently closed.

(2) That the hypochlorite treatment which has been installed by the Engineer be continued, and that until a better water supply such as that recommended by Mr. Hazen be established this treatment be continued; and since hypochlorite treatment is not completely effective in case of much turbidity of the water that the people of Ottawa be advised to boil all water used for domestic purposes.

(3) That a systematic inspection be made and records kept of all the plumbing of the city, and that in all new plumbing installed it shall be required that proper plans thereof be filed with the Medical Officer of Health.

(4) That in the Hintonburgh portion of the city, which has a water system but no complete sewerage system, there shall be started without a day's delay the establishment of proper sewerage and sewage disposal; and that in the meantime all householders shall be required to thoroughly clean and dispose of the contents of their closets, and in the future until such sewerage system is completed be required to use dry earth closets. The fact that Hintonburgh has a number of cases of typhoid with its open sewer (the stream mentioned) will, unless proper precautions are taken surely induce a further spread of the disease when warm weather and flies make their appearance.

(5) There should be established a proper bacteriological laboratory for the city wherein daily examinations of the water should be made. In addition such laboratory might examine sputum, diphtheria swabs. etc., for local physicians. All this work is cheerfully undertaken by the Provincial Laboratory free of cost. but the distance to Toronto or Kingston is too great to make our service of the prompt character required by a large city. Such laboratory should be under the control of a competent man who should have supervision of the treatment of the water.

(6) A city of the size and importance of Ottawa should have a Health Officer who gives his entire time to the work of caring for the health of its inhabitants. If Ottawa is to continue to maintain its reputation as a health resort it cannot afford to have a repetition of an epidemic such as this one.

If it is desired by the City authorities, the Provincial Board of Health will undertake in conjunction with the Board of the Province of Quebec a more detailed examination of the source of its water supply as soon as climatic conditions will allow.

An epidemic of typhoid fever with the number of deaths which have already occurred is a severe lesson for the authorities of the city. Typhoid fever is a preventable disease.

In view of the present conditions and of the oft repeated warnings given this city which are on record in the office of the Provincial Board of Health, I have no hesitation in affirming that the responsibility for the present epidemic is upon the authorities of Ottawa. Theirs is the well-known experience of scores of places which cannot be induced to spend money for the protection of human lives until they receive such a lesson as your city is now experiencing. I trust this experience will be of value to your authorities and that they will not repeat the folly of further neglecting the precautions necessary for the health of the city.

Trusting that you shall have seen at an early date the termination of your difficulties,

I have the honour to be,

Faithfully yours,

John W. McCullough,

Chief Health Officer of Ontario.

J. A. Pinard, Esq.,
Chairman Local Board of Health, Ottawa, Ont.

Ontario Public Health Exhibit. Canadian National Exhibition, 1911.

Ontario Public Health Exhibit. Canadian National Exhibition, 1911.

Ontario Public Health Exhibit.   Canadian National Exhibition, 1911.

Ontario Public Health Exhibit. Canadian National Exhibition, 1911.

DEATHS IN ONTARIO FROM TUBERCULOSIS BY AGES, 1903-1910.

Year	Under 5 years 0-1	1	2	3	4	5-9	10-14	15-19	20-24	25-29	30-34	35-39	40-44	45-49	50-59	60-69	70-79	80 and over	Not given	Total	Total from all causes
1903	140	66	31	16	14	55	78	255	415	358	281	227	182	141	209	167	51	13	24	2,723	29,664
1904	7	52	26	9	17	52	78	278	417	409	320	267	211	163	257	175	104	13	21	2,877	31,290
1905	...	55	31	21	18	47	85	266	424	389	277	232	180	161	212	144	79	16	30	2,667	31,371
1906	251	72	23	14	14	38	74	234	362	362	342	262	201	166	228	169	66	19	14	2,911	32,782
1907	74	41	27	20	15	44	62	206	745	...	499	...	311	...	227	173	64	9	13	2,530	33,502
1908	68	46	20	13	13	43	67	216	764	...	479	...	315	...	217	136	70	14	30	2,511	32,714
1909	47	27	25	9	15	54	54	179	687	...	487	...	290	...	2	163	66	15	38	2,378	32,628
1910	38	35	19	15	6	36	55	184	652	...	463	...	293	...	2	160	71	18	24	2,291	33,593
	625	394	202	117	112	369	553	1,818	4,466	......	3,148	......	1,983	......	1,794	1,287	571	117	194	20,888	257,544

CASES AND DEATHS FROM CONTAGIOUS DISEASES REPORTED WEEKLY BY LOCAL BOARDS OF HEALTH FOR THE YEAR 1911.

Month	Infantile Paralysis		Cerebro-spinal Meningitis		Smallpox		Scarlatina		Diphtheria		Measles		Whooping Cough		Typhoid or Malaria		Tuberculosis	
	Cases	Deaths	Cases	Deaths	Cases	Deaths	Cases	Deaths	Cases	Deaths	Cases	Deaths	Cases	Deaths	Cases	Deaths	Cases	Deaths
January	2		6	6	50		413	21	175	14	203	6	20		375	25	90	74
February			4	4	80		619	32	213	31	204	4	19	2	476	37	131	14
March	4	2	7	7	57	1	711	25	176	24	369	8	22	4	300	41	127	91
April	9	9	13	13	58	1	593	41	229	28	391	13	25	2	84	16	150	10
May	1	1	4	4	44		438	28	171	20	254	9	42	2	41	11	135	09
June	4		4	4	45	1	310	13	211	28	116	19	29	4	81	20	129	18
Ju y.l	6	3	1		35		164	9	176	20	129	10	35	10	101	16	73	52
August	5	2	2	2	14		112	3	141	12	7	1	40	4	210	27	82	67
September	5	2	1	1	9		174	2	225	26	17	1	31	6	327	34	94	75
October			9	9	20		155	8	315	26	65	2	35	8	182	26	68	49
November	3		3	3	28		188	9	244	20	108	2	28	2	103	13	72	49
December			2	2	41		264	19	355	31	112	2	5	1	197	21	113	68
	39	19	56	54	481	3	4,141	210	2,631	280	1,975	77	331	45	2,477	287	1,272	976*

*Only 42 per cent. of these deaths are reported weekly by Local Boards of Health. See correct number in Tuberculosis table by ages.

2 B.H.

Reports of Medical Inspector, R. W. Bell, M.D.

REPORT *RE* PROPOSED SEWER SYSTEM TOWN OF SIMCOE.

June 19th, 1911.

To the Chairman and Members of the Provincial Board of Health.

GENTLEMEN,—Application having been made by the Town of Simcoe for approval of a plan for sewers prepared by Chipman and Power, Engineers. I visited that Town on June 12th inst. and looked over the situation with Mr. McColl, Town Clerk. The town has a population of 4,000 and has a good water supply with a consumption of 150,000 gals. daily, but no sewers to take charge of the polluted output. A few drains exist for surface or cellar drainage only, but I am assured there are several house and closet connections with them, and they discharge into the River Lynn in a raw state close to the east centre of the town. Several parties have private septic tanks with subsoil distribution tiles, and numerous cesspools exist. The former are not sufficient and the latter with the polluted drains are an abomination and should be at once abolished. A well constructed sewarage system with proper disposal plant is absolutely necessary for the health safety of the town.

According to the plans submitted the sewage of the town can be readily taken care of, and the only·question is as to the best location of the disposal plant and how reached. After considering several plans and places submitted by the Engineers, I am of the opinion that the best location for the disposal plant is the one on the east side of the river and north of the railway track, as more ground and a better site is available for sedimentation tanks. I would prefer the pumping station located at the site of the disposal works instead of at Victoria St., although the main difference as the engineers say will be in the cost of maintenance and that is in favor of the disposal location.

I fear there is likely to be delay in carrying out the scheme owing to indifference on the part of the citizens who have already provided for disposal of their sewage, but I feel the town should be urged to proceed with the work without delay. and wherever connections with present drains have been made for domestic sewage they should be at once cut off. and all cesspools established without civic consent should be abolished and connection with the proposed sewers made compulsory.

REPORT *RE* WATER WORKS AND SEWERAGE SYSTEMS, TOWN OF COCHRANE.

June 22nd, 1911.

To the Chairman and Members. Provincial Board of Health, Ontario.

GENTLEMEN,—The Town of Cochrane having applied for approval of contemplated water supply and also sewage disposal, I visited the proposed locations on June 15th with Mayor McManus and Engineer Neelands. The town situated at the junction of the G. T. P. and T. & N. O. railways is only two years old, but has a population of about 1,200 with every prospect of a rapid growth. The town is well laid out by the T. & N. O. Railway Commission and has within a few yards of its Southern border two small lakes, viz., Norman and Hector, while Commando, a little larger, lies to the north-east and within the town limits. The intention was at first to sink artesian wells to the north, but as the drainage is principally in that direction and the sewers must find an outlet to the north, another source of supply was sought, and samples of water from Norman and Hector lakes were sent to your laboratory for examination. The one from Norman Lake has proved satisfactory, while the one from Hector Lake shewed some pollution, easily accounted for as the T. & N. O. Ry. round house, &c. drains into it, but otherwise it should be free from pollution. It is now the intention with your approval to ask permission from the T. & N. O. Ry. Commission to use one or both of these lakes for a civic supply, and also to ask your Board to grant the municipality control of the watershed which is very small.

Norman Lake is only about 200 x 300 yards across but is deep, having a maximum depth of 93 feet. Hector Lake situated a few feet lower and only a few yards distant with no connection between, has a maximum depth of 71 feet. These two lakes it is believed by the Engineer will furnish an ample supply of water for years to come but, in the event of failure, wells can be sunk in the immediate vicinity.

I suggest approval of the Norman Lake source with control of the watershed of both lakes at once, and also of Hector Lake when its water proves satisfactory after the diversion of the railway drainage takes place, which it is hoped will be done by the railway commission. If it cannot be readily turned into the town sewers, I believe a separate sewer for it can be run down between the two lakes and discharged to the south-west beyond any possibility of contamination of these waters. This might be done by the town if the Commission does not feel disposed to bear such expense, so as to secure control of Hector Lake. From interviews, however, with the Chairman and one of the members of the Commission I have reason to believe they are prepared to aid the town in every way possible in securing an ample and satisfactory supply of water.

Sewers. The plan of sewerage contemplates carrying all sewage in a northerly direction around both sides of Commando Lake (the pipes now being laid in lanes through the centre of each block) in which direction there is ample fall to temporary sedimentation tanks from which the effluent will be discharged into a marshy lake, but the permanent plan provides for tanks much further away, the effluent reaching Lillabella Lake, and ultimately the Abitibbi River.

This scheme I suggest approval of, subject to any necessity arising for a change in the future should the pollution prove a nuisance.

REPORT *RE* EXTENTION OF WATER WORKS AND SEWERAGE SYSTEMS OF COBALT.

June 22nd, 1911.

To the Chairman and Members, Provincial Board of Health, Ontario.

WATER.

GENTLEMEN,—Because of the excessive quantity of water used by the mines from Sassaganaga Lake—the source of Cobalt's civic supply—the lake has been lowered about two feet, causing alarm for the future. That this may not be endangered it is now proposed by the town with your permission to get control of the watershed of Sharpe Lake and obtain from that lake an auxiliary supply by pumping it into Sassaganaga Lake. Sharp Lake lies about a mile west of Sassaganaga and is a long narrow lake extending over two miles north. It is proposed to pump several hundred thousand gallons per day for seven or eight months in the year and so keep up an ample supply.

Samples of water have been examined at your Laboratory some months ago. One proved satisfactory, the other not. On June 17th inst. with Dr. Hair, M.H.O., I visited Sharpe Lake. We found the one settler on its shores with a hennery and piggery, the hogs from the latter having access to a pond some 200 yards across and now found not apparently to have connection with the lake. From here the contaminated sample had been taken supposing it to be a bay off the lake. The owner, however, offers to remove his hogs beyond any danger zone, if Sharpe Lake is to be used.

If further samples of water prove satisfactory and the town is given control of the watershed. I see no reason why permission to use Sharpe Lake should not be granted.

SEWERS.

An application for permission to extend the sewer on Lang St. (formerly Haileybury Road) is about to be made. I may, however, to begin with say that the sewer system approved of by your Board over two years ago has not been carried out in its entirety. The disposal plant provided for in the north end of the town close to the athletic grounds has never been installed, and now that location is covered with deposit from the washings or tailings from the mines. I believe your permission will be asked to so change the plan as to provide for carrying the sewage, mixed, I understand, with the mine tailings, in an open flume to a point a mile to a mile and a half further away, there to be disposed of with a plant as formerly agreed upon and into the same outlet—down Sassaganaga Creek. Some further information as to the effect of the mixture of the tailings and sewage may be necessary before decision as to its ultimate treatment or disposal.

Re Lang Street. A short sewer now serves the southern end of this street being connected with Argentite St. The next couple of blocks being on hill sides must drain to bottom where they will meet, and it is here proposed to place a sedimentation tank in rear of the T. & N. O. Ry. freight shed, the effluent being discharged into Cobalt Lake a few yards distant. To this I can see no objection, as the lake is now little better than a cesspool receiving several sewers, and never was at best fit for use. Beyond the northerly end spoken of the sewer will run north along the street to the railway track where it is proposed to place a sedimentation tank between the sidewalk and the creek from Cobalt Lake, and into this creek discharge the effluent. I advise that the sewer be extended further alongside the railway track and the tank be there placed so the effluent will discharge into the main sewer and mine tailings on the flat below.

I may say I went over the ground on Friday, 16th inst., with Mr. Barton of the Board of Works and next day before going to Sharpe Lake met Mayor White, Dr. Hair, M.H.O., with Messrs. Jones, Watson and Barton, members of the Board, and discussed the whole situation.

The applications with proposed plans and specifications for both water and sewer extensions will be sent you shortly.

REPORT *RE* NUISANCE AT JACKSON'S POINT.

June 22nd, 1911.

To the Secretary, Provincial Board of Health, Ontario.

Sir,—As instructed by you I proceeded to Jackson's Point on the 20th inst. to investigate a complaint *re* a nuisance thereat. It is too bad that the time of your Board or its officials should be taken up investigating such minor matters of importance. The local board of health could have, and should have, dealt with the complaint as advised in your letter of March 28th last. The matter is purely a personal one between two adjoining cottage owners on the shore of Lake Simcoe— Messrs. Malone and Wheler. These cottages are only a few feet apart and a few yards back from the water. A lane runs across the back of the lots, and in the lot in the rear Mr. Wheler has three small cottages for tenants. Across the corner of this rear lot runs a small gully a couple of feet deep, and I fancy a natural water course to the lake formerly across Mr. Malone's lot, but now with a box drain and covered over through the latter until it opens in the edge of a low bank onto the sand beach a few feet from the front corner of Mr. Malone's cottage. All is perfectly dry at present but after a heavy rain there may be some flow. Into the gully in rear I understand the tenants of Mr. Wheler and possibly others dump their kitchen refuse, slop and laundry water. This without doubt will create a nuisance offensive to the eye and nostril in warm weather both at the point of dumpage and outlet of box drain, and should be abated. All this can easily be remedied by having the water scattered over the higher ground where it will readily soak away in the sand, and collecting the kitchen garbage in covered cans or boxes and disposing of it at frequent intervals in a sanitary manner. In this way the gully will remain dry unless from surface drainage after rain, which should not create any nuisance.

I would here recommend the abolition of all pit closets in connection with these cottages and the installation of buckets or boxes with use of dry earth, thereby adding greatly to the convenience and comfort of the occupants.

REPORT *RE* POLLUTION OF CEDAR CREEK AND RIVER THAMES AT WOODSTOCK.

June 22nd, 1911.

To the Chairman and Members, Provincial Board of Health, Ontario.

Gentlemen,—Complaint having been made by the Townships of North and West Oxford regarding pollution of the river Thames running through these municipalities. from the City of Woodstock. I undertook an investigation on June 21st inst. The river Thames runs in a southerly direction through the western section of the city which is low and flat. Cedar Creek runs across the city in a north-westerly direction and joins the Thames a little south of Dundas Street. A year or two ago several manufactories discharged much sewage into Cedar Creek, frequently coloring the water almost black and destroying the fish rapidly. However. most of these factories are now connected with the civic sewers, and only occasionally is the creek polluted to any great extent, but this has not relieved the situation, as the *raw* sewage is largely poured into the river a few yards below the mouth of the creek. There is a civic sewer system with a sedimentation tank and four filter beds each about 100 feet square located on a low flat close to the east bank of the river. This location I visited with Mr. Cook, Reeve of West Oxford. We found the tank full of sludge into which we pushed a piece of board to a depth of at least six feet and then were not through it. Both compartments were the same and under this sludge the sewage evidently had a channel, as it was pouring into the well beyond, and there was shut off from the filter beds, and was running in a raw state into the shallow river, excreta being quite visible at the sewer outlet.

One filter bed had a few inches of sewage on it, the others were quite dry and did not look as if in use, all were covered with dry scum, leaves, &c., matted and utterly useless as filters. The whole condition was disgraceful, apparently no effort whatever being made to treat the sewage, and the complaint of the municipalities further down stream is well founded.

Later, in an interview with Mr. Morrison, City Clerk, Mr. Hobson, Chairman Board of Works, and Mr. Ure, County Engineer, I learned that there was really no responsible party in charge of the situation, the tank had not been cleaned out for at least two years, possibly longer, the main sewer from near the tannery a short distance south of the G. T. R. station to the tank one and one-half miles, only having a fall of ¾ inch in 100 feet, was full of sludge which was forcing its way up the manholes, the liquid sewage eating its way, as best it could, through this sludge. Where the sewer crosses the creek, the man nominally in charge, occasionally at night opens a valve, letting the sewage into the creek for the night and sometimes forgets to close it in the morning, thus polluting the creek and giving the near residents an object lesson of what the rural municipalities are suffering from.

Mr. Ure, only occasionally being employed by the city, has no control over the situation.

I urged the cleaning out of the sewer pipe and sedimentation tank at once, also cleaning off the filter beds and adding fresh layers of sand to them, and that a competent person be placed in charge who shall see daily to the proper working of the tank and beds. Mr. Ure urges and I believe has previously advised the preparation of two more filter beds, as the area of the present ones is not sufficient, also that another sedimentation tank be installed near the west side of the tannery to collect as much as possible of the solid matter before the remaining effluent passes into the almost level sewer.

These suggestions I think should be approved of, and, if carried out, will go a long way to relieve the present condition. I understand the City Council considered them favorably a year ago, but have so far neglected to act on them, and have allowed matters to go from bad to worse until now it is imperative for the city's own safety as well as adjoining municipalities, that speedy action be taken to prevent the possible results of such unsanitary conditions. Woodstock is sleeping to-day over an unsanitary mine which may explode any time with most horribly fatal results. May she speedily waken up and cleanse her hidden parts ere such occurs.

All of which is respectfully submitted.

REPORT *RE* UNSANITARY CONDITIONS SARNIA.

June 30th, 1911.

To the Secretary, Provincial Board of Health, Ontario.

SIR,—As instructed by you I visited the Town of Sarnia on June 28th inst. to enquire into a number of matters affecting its Sanitary Condition. I had interviews with the Mayor Dr. Henderson, Dr. Pousette, M.HO. and Mr. Stewart, Secretary of the Local Board of Health, and accompanied by Sanitary Inspector Crosbie I visited many places, as the water intake, sewer outlet, source of ice supply, ice houses, livery stables, Junk shops, bakeries. &c., and inspected delivery wagons and baskets, also saw how garbage was collected, so I can speak from personal knowledge on most points.

1st *Water supply*. This is taken from the St. Clair River, an intake pipe extending out 700 feet from the foot of George Street until clear of the bay and into the current. The bay water is certainly polluted and not fit for use. There is a reverse current from about a block south of the pump house frequently, and this will either retain pollution in the bay or carry it around the outer side to the current. The intake is liable to pollution from this source or at least from Point Edward a mile or two above. An average of 3,000,000 gallons per day is pumped and should be taken from the lake above Point Edward. This is admitted as the proper source of supply and should be. resorted to as soon as possible.

2nd *Sewers*. The main sewer outlet is at the ferry dock foot of Cromwell Street, in the very heart of the town, two blocks south of the water intake. It is into very deep water and but little sewage perceptible on the surface. The current is swift and no probability of contamination of water supply. The Port Huron Sewer outlet on the United States side of the river, Dr. Henderson told me, was 500 yards further down than the Sarnia intake, so no danger from it. The town is well sewered and connections therewith are or will be compulsory on all sewered streets by the end of 1912. I regret, however, that in other sections of the town the vile pit closets are still in use. I advised that they be abolished and buckets with dry earth system be substituted until sewers are provided.

3rd *Livery Stables*. These were as a rule comparatively clean and manure removed once a week or oftener.

4th *Junk shops*. Here I found very unsanitary premises from manure and garbage, while the rooms in which rags were stored were vile, positively sickening, and employees were at work packing the rags, where no ventilation but the door, and breathing the most horribly smelling dust, &c.

5th *Garbage*. Night soil is collected within limited hours and carted out of town by authorized parties who have tendered for the job, but paid by the parties served.

Kitchen .garbage and swill, however, is collected at all hours for hog feed by parties who go about the streets with horse and wagon with from one to four or five barrels. This is neither very pleasant to the eye or nostril as I saw it on a hot summer day, and certainly very unsanitary. This should be collected within limited hours. say very early in morning before many citizens are on the streets.

6th *Foods.* (a) Ice. As one man has a monopoly of the ice supply and owns a large section of the bay shore, he takes his ice from nearby in the bay where the water can scarcely by any possibility be free from contamination. As the bay was full of saw-logs last winter he had to go further out near the current, but still not free from risk. His ice houses are old ramshackle buildings, about ready to tumble down, and much of the sawdust used is old and has been in use for years, being dumped during the summer on the roadside where it gets all the dust and manure blown by the winds off the street. Plenty of fresh clean sawdust is to be had from the mills close by and should be used. The ice is delivered from wagons none too clean and the bulk of it thrown on the sidewalks, washed to be sure before being used, but still cleaner and more sanitary packing, &c. would be more satisfactory.

(b) *Meat.* The butchers as a rule are pretty careful and clean about their shops and in the delivery to customers, meats being wrapped or covered, but in bringing the meat in bulk from the slaughter houses to their shops the same care is not taken and frequently it is exposed on open rigs to the dust, etc. of the street.

(c) *Bread.* All bakeries visited I found comparatively clean and the output being handled there in a cleanly manner. One, however, had very unsanitary conditions within a few feet of the door which is wide open during warm weather. There was an open closet, stable manure and garbage heap within about 15 feet of the door, while barrels of empty fruit tins were within 4 or 5 feet breeding flies. Another bakery mostly pastry was in a basement with but little ventilation, a low long window opening level with the sidewalk, through which street dust was blown or swept by passers-by.

The delivery wagons were fairly clean, but the baskets used were in several cases very dirty at least on the outside, and were pushed against the bread in the wagon boxes or cupboards. The drivers who handle the harness and wagon with bare hands and then the bread can not help but dirty it to some extent. All bread should be wrapped in light paper.

These are the conditions as I found them and are similar to what may be found in any of our cities or towns, but two or more wrongs do not make a right, and it is a pity to find any of the unsanitary conditions mentioned permitted in an otherwise pleasantly situated town with fine streets, clean and well-shaded with trees, comfortable dwellings and prosperous citizens. All, however, can be remedied by the local Board of Health under the Public Health Act and I hope it is only necessary to call the attention of the authorities to these conditions to set the wheels in motion to bring about the desired improvements.

REPORT *RE* PROPOSED CHANGE IN WATER INTAKE AT WELLAND.

April 26th, 1911.

To the Chairman and Members of the Provincial Board of Health, Ontario.

GENTLEMEN,—On April 25th inst. accompanied by Mr. Cooper, Mr. J. R. McCallum and Dr. Howell, M.H.O., I looked over the location of the proposed new water supply for the Town of Welland. It is situated about 100 yards below the aqueduct where the hydraulic power house is to be placed and water from the canal pumped directly through the mains. The fall from the canal to the river is about 10 feet, and 250 h.p. will be developed.

The present supply is taken from the canal a short distance above the aqueduct, and runs to a power house on the feeder where there is not sufficient power furnished for present needs. The intake is only 24 in. and is too small. In low water it also occasionally fails, and water then has to be pumped from the feeder, hence the necessity for a change in location.

There is no change in the *source* of supply, it being taken a short distance further down the canal and all from Lake Erie on the same level, with considerable current. There is no pollution from above unless from Port Colborne and it is well provided against. Welland town sewage is discharged into the Welland River mostly below the aqueduct—(See previous report in 1906). I recommend that the proposed change be permitted.

REPORT *RE* MAPLE LEAF MILLING COMPANY'S SEWAGE DISPOSAL AT PORT COLBORNE.

February 16th, 1911.

To the Chairman and Members of the Provincial Board of Health, Ontario.

GENTLEMEN,—By instructions of your Secretary I visited the premises of the Maple Leaf Milling Company, Port Colborne on 15th February, to look over proposed location of septic tanks and distributing tile. I was accompanied by Dr. J. B. Neff, M.HO. I found the building erected over a pier east of the Governmen Elevator. It is proposed to put septic tanks in the mill and storehouse, with subsoil tile for distribution of effluent, between these buildings which are only 42 feet apart, and between which two railway tracks are to be laid. This pier is all filled in with large broken stone. Under a strip 8 feet wide on each side of the tracks a base of 3 feet of sand is to be laid, and over this 2 feet of broken stone. The soil pipes are to be laid on the sand, and through it the sewage will percolate into the water between the large broken stone in sides of the pier.

This pier forms the west side of the entrance to the Welland Canal into which a current of $1\frac{1}{2}$ miles per hour runs. 1,400 yards down the canal is the intake of the civic water supply and a polluted current would reach it rapidly. 150 men are to be employed in these two buildings, therefore the quantity of sewage will be considerable every day. I do not think the civic water supply would be at all safe from pollution from this source.

REPORT *RE* PROPOSED WATER SUPPLY AT HARRISTON.

April 28th, 1911.

To the Chairman and Members of the Provincial Board of Health, Ontario.

GENTLEMEN,—On April 27th inst. I visited Harriston to inquire into a proposed water supply for the town. It is proposed to obtain it from an Artesian well at a depth of 150 to 160 feet by a ten inch pipe, and a sufficient and inexhaustible supply is expected judging from several similar private wells in town.

With Dr. S. M. Henry, M.H.O., and Mr. A. J. Stewart. Secretary of the Board of Health, I visited the location on a lot south of Young St. two blocks east of Elora St. near the centre of the town (which is rather a hollow) and a few yards north of a branch of the Maitland River. Preparations with an engine in place were being made to commence drilling within a few days. The water is to be pumped to a stand pipe at the north west part of the town on higher ground north of William Street, near the over head C. P. R. bridge. There does not appear to be any liability to pollution. There are no sewers in town, but no privy vaults are allowed, the box and dry earth system being compulsory, but cleaning is done at private expense and the burial of excreta was recently discovered and stopped, its removal to farms being ordered.

Samples of water are to be forwarded to your Laboratory for examination when reached by the drillers.

All of which is respectfully submitted.

REPORT *RE* SMALLPOX.

May 1st, 1911.

To the Chairman and Members of the Provincial Board of Health, Ontario.

Gentlemen.—Since the beginning of the year smallpox mostly of the milder type has been reported from numerous places, and in several instances complaint made that the outbreak was not being properly handled, or was being treated as chickenpox and unfortunately the complaints were justified.

In most cases, however, the outbreaks were handled satisfactorily by the local M.H.O. and Boards of Health. In the unorganized districts a few cases developed in lumber and mining camps, but all were promptly looked after by your inspector, Mr. Geo. Young, with headquarters at North Bay.

The following places were visited by me and all necessary advice and aid given to the local authorities:—

Jan. 4. *Village of Lucan,* where several typical cases were seen, but had previously been mistaken for chicken pox. A conference with the M.H.O. and Secretary of local Board of Health started things right.

Feb. 13. *Tp. of Raleigh*—Co. Kent—Here the same error had been made, and children allowed to attend school with rash out on them. I visited one school and several families and afterwards advised with the M.H.O. also the Reeve.

Feb. 25. *Madawaska*—Here cases had developed in the G. T. R. bunk house. A van car was secured and fitted up for hospital purposes and all necessary precautions taken to stamp out the disease, Mr. Donaldson, Supt. of the Ottawa Division, responding promptly to our requests.

April 5. *Ottawa.*—I was hastily called here on April 4th and requested to take steps to protect the city from smallpox cases in the lumber camps, as men from the camps were reported to be walking the streets covered with smallpox rash. These reports I soon found were absolutely without foundation, and the trouble was principally within their own doors, where there was exhibited the grossest ignorance, negligence, carelessness or indifference, or all combined. There was no proper effort to cope with the disease or protect the public, and no adequate provision made to care for the patients. Two weeks previous, while in Ottawa *re* the typhoid fever epidemic, I heard the M.H.O. tell the Chairman of the Board of Health there were then eight smallpox patients in the hospital and only two more could be accommodated unless a temporary building was erected. I then advised the erection of a double walled tent at once, as being quickly obtainable and more comfortable. Two or three days later by request of the M.H.O. I visited the Protestant Orphan's Home and there found two well marked cases. The Matron informed me that during the past few weeks there had been 18 or 20 similar cases, but all supposed to be chickenpox. The present cases were at once removed to hospital, the remaining inmates vaccinated and the premises placed under quarantine.

About this time a case had been discovered in the Medford Apartments over one of the busiest corners (Cor. Spark and Bank Sts.) in the city. The patient had been removed, most of the occupants vaccinated, premsies disinfected and quarantine raised in two days. Now on my return I found 26 cases instead of 10, all down at Porter's Island Hospital, and instead of being imported cases, 24 were admittedly of local origin. Of the other two, one came from a restaurant in North Bay, and the other two days previously from Tupper Lake 130 miles distant in N. Y. State where he had been for over two weeks. He had been in a lumber camp during the winter, hence the camp scare. Five more cases had developed in the Orphan's Home and the sanitary police guard placed there had been deliberately taken off duty the previous week for nearly 24 hours, (because the Matron disliked having him on the street in front of the Home) thereby affording the attendants and maids handling these patients an opportunity to go out.

At the Medford Apartments another case had developed and been removed by order of the M. H. O. at 1 a.m. on Monday morning last (to-day Wednesday) a sister of the housekeeper, and who had been sleeping with her, and no quarantine placed on the premises, while since Monday this housekeeper and a maid also closely in contact with the case had been doing the chambermaid's work in the forty rooms of the Apartments, thirty-seven of which were occupied by young men and women employed in offices and shops, and who were kept in ignorance of the situation. The excuse for this neglect was that the occupants had been vaccinated and premises disinfected two weeks before, quite ignoring the new outbreak shewing the place was still infected, and on enquiry and examination I found some previous occupants were gone and new ones in, some were not vaccinated and on others the previous vaccination had failed. These were at once done again, and the premises ordered under an effective quarantine for at least two weeks.

On Porter's Island about 300 yds. long and 50 to 100 yards wide lying in the Rideau River just below the St. Patrick St. bridge, and used as a dumping ground for city refuse (dry) was situated the Smallpox Hospital, a miserable old clapboard shack 20 x 24 ft. and 1½ stories high, with stove pipe running up the stairway so one had to go down on hands and knees to get underneath it to go upstairs.

In this building were housed 20 people, 17 being patients and sleeping 3 in a bed. Cooking, eating and sleeping were going on, all in one room. One tent only had been erected and in it were 10 patients fairly comfortable. Immediately in the rear was a small store room, in a corner of which was a bed for the two trained nurses in charge. Here also suspects were sent and patients bathed. As these conditions were disgraceful I urged prompt measures to remedy them. In the evening of the following day I met the Board of Health when matters were still in the same condition. I insisted on immediate action in connection with further tent hospital accommodation, and prompt measures for public protection with any further patients, as the situation under the circumstances was serious and alarming. Various excuses were made for dilatoriness in action, until I finally had to threaten that if proper precautions to protect the public from exposure to the disease were not promptly taken, it might become necessary for the Provincial Board of Health to quarantine the city. Two days later extra tents were up for the patients and suspects. The Local Board of Health by resolution applied to your Secretary for permission to have me remain in Ottawa for a month to help them out of the trouble, but this was declined as it was considered I had done all required by an official of your Board, and there were other duties demanding my attention. When I left Ottawa the following week the number of cases had risen to 40, and afterwards went a little higher, then rapidly declined under, I believe, extra vigilance.

I regret to say much of the neglect and lack of prompt action arose through want of harmony amongst the health authorities. With a change in the M. H. O. who seemed to be a bone of contention between the different parties, it is to be hoped all differences will be removed and the whole Board, etc., will work in unison for the local and public safety.

April 7th. *Carleton Place*—Lanark Co.—By instructions from your Secretary I visited this Town and found 13 cases of smallpox. Eight were in an excellent isolation building, erected during a former epidemic several years ago, outside the town and were comfortable and well looked after. The others were quarantined in their own homes. All cases were traceable to a worker in a mica factory, who brought the disease from a locality where it was prevalent and where she had been visiting. A very pleasant meeting was held with the Board of Health and the M. H. O. where all was harmony, and the utmost desire to receive advice and act on it was expressed. When once the disease was recognized in this town the promptest possible action was taken to deal effectually with it and stamp it out.

April 10th. *Embrun*—Russell Co.—While in Ottawa cases from this neighbourhood were reported to me and as only 24 miles distant I visited the place on April 10th and interviewed Dr. Chevrier, also Father Forget P.P., and Mr. St. Onge, Reeve, and visited the village school. There had been cases in the village but all now well. I learned, however, of cases at Cambridge, a few miles south, and these I reported personally to Dr. McDougall, M.H.O., at Russell Village for necessary investigation and action, he being the M. H. O. for the Township of Russell. Some of these cases being quite mild had not been seen professionally by a physician and were only accidentally discovered.

April 21st. *Township Augusta*—Grenville Co.—I visited this township to-day and, with Dr. Waddell of N. Augusta, saw several cases in the neighbourhood of Roebuck 9 miles north of Prescott. Here the Post Office had been closed for several days and extra precautions taken. I found my visit had been requested to a great extent for diagnostic purposes and to advise *re* reopening of P. O. In Prescott the postmaster, on behalf of the Post Office Inspector, obtained from me written suggestions regarding the matter. I also advised with Dr. McPherson, M.H.O. of Prescott, regarding the situation.

A telegram from your Secretary suggested a visit to Lyn, but on communicating with Reeve Checkley also Dr. Judson of Lyn, M.H.O. of Tp. Elizabethtown, I found the cases were nearly well and about to be released from quarantine and being 14 miles distant quite unnecessary to visit. The question was fear of damages if there had been a mistake in diagnosis, but that had been settled by a consultation with and diagnosis confirmed by Dr. Macauley, of Brockville

This completed my smallpox visitations to the present date.

REPORT *RE* TYPHOID FEVER IN OTTAWA.

May 15th, 1911.

To the Chairman and Members of the Provincial Board of Health, Ontario.

GENTLEMEN,—In the early part of the year a very serious outbreak of typhoid fever began in Ottawa. Your Secretary being notified of it visited that city and reported thereon. Later as the epidemic was not abating, the Conservation Commission of the Dominion offered the city the services of Dr. Hodgetts, late Secretary of this Board, to make a thorough investigation as to the origin of the outbreak. The offer was accepted and Dr. Hodgetts asked for assistance from your Board. Your Secretary delegated me for that work. I proceeded to Ottawa on March 5th, and for three weeks devoted my best energies to it.

Col. Jones, D.G.M.S., and Major Drum, P.A.M.C., with a staff of assistants from the Militia Department also aided in the investigation.

Between Jan. 1st and March 18th we found 1196 cases and got a complete record of over 900 of them. I personally investigated over 300 of these in the different hospitals of the city, convents, colleges, orphanages, etc. Our report is now in the printer's hands a proof copy of which is hereby attached. The finding agrees with that of your Secretary made the first week in February, and is that it originated from the pollution of Nepean Bay from which water was drawn for the civic supply on several occasions and its continuance arose from contact, unsanitary conditions, etc., some of the latter being the most horrible imaginable in the suburbs of Hintonburg and Mechanicsville. Photographs shewing some of these will be in the complete report. Further details are here unnecessary as all will be found in the report to the Conservation Commission.

REPORT *RE* POLLUTION OF WILBER PARK LAKE, VILLAGE OF GEORGETOWN.

May 31st, 1911.

To the Secretary of the Provincial Board of Health.

SIR,—As instructed by you I proceeded to Georgetown on May 30th to investigate a complaint *re* pollution of Wilber Park Lake, a small body of water situated within the village limits and used for boating, fishing, bathing, power and ice supply. The principal source of pollution is from the Canada Coating Mills situated close to the G. T. Ry. station and consists of waste coloring material from the washing of brushes used in coloring paper, together with their domestic factory sewage. In the village, I understand, two hotels also discharge their sewage into this water. The material from the Coating Mills is discharged frequently into a tank which is full and overflows into a small creek leading into the lake. It is thick and of various colors, and adheres to boats which sail in it for a short time so it is with difficulty rubbed off. I saw Mr. Parker, Manager of the Mills, and he informed me the company were now preparing a sedimentation tank at the west end of the mill which he hoped shortly would be in operation and remedy the matter so nothing but a harmless watery effluent would escape into the creek. He however, admitted that the tank would rapidly become coated over with the same sticky scum which adheres to the boats and then filtration would cease, unless frequently cleaned off.

I asked him to furnish you at once with a statement shewing what the pigments used consist of, and he offered to send samples of them for analysis, claiming none of them were in any way injurious. His statement and samples should reach you without delay.

I also called on Mr. Kennedy, Village Clerk, re pollution from the hotels, etc., and urged the necessity for a civic sewerage system. This I believe is admitted by the citizens generally, but finances will not permit of it for the present year at least. I advised the cutting off of closet connections with this lake, as without pollution it would be a thing of beauty and pleasure as well as a healthy resort for the citizens. The local authorities, however, can under the Public Health Act have the pollution nuisance abated as pointed out in your letter of November 24th, 1910.

Report of Sanitary Inspector, George E. Young,

For Six Months, ending October 31st, 1911.

On your notice to me of a complaint having been sent in from Sellwood of the unsanitary condition of that village, I visited it the first week of May.

This town is owned by the Moose Mountain Company, Limited, and consists of a population of about 500 persons. This camp is practically new, exposing decayed timber and other matter to the sun, also a low swamp runs through it, having no drainage so far, the settlers using it to throw all sorts of refuse, etc., into.

The village is situated on a level, sandy plain lying along the Vermilion River. The lots are small consequently the wells are too near, the pit closets that the people have been using and the yards generally dirty.

Dr. Lockwood, who is the resident doctor for Doctors Arthur and Cook, of Sudbury, who have the medical contract accompanied me in a house to house inspection. Where houses were large and a number of people congregated I ordered cesspools to be put in, and all the citizens to use dry earth closets instead of the pits now in use, removing garbage, etc., to a safe distance and burn.

I also asked the company to have a 1 ft. tile laid from the river to this swamp making a well at the upper end and then an open drain may be used above this point for the present, also to remove some old log buildings which are filthy and to furnish a supply of good water from a higher level for the use of their employees.

I was here a week, and when I left a good many of my instructions had been carried out, the doctor promising to see to the rest. Two cases of typhoid had occurred at a house where water was taken from a polluted well. I have learned of no further cases.

May 13th.

On information I visited a family by the name of Langlad living at Moon River, on the Georgian Bay, about 30 miles below Parry Sound, who were reported to have smallpox. The children had some skin affection on their faces only. As a precautionary measure I quarantined the house until the trouble disappeared. I could not learn of any other cases in the neighborhood.

May 18th.

A case of smallpox being reported to me from Bonfield, I found on arrival there that it had been quarantined by the doctor. I believe a number of cases had been concealed in this neighborhood. I drove out into the township and visited a number of suspected houses but could find nothing further, the people being very reluctant in giving information.

May 20th.

Accompanied by Dr. Shaw, of Callander, who is M.H.O. for Ferris Township, I paid a visit of inspection to Nosbonsing, Corbeil and Asterville in that township, where we quarantined Audette, Post-Master of Nosbonsing and E. Tremblay of Astorville. Two other families appeared to have recently recovered from the disease but the doctor thought the evidence not strong enough to secure conviction. However, I notified Ferguson and McFadden, of Tomiko, that a man by the name of Xavier Genest had been visiting at one of these suspected houses. The company kept him isolated as much as possible and in two weeks he took the disease.

May 23rd.

Acting on your telegram I visited Madawaska and learned that two men coming by train from Ottawa five weeks ago were employed by the Fraser Lumber Company, one dying a few days after, without medical attendance. Dr. Mason of Kearney gave a burial permit, cause delirium tremens, without seeing him, so I am told. The body was shipped to his family at Guyon, Quebec, where they reside. The other man, Sullivan, told before he died that he took sick about ten days before, went to Dr. Mason who pronounced the trouble diphtheria but out of danger and sent him back to camp. Getting worse he came out two days afterwards to Dr. Davis of Madawaska on the 19th inst. and died in about 48 hours afterwards. This man in coming to Madawaska was put in a box car down in a low, wet switch end where smallpox had previously been. This car was in a very filthy condition, windows broken and not a fit place for a sick man to be. He had no attention other than the doctor. I believe that the condition of the premises and want of attention were largely contributory to this man's death. Dr. Fraser has disinfected all the clothing, bedding, etc., in the camp, administered anti-toxin to the few men in camp. I have ordered the lumber company to burn the camp which is now closed. I have also ordered Mr. Donaldson, Divisional Superintendent, to burn the infected car and build an hospital for the use of the large number of men at this divisional point.

The Fraser Lumber Company, of Brule Lake, made a medical contract with Dr. Hand, of Whitney, of which I enclose a copy received from him. This occurred just before the doctor got sick last fall and I believe the men in camp were not attended to very well.

Accompanied by Mr. Whitten, Provincial Constable, we gave the town a sanitary inspection, having hogs, stables, manures, etc., removed and a number of dead carcasses buried.

May 31st.

Receiving your enclosed letter of complaint from Englehart respecting the dairies there, I enclose copy or report given to the local Board of Health.

" ALLEN CONNELL, ESQ.,
Chairman Board of Health, Englehart.

" DEAR SIR,—When I inspected the dairies of A. W. Skinner, Mrs. Philip Levine and Sam Vertliebe in April, I condemned all the premises at that time. On the strength of a complaint sent to us I have again visited them. Mr. Skinner has moved his cows to different premises and, with the exception of manure near the stables, the conditions are fair. Your constable and I took samples of milk from wagon on street and after keeping it 24 hours, the quality which was complained of was satisfactory to us, having a heavy cream.

" At the time of my previous visit there was a quantity of snow and ice so that we could not see it under all conditions. I now find the premises of Mrs. Levine and Vertliebe, low and wet and the water supply poor. I would advise

our Board to stop the sale of milk coming from these premises. We also tested
he measure of the glass bottles used by the different dairies and found them
correct."

June 3rd.

I visited and inspected the camps Diliona and Orlando, Gentila and Fera,
Angelo Santilino, Carlos Carmiel and Murdoch Bros., Camp No. 1 on the Mani-
toulin and North Shore construction work. The camps that I visited last winter
have taken a lesson from their prosecution as I found everything sanitary and the
men reasonably healthy.

The camp of Murdoch Bros. was well built and clean inside, but the location
poor, also poorly laid out and unsanitary surroundings. I served them with written
notice instructing them as to disposal of slops and garbage from kitchen, closets,
water supply, manure, etc. The foreman was starting a gang of men to do the
work when I left.

Dr. F. C. Kidd, a licensed physician, has been on the work about one month
going over the work regularly and the people tell me he is very attentive and quite
satisfactory. He is using a launch to go from one camp to another. I unfortunately missed him among the islands. The balance of this work will be reached
from Espanola, which I will visit as soon as possible.

As there has annually been a number of cases of typhoid fever at Little Current,
the place being apparently healthy looking and well situated, I took a look around
town while there. Along the water front, I found flush closets running direct into the
lake where they were drawing their water supply from, public closets of mill built
over the water, a laundry draining direct, also old clothes, cans and rotten vegetables scattered along the front. A well that was complained of last year as
dangerous has had nothing done in the way of testing the water or closing it up.
I went over the different matters with Dr. McDonald, Mayor and Chairman of the
Board of Health there, but they are apparently slow movers in matters of health
and will likely pay further toll in lives before it is corrected.

June 22nd.

On instructions received from you, I visited the railway construction camps at
Coniston and enclose copy of notice to Mr. C. J. Labreche, the man whom I found
in charge, which will speak for itself.

"DEAR SIR,—As you are the man I found in charge of Angus Sinclair's Railway Construction Camps numbers 1, 1½ and 2 at Coniston, I beg to report to you
on my inspection yesterday. At camp No. 1 the bunk house has air space for 30
men with bunks for 70. Another bunk house or tents must be provided at once
to give proper accommodation for the men, making tight floors, so dirt or slops
cannot run through. The kitchen is dirty. This must be scrubbed out at least
four times a week, a covered drain to be constructed for the bunk house and kitchen
running to a covered cesspool. If a cesspool is not provided, all liquids, garbage,
etc., must be tanked away to a safe distance.

"The tent belonging to the bridge gang was filthy and must be cleaned out at
once. The premises must be thoroughly cleaned up of all garbage, cans, old clothes,
etc.

"At camp 1½ I found the slops running over the level ground from kitchen.
This must be remedied at once the same as ordered at camp No. 1. This kitchen
was dirty also and must be scrubbed out four times a week.

3 B.H.

"At camp No. 2 the yard and kitchen were reasonably clean but slops from kitchen, cans, etc., must be provided for as ordered at the other camps. This camp was using swamp water for cooking purposes. In all these camps a sufficient supply of good water must be provided for all purposes.

" In none of these camps are closets provided for the use of the men. These must be built at once making them close and with tight fitting doors so that the flies canot enter, using disinfectants liberally around the premises especially around the closets and kitchen.

" An hospital building or tent must be provided at once at a point convenient to all the camps.

" None of the sleeping accommodations were fit for the use of men, and my observations are that these camps have not complied with the Camp Regulations in any one point."

I served Dr. Cameron of Victoria Mines with a copy of the above. I afterwards quarantined this camp for smallpox and revisited it several times before I got my orders all carried out.

July 6th.

While at Sudbury looking into the smallpox situation there, I learned that the Sauble and Spanish Boom Company, Limited, had been quarantined for smallpox by Dr. Burd, of Blind River, their contracting physician. I visited their camps situated on some islands at the mouth of the Spanish River.

A man by the name of H. Sauve, coming from Ottawa, developed the disease a few days after his arrival on June 21st. He was well isolated the premises disinfected and the disease has made no further spread.

I inspected the company's camps where nearly 300 men are employed. I advised removing the partition and making more ventilation in bunk house No. 2. The camps were well built and complying with the regulations, everything thoroughly clean, disinfectants being used freely around closets and premises. I saw very few flies and the men were all healthy.

Mr. C. A. Williams, the manager, and the company deserve credit for the thoroughly sanitary condition in which they have kept their camps.

July 20th.

Following your instructions I reached Porcupine on the 16th instant and found a Relief Committee established in the three towns with a supply of provisions sufficient for immediate use. A consignment of 500 tents and 5,000 blankets reached here the same day from the Dominion Government which gave ample shelter and comfort to all.

Our six tents, blankets, etc., which were stored here were distributed by Mr. Piercy, O.P., at the first, and were very acceptable.

All dead animals have been buried, disinfectants used. The Ontario police have maintained good order and everything is quiet and the inhabitants doing the best they can in a cheerful manner, under the circumstances.

Louis Smith, the junk man, who has been fighting the Board of Health at North Bay, was fined under two complaints laid by me and has been ordered by the Court to move to an isolated position. I expect we will have no further trouble from him.

August 1st.

I inspected the hotel, mines and boarding houses at Swastika. This town is just starting. I found very few closets. Wherever lacking, I ordered installed forthwith. Garbage, etc., has been taken from the hotel and mine to the edge of the river, partially burned and left. This I ordered to be cleaned up and removed to a safe distance.

Water for cooking purposes is taken from river above the town, drinking water from a spring above the town also.

There was no sickness of a serious nature, doctors Dorsey and Campbell are residents at present.

The Swastika Mining Company are employing about 55 men at present charging them $1.00 for hospital and medical attendance. Dr. Dorsey has the contract.

August 10th.

While en route to Porcupine, I stopped off in Cobalt and took a run around town. As a consequence I drew the attention of the Board of Health to several matters which came under my notice. I enclose you copy of letter which I gave the Chairman, Mr. R. S. Taylor.

" DEAR SIR,—In walking around town to-day I noticed that in the north end of the town not more than one in three closets had buckets in them, ninety per cent. imperfectly built being open both back and front with myriads of flies having access to same. In several cases no closets were provided whatever. At Luios Ignace's an open closet ten feet from kitchen window. At 94 Earl Street a stable underneath the house and used for closet was very filthy. Excreta was lying around the yard at the rear of The Cobalt Household Furnishing Company on Lang Street, no closet being provided.

" Hogs might as well be penned underneath the houses as horses and hens, which I found in several cases. In a bakery on Lang Street, the floors looked as if they had not been cleaned for six months, hens roosting over the oven, stable and closet just outside the door. An open sewer coming from the rear of the Bijou Theatre runs across Peter Street. A quantity of manure from stable on Lang Street covers the ground down to the railway track.

Covered cesspools should be installed where the rocky conformation does not allow sewers to be put in. Some relief should be given Galena Street, as it is in a very congested district without sewerage and creating a nuisance which may be far reaching.

Two years ago your Council Board passed very strict By-laws for the enforcement of sanitation, which had a beneficial effect, and while there is not nearly the filth in the town that there was then, vigilance has been relaxed and there is enough now to cause your town serious trouble."

I came to Porcupine on August 12th and stayed until September 1st. As I could not procure men or teams here to do scavenger work, I brought two experienced men from Cobalt with teams and other appliances, I had them repair the road to the last winter's dumping ground and they have been actively at work since, moving from four to eight loads per day.

You cannot imagine the conditions here, back yards covered with stagnant green water and crawling with maggots, flies everywhere, the ground so soft that the team could not reach the yards. I notified the property owners on the principal streets to have their properties drained and succeedeed in getting inexpensive open drains put in by them. I got the contractor, who did this work for the owners, to continue one drain across a fraction of unpatented mining claim that intervened to the outlet at the same cost as the others had paid. Mr. Chalmers, Inspector of Colonization Roads brought on a gang of men on the 27th and completed the work across the balance of Government property which I had asked for.

At my leaving I have had over 100 loads of garbage, etc., removed, distributed most of the disinfectants that I brought in and the streets and lots are taking on a cleaner appearance. The odors are disappearing also.

The township is organizing in a few days and, as no great amount of sickness has occurred so far, we hope they will be able to handle the situation themselves in the spring.

I visited Mond Village on the request of Dr. Cameron, of Victoria Mines, who is contracting physician for the Mond Mining Company, where they had an epidemic of typhoid fever. Between 50 and 60 cases have occured this fall in a population of about 400. We closed all doubtful wells, sent samples of the balance, 17 in number, for analysis. Out of that number only two were anyway pure. We had them all chlorinated. Half the village is composed of log shacks no person knows how old. I had eight destroyed and several renovated. All the usual causes were present for causing disease. I will attach the notice given by me to the Board of Health in the Township of Drury, Denison and Graham which will cover the whole case:—

" Gentlemen,—Accompanied by the Mining Foreman and Sanitary Inspector, we gave the village a very thorough inspection to-day. In houses where typhoid had occurred, it was not hard to find the causes of the outbreak, namely, open closets, leaving slops from the sickroom exposed, hogs adjacent to dwelling houses and public highways and generally unsanitary conditions. These are some of the steps that require to be taken:

1.—All closets must be built of good lumber being made close to exclude the flies, using buckets or drawers, disinfecting regularly and having emptied when required.

2.—That all garbage, cans, etc., etc., be collected in covered boxes or barrels and removed by a scavenger to a safe distance and destroyed.

3.—That all houses and yards that require it be thoroughly disinfected.

4.—Where typhoid occurs the slops must be disinfected and buried. Dig a pit, say 2 feet square and 4 feet deep and every time anything is emptied into it, after disinfecting, add a shovelfull or two of earth. When the pit is filled within one foot of surface, fill up entirely and dig a new one.

5.—Where buildings have become decayed, they should be destroyed as they must be saturated with disease after all those years of use.

6.—That all old cloths around the mines be burned, that the public change or wash house be fumigated once a week during the epidemic with 16 oz. of formaldehyde, 7 oz. of permanganate of potash to each 1,000 cubic feet, that all drains and floors of same to drenched regularly with sulphate of copper with a strength of 1 lb. to 1 gallon of water. It appears to me this building is too small to accommodate the 170 men who use it.

7.—I would also draw the Mining Company's attention to Sections in the Mining Act requiring them to furnish portable closets in mines where they are deeper than 100 ft. Some men will not always or cannot come to the surface and I understand this mine is over 1,300 ft. deep.

8.—All milk should be sterilized before using, as the cows are wandering everywhere and drinking questionable water from the little creek and picking up garbage from back yards. That a settling basin be made in the creek below the town and chlorinated, as this stream eventually reaches the Victoria Mine water supply."

I remained in the village 13 days and saw these instructions carried out, and at my leaving there had been no new cases for several days. I revisited later and found conditions becoming satisfactory.

September 28th.

I again revisited Porcupine and found the new Council of Whitney had made important improvements in draining and grading. Mr. Bachon, the scavenger I took up, is still busily at work.

Tisdale Township is now legislating a road to their dumping ground and have employed Mr. Bachon to do their scavenger work also. A few isolated cases of typhoid from the bush and town have occurred but no serious outbreak is anticipated. I secured a conviction while there against the Gordon Davies Abattoir Company, for having decayed poultry and meat on their premises and that their premises were unfit to carry on that business.

October 5th.

I visited the depot camps and camps 4, 5 and 6 of the Hettler Lumber Company, Railway Camp, J. B. Smith & Sons., and Camp No. 1 of the Georgian Bay Lumber Company, all on the Dokis Reserve. The camps of the Hettlers are all new and well built, and after having cesspools put in and better protection to their water supplies I see no reason why the men will not be healthy.

Smith's railway camp had too small a bunk house. This will have to be enlarged and the closet moved further from the Restoule River. Their water comes from a spring and is good. Camp No. 1 of the Georgian Bay Lumber Company is new. It is poorly situated, being overcrowded and on the banks of the French River, manure from stables and slops from kitchen running directly into it. The bunk house is also too small. I have now ordered them to move to a better location after consulting with you in the matter.

October 14th.

While at Burk's Falls looking after Mr. Gourlay, an indigent and helpless old man from an unorganized township, I noticed the public closets of the Knight Bros., factories, where between 75 and 100 men work, were over and polluting the Magnetewan River. I have given them notice to remove the same within thirty days. I have since revisited and found them working at the necessary improvements.

October 27th.

I inspected the camps of George Gordon on Weshigami Lake back of Markstay about 30 miles. I found several objectionable features in them, especially at camp

No. 4, but I see by Dr. McKee's plans and report of camp since, that improvements have been made and hope when I revisit to find all my orders carried out.

I have had to do with very few cases of smallpox this summer and with the exception of an outbreak of typhoid in a few places the people have been reasonably healthy in Northern Ontario this summer. I notice as a rule that new built camps this winter are conforming more to the regulations, some of them peeling the logs before building, plastering with sand and lime, roofing with paroid making better ventilation, etc., but there is a tendency to build too close to the streams or lakes, where slops, etc., will reach the water. I believe it should be definitely mentioned in the Camp Regulations that they should not be located closer than 100 feet to any lake or navigable stream.

Another matter that comes under my observation is that some of the doctors in the camps do not always report the true state of affairs apparently for fear they lose their contracts, the companies having the power to terminate the medical contracts. Legislation should be made to cover this matter, as it is impossible for an Inspector to visit the large number of camps in this country.

The Blanche River District, Province of Quebec.

The main lot numbers refer to those registered claims. The claims that have been formally taken up only are marked.

REPORT ON INVESTIGATION OF THE McGREGOR LAKE DISTRICT
AND THE OTTAWA RIVER WITH RESPECT TO GROWTH
OF ALGAE.

By GEORGE C. WHIPPLE, CONSULTING ENGINEER.

August 1st, 1911.

To the Water and Sewage Disposal Commission, Ottawa, Canada.

GENTLEMEN,—The following is a report of an investigation of the algae conditions in the lakes of the McGregor Lake district, made during July, 1911:—

Itinerary.

The party, consisting of Dr. C. A. Hodgetts, Dr. J. W. S. McCullough, Dr. John A. Amyot, and G. C. Whipple, went to McGregor Lake from Ottawa on the afternoon of July 5th. Headquarters were made at Percy Hamilton's, on McGregor Lake, from which point daily trips were made to the other lakes. In addition to making a general inspection of these lakes, samples of water were collected and examined physically and microscopically. Temperatures of the water were taken at various depths by means of a weighted thermometer inserted in a bottle so arranged that it would be filled at any desired depth.

The forenoon of Thursday, July 6th, being rainy, was devoted to the collection of samples from McGregor Lake, near Hamilton's. In the afternoon the party drove to Wakefield Lake, and took samples of water at two places. On Friday, July 7th, an all day trip was made to Lake St. Germain, by team and boat. Anatole Barbeau accompanied the party. Samples were collected from both arms of the lake. On Saturday, July 8th, an all day trip was made by launch and team to Battle Lake and to Lake Rheaume. Samples of water were collected from both lakes. Sunday forenoon was spent analyzing the samples collected. In the afternoon a trip was made around the entire shore line of McGregor Lake in Mr. McLaurin's motor-boat. Notes were kept as to the character of the shore. On Monday, July 10th, an all day trip was made by boat to Grand Lake, Green Lake and McArthur Lake. There was a severe thundershower in the afternoon about four o'clock. On Tuesday, July 11th, an all day trip was made by boat to Grand Lake and Double Dam Lake. On Wednesday, July 12th, samples were collected from various parts of McGregor Lake in the forenoon. The afternoon was devoted to analyzing the samples and tabulating results. On Thursday, July 13th, a trip was made to the lower end of McGregor Lake, including Mud Bay, in Mr. McLaurin's launch. Various samples were collected and analysed early in the afternoon. The party left for Ottawa Thursday afternoon.

Friday, July 14th, was devoted to a trip on Lake Deschenes, from Ottawa to Quio. Prof. W. M. Edwards accompanied the party. Twelve samples of water were collected. On Saturday, July 15th, an inspection of the waterworks was made in the forenoon, with special reference to the disinfection plant. In the afternoon the samples of water collected on the previous day were examined microscopically in Dr. Hollingworth's laboratory in the City Hall. Dr. McCullough and Mr. Parsons made a trip to Wright's Bridge on the Gatineau River and collected a sample there. Sunday, July 16th, was devoted to a tabulation of records.

On Monday and Tuesday, July 17th and 18th, Dr. C. A. Hodgetts, Mr. N. J
Ker, City Engineer, and G. C. Whipple, went to Ogdensburg and Watertown and
examined the filters in both places. Dr. McCullough went from Toronto to Water
town on Monday.

During the trip sixty-one microscopic examinations were made of samples collected from the McGregor Lake district, and twelve samples were collected from
Lake Deschenes. Five samples were collected for chemical analysis. These were
analyzed in the laboratory of Hazen and Whipple at the Brooklyn Polytechnic Institute, Brooklyn, N.Y. In addition to these analyses, observations of the temperature of the water were made at various depths at eleven different places in the
lake.

McGREGOR LAKE DISTRICT.

Temperature Conditions.

Just preceding the trip to McGregor Lake, the country experienced an unusually severe period of intense heat. The following records, obtained from the
Agricultural Experiment Station at Ottawa show that during the first two weeks
of July the maximum temperature was almost continuously above the average
maximum for the month of July, 1910. At McGregor Lake temperatures above
90 deg. were observed on July 9th and 10th.

Fig. 8 shows a comparison between the monthly air temperatures at Ottawa
from July, 1910, to June, 1911, and the corresponding average temperatures for
New York and Boston. Apparently the summer maximum is about as high for
Ottawa as for Boston, and almost as high as for New York. The maximum is
reached earlier in the season. The winter temperatures are, of course, much lower
than for the other cities named, and the change is somewhat more abrupt.

OTTAWA, ONTARIO.

TEMPERATURES OF AIR.

July, 1910—June, 1911.

—	Mean maximum.	Mean minimum.	Mean.
1910			
July......................	31.88	58.93	70.40
August.....................	77.94	55.56	66.74
September...................	26.56	44.84	55.70
October	55.21	38.32	46.92
November...................	36.98	27.56	32.27
December..................	20.13	3.49	11.80
1911			
January....................	22.99	0.20	11.38
February...................	21.38	3.31	12.34
March......................	21.36	11.99	21.67
April......................	50.29	28.59	39.44
May.......................	76.14	49.82	62.98
June	74.75	54.50	64.62

OTTAWA, ONTARIO.

MAXIMUM AND MINIMUM TEMPERATURES.

July 1st—July 15th.

	Maximum.	Minimum.
July 1	91.6	56.0
2	95.5	68.0
3	97.8	70.0
4	89.8	73.2
5	96.8	66.2
6	84.8	70.8
7	78.0	56.8
8	86.0	52.0
9	96.4	60.0
10	97.0	70.0
11	92.0	66.9
12	79.4	65.0
13	76.8	58.4
14	81.4	53.8
15	81.5	57.8

Temperature of the Water.

In consequence of the hot weather, the temperature of the water at and near the surface was found to be unusually high for this latitude. On almost every day the temperature of the surface water was above 80°F. The highest recorded surface temperature was 34.5 and the lowest 79°.

The temperature of the water at depths below the surface is shown by figures in Table 1 and by diagrams in Figures 3 to 5. The observations showed a striking similarity in temperature conditions in all lakes examined. Generally speaking, the depth of water in active circulation below the surface was about 8 or 10 feet. Within this upper layer the temperatures were practically the same. Below this depth the temperature decreased rapidly down to a depth of 25 to 30 feet. Below this depth the increase in temperature was much slower. The region between 10 feet and 25 feet below the surface, within which the temperature fell rapidly, is commonly known as the *thermocline*. The temperature at the foot of the thermocline was found to be about 50°. The temperature of the water at the bottom of the lake, where the depth was less than 100 feet, was from 46° to 48°. The deep water temperature was sometimes found as low as 45°, which was the lowest figure recorded. No temperature observations were made below a depth of 100 feet, as this was the limit of the cord attached to the apparatus.

Between the first and last sets of observations at McGregor Lake there were several days on which the wind reached a considerable velocity. This caused the water to be stirred up to a slightly greater depth than when first observed. This is illustrated by Fig. 3.

Fig. 4 shows the temperature observations made at different places on Grand Lake, in which it was observed that the surface temperatures were generally higher on the windward side. This lake receives a greater sweep of the wind than most of the other lakes. Consequently, it is stirred to somewhat greater depths than the others, and its bottom temperatures during the summer season are slightly higher.

The conditions at the time these temperature observations were made were unusual, and it is not likely that in ordinary years the temperature of the water near the surface will become as high as during the present season. Apparently. also, the depth to which the water was found to be stirred was somewhat greater than would be ordinarily observed. In general, the temperature conditions were found to be similar to those of the lakes of New England, but a comparison of the data appears to indicate that the change at the foot of the thermocline is somewhat more abrupt in McGregor Lake than in the New England Lakes. The most marked difference, however, between the Canadian lakes and those farther south is probably the shallowness of the layer of warm, circulating water near the surface in the northern waters.

Stagnation.

Although the water in all of the lakes was thermally stratified, in no case was there found any indication of a lack of oxygen in the bottom water. None of the samples from the bottom had a disagreeable odor or. with one exception, an increased color. The exception referred to was Double Dam Lake, where the sample from a depth of 45 feet had a color of 45 as compared with 20 at the surface. Wherever possible, the character of the bottom was observed by stirring up the deposit and collecting the sediment in the bottle. The deposits thus collected were examined microscopically and found to consist, for the most part, of peaty material with some microscopic organisms. In no case was there any evidence of putrefaction. In some cases the bottom was comparatively hard.

Color of the Water.

The water was found to be relatively light in color at all points. The lowest recorded color was observed in Battle Lake and Lake Rheaume, *i.e.*, 12. In Wakefield Lake the color was somewhat higher, being 30 in the south-west arm. In Mud Bay the apparent color was 45, but this was due in part to the presence of suspended matter in the water. The water in the various brooks and small lakes varied in color from 30 to 50. In McGregor Lake the colors varied from 15 to 20, the average being approximately 18.

Practically speaking, the water in the lakes of the McGregor Lake District may be considered as colorless. The fact that the lake water is less colored than that of the tributary streams is due to the bleaching action of the sunlight during the long storage of water in the lakes.

Odor.

Nearly all of the samples examined have no taste or odor. A few had a faint vegetable odor,. and in one or two cases the samples collected within the thermoeline had a very faint aromatic odor, due to the presence of microscopic organisms. These were not strong enough to be observed by the ordinary water consumer drinking the water. The water in Mud Bay had a grassy odor, due to the presence of algae.

Speaking generally, and from a practical standpoint, all of the lake waters may be regarded as tasteless and odorless. Samples of the cool, deep waters were used regularly by the party for drinking, and in no instance was the slightest objectionable taste or odor detected.

Turbidity.

The water in all of the lakes was clear. In many instances the turbidity was recorded as 0. Owing to the presence of microscopic organisms in small numbers, however, the turbidity was occasionally reported as 0.5 or 1, merely to indicate that some suspended matter was present. These figures are so low as to be entirely without practical significance. One exception only is to be noted, viz., in Mud Bay, where, on account of the growth of Aphanizomenon, the samples of water had turbidities between 8 and 24, as determined by the U.S. Geological Survey measuring rod.

Microscopic Organisms

A general similarity was found in the microscopic flora and fauna of the various lakes. The only diatom present in large numbers was Tabellaria, an organism that seldom or never causes trouble even though present in quite large numbers. In McGregor Lake this diatom was found most abundant near the surface of the water, the number present being generally between 100 and 300 per cubic centimeter.

Few green algae were found, and none in large numbers.

Several species of important blue-green algae were met with, namely, Anabaena, Clothrocystis, Coclosphaerium, Microcystis, Aphanizomenon and Cylindrospermum. These algae, should they be present in large numbers, might give rise to objectionable tastes and odors. While found generally distributed through the lakes, in no case were they found in numbers sufficient to cause a noticeable odor, except in Mud Bay. These algae could be seen as minute specks floating in the water near the surface, and while these specks on close inspection were in some instances conspicuous, the actual amounts of algae present, as shown by microscopical analysis, were small.

In Mud Bay, Aphanizomenon was found in large quantities. Here one sample, collected on July 9th, contained 1,080 per c.c., and another sample, collected on July 13th, contained 15,000 per c.c. This water had a noticeable grassy odor, due to the presence of the algae. The water of McGregor Lake at the lower end, below Mud Bay, showed an increased number of Aphanizomenon, but the number was not sufficient to produce a taste or odor that could be detected by drinking the water.

The most important protozoa observed were Dinobryon, Synura and Ceratium. In almost every case the numbers were too low to cause a noticeable odor, but a few of the samples collected within the thermocline contained Dinobryon and Synura in quantities sufficient to give the water a very faint, aromatic odor, as mentioned above.

Vertical Distribution of Microscopic Organisms.

A number of samples were collected from McGregor Lake at different depths in order to determine the vertical distribution of the microscopic organisms. These results have been plotted and results are shown in Fig. 6. From this it will be seen that the Tabellaria were most abundant near the surface, within the region of the circulating water. This was also true of the blue-green algae, such as the Anabaena. The Synura and Dinobryon, however, were concentrated within the region of the thermocline, the apparent reason being that these organisms are dependent upon light, yet tend to shun warm water. They have powers of locomotion and apparently chose a position as near the surface as possible, yet within the region of the comparatively cool water.

Growths of Algae at Other Seasons

Generally speaking, the numbers of microscopic organisms found during the investigations were low, and when the unusually high temperature of the water is taken into account, it does not seem likely that greater growths than these will often occur during the summer. It is not unlikely that growths of diatoms may occur in these lakes during the spring and fall. Examination of the sediment at the bottom of the lakes shows that they are seeded with Asterionella, Melosira, Synedra, etc. Owing to the great depths of the lakes and the absence of putrefaction at the bottom, it is not likely that these spring and fall growths of diatoms will ever reach large proportions. The conditions for such growths are not favorable.

It would be advisable, however, to continue the microscopical analysis of samples of water from McGregor Lake through the autumn, and preferably, through an entire year, in order to ascertain if, by any chance, heavy growths of diatoms should follow the spring and fall overturning of the water.

Chemical Analysis.

Chemical analysis shows the water of McGregor Lake to be soft. Such hardness as there is is due to the carbonates of calcium and magnesium. Sulphates were practically absent. The amount of chlorine was also low, as was also the iron and other mineral matter. The amount of nitrogen as nitrates was low, and this is a further reason for believing that large growths of algae will not be likely to occur in the lake. The samples of water were somewhat delayed in transportation to Brooklyn, and therefore the amounts of nitrogen as free ammonia were somewhat higher than would have been obtained had the analysis been made more promptly.

Possibility of Algae Growths in Sheltered Coves.

McGregor Lake has a broken shore line, and there are numerous coves within which the water does not circulate as thoroughly as in the open reaches. The possibility of algae growths within these coves is one that was observed carefully. In no case, however, was there found any large accumulation of algae. The only exception was Mud Bay, already referred to. This bay has a soft bottom and is relatively shallow; considerably more than half of its area was found covered with lily pads. The stream entering this bay flows down from Blackburn Mines. It is possible that the washings from the phosphate rock tend to increase the algae growth in this bay, but it is more likely that the growth is due chiefly to the shallow water and the deposits of organic matter at the bottom.

Conclusions as to the Possibility of the Growths of Algae in McGregor Lake.

From the inspection of McGregor Lake and its watershed and from the analyses of the water itself, the conclusion reached is that at the present time the water does not contain algae in sufficient amounts to cause any noticeable taste or odor to the water consumers, while on account of the unusual weather conditions the present season must be regarded as an especially severe one. The effect of raising the water level of McGregor Lake would be to reduce the growths of algae in the water. The shores of the lakes are generally rocky for a considerable distance above high water mark, and the strip of land that would be flooded if the water were raised is chiefly rock, covered with a thin top soil and wooded. With the timber cut and the stumps removed or burned around the margin of the lake, there ought to be no substantial increase in the amount of organic matter in the water. The deepening of the water in itself would tend to lessen the growths of algae, especially in the lower arm of the lake near the outlet and for a few miles above the site of the proposed dam.

The only places where algae would be likely to occur in large amounts are Mud Bay and Martin's Bay. With the water raised, the growths of algae would probably be less in Mud Bay than we found them. In Martin's Bay. where the water would be set back into Pelissier Creek for some distance, there would be created an area of shallow flowage where algae might develop, but this point is more than six miles from the proposed dam site and its effect upon the general body of the lake would be negligible. Mud Bay is separated from the main body of the lake by a narrow channel and its waters do not readily mix with the broad waters of the lake. Little danger need be feared, therefore, that algae growths in this bay will affect the water of the lake to any serious extent.

Even if algae growths should occur in Mud Bay, or in some of the coves, their effect on the water would be practically nullified by the use of copper sulphate applied locally. This same treatment could also be applied to the waters of the lake at the lower end, should occasion require. It does not appear likely, however, that it will be necessary to resort to the use of copper sulphate except at very infrequent intervals. A comparison of the analyses made with those that have been made for many years at the reservoirs of the Boston Waterworks and the waterworks of the City of New York, and of many lakes in New England, shows that a water supply derived from McGregor Lake would be superior in quality to most of the water supplies of New England and New York, so far as growths of algae are concerned.

Sanitary Qualities

Attention was given to the possible danger of pollution of McGregor Lake supply. The population on the watershed was found to be very sparse and very much less than in most of the water supplies of New England used without filtration. There are a few places where the water of the lake might become slightly contaminated but these can be removed at little cost. Furthermore, the amount of storage in McGregor Lake and the other lakes on the watershed is so great and there are so many constrictions in the lake preventing active circulation and rapid cross-currents, that, even though the water should be slightly contaminated, the effects of such contamination would be lost before the water reached the pipe line. From the sanitary standpoint, therefore, McGregor Lake supply can be made thoroughly safe at very slight expense and without the necessity of filtration. Any design for utilizing the supply would, however, naturally provide opportunities for filtration should this ever become necessary through increase of population on the watershed or because of unexpected growths of algae.

OTTAWA RIVER

Temperature.

The temperature of the water in the Ottawa River on July 14 was found to be practically 76°F. at all depths. On account of the comparatively shallow water in Lake Deschenes and its long reach, the wind apparently stirs the water throughout its depth, so that the conditions of stratification observed in Lake McGregor were not here found.

Turbidity and Color.

The turbidity of the water was found to be from 12 to 30, an average figure for the entire lake being 15. The color of the water was found to be about 92 and was about the same at all points. The water had the distinct vegetable taste and odor characteristic of colored waters.

Algae in Lake Deschenes.

All of the samples of water collected from the Ottawa River in Lake Deschenes contained algae in small numbers. The diatoms and rotifers predominated. The numbers were lower than in the Lake McGregor District, and were too low to be of practical significance. So far as they were present, however, the species appeared to be the same as those found in the other lakes.

Chemical Analysis

Chemical analysis showed that the water of the Ottawa River is exceedingly soft, somewhat softer, in fact, than the water of Lake McGregor. Such hardness as there is is due chiefly to the carbonates of calcium and magnesium. While this softness of the water is in itself an excellent quality, it is not so when considered in connection with the use of alum. In order to properly decolorize the water of the Ottawa River, it would be necessary to use sulphate of alumina as a coagulant. This chemical gives better results when used in hard water than in soft water. A certain amount of alkalinity in the water is required to decompose the sulphate of alumina, and if the necessary alkalinity is not naturally present in the water it is necessary to add it in the form of lime or soda ash. It would be necessary to do so in this instance in order to provide a safe margin of residual alkalinity after the alum has been added. If this were not done, the filtered water would acquire certain troublesome corrosive properties, that should, if possible, be avoided. Therefore, while the water of the Ottawa River in its natural state is softer than that of lake McGregor, the river water, after treatment with alum, would be found more troublesome in actual use than the lake water.

The amount of organic matter as shown by the nitrogen as albuminoid ammonia, was about the same as that found in McGregor Lake, but the oxygen consumed was nearly double that in McGregor Lake. This apparently is due to the presence of organic matter containing a rather large percentage of carbon, this organic matter producing the color. From the sanitary standpoint, there seems to be no doubt that the water of the Ottawa River can be filtered and rendered safe for drinking. Without filtration, however, it would not be as safe for use as the water from McGregor Lake. The storage in Lake Deschenes is large, but the lake is a broad expanse of water, down which the wind may readily force a quantity of surface water in a comparatively short time. Practically, therefore, the storage in this lake is less efficient than that of McGregor Lake, so far as the elimination of pollution is concerned.

GATINEAU RIVER.

The water of the Gatineau River is similar to that of the Ottawa River. It is, however, somewhat less colored and is slightly softer. It contained algae in small numbers. This water could not be safely used without filtration, which would be necessary both from a sanitary standpoint and from that of making the water acceptable to the consumers. Its decolorization would require the use of alum and its softness is such that alum alone could not be safely used. Either lime or soda would be required in addition to alum.

TABLE 1.

OTTAWA, CANADA.

TEMPERATURE OBSERVATIONS TAKEN IN THE McGREGOR LAKE DISTRICT.

July 5-13, 1911.

Depth in feet.	McGregor Lake. Stations. 3 July 6 11.00 A.M.	Wakefield Lake. 6 July 6 3.45 P.M.	Stadermain Lake. 13 July 7 2.00 P.M.	Battle Lake. 15 July 8 1.45 M.	Rheaume Lake. 16 July 8 2.20 P.M.	Grand Lake. 22 July 10 2.00 PM	Grand Lake. 24 July 10 2.50 P.M.	Double Dam Lake. 29 July 11 2.15 P.M.	McGregor Lake. 34 July 12 10.20 A.M.	McGregor Lake. 44 July 12 12.15 P.M.	McGregor Lake. 35 July 12 12.15 P.M.
0	81.0	81.0	79.5	82.5	81.0	84.3	81.5	83.0	79.0	79.5	79.5
5	80.8	79.0	77.5			84.0	81.5	82.0	79.0	79.5	79.5
10	740	71.0	75.0	77.0	75.0	82.8	79.0	76.8	75.2	77.0	77.0
15	63.2	62.0	65.2	61.5	61.0	70.0	70.0	65.8	62.0	67.0	67.0
20	55.0	54.5	54.0	55.0	54.0	62.0	58.0	58.5	54.0	54.0	54.0
25	51.0	52.0	51.2	51.5		54.0	54.0	52.5	50.0	50.8	50.8
30	50.0	49.2	50.5	49.5	49.5	51.8		49.0	48.5	49.5	49.5
40	48.0	48.2	47.5	48.0	47.5	50.5	49.5	47.5	47.0		
50	47.5	48.0*	47.0*	46.0	Bottom	48.5		46.5	46.0	47.5	47.5
60	470	*Bottom 45 ft.	47.0* *Bottom 55 ft.					Bottom 45 ft.	Bottom 46 ft.		
70	440										
80	46.0										
90	460			45.5 Did not reach bottom		47.5 Bottom 95 ft.	46.0 Did not reach bottom			45.0 Did not reach bottom	45.0 Did not reach bottom
100	Bottom										

TABLE 2.

PHYSICAL EXAMINATION OF SAMPLES OF WATER FROM THE McGREGOR LAKE
DISTRICT, COLLECTED JULY 6–13, 1911.

Station.	Depth in Feet.	Temperature.	Turbidity.	Color.	Odor.	Date.	Hour.	Location of Sample.
1			0.5	20	2v	July 5	8:00 P.M.	Blanche River, outlet to McGregor Lake.
2			0.5	20	2v	" 5	8:30 P.M.	Blanche River, Dufresne Bridge.
3		81.0	0.5	20	......	" 6	11:00 A.M.	McGregor Lake, opposite Marcelais Point.
3	25	51.0	....	17	1a	" 6	11:00 A.M.	McGregor Lake, opposite Marcelais Point.
3	50	47.5	....	17	1a	" 6	11:00 A.M.	McGregor Lake, opposite Marcelais Point.
3	80	46.0	....	19	2v	" 6	11:00 A.M.	McGregor Lake, opposite Marcelais Point.
3	90	46.0	....	17	2v	" 6	11:00 A.M.	McGregor Lake, opposite Marcelais Point.
4			0.5	15	2v	" 6	1:50 P.M.	Outlet to Lake Bonin.
5		74.0	0.5	50	2v	" 6	1:50 P.M.	Pelissier Creek at Dubois Bridge.
6		81.0	1.0	30	1v	" 6	3:45 P.M.	Wakefield Lake, southwest arm.
6	20	54.5	0.5	35	1v	" 6	3:45 P.M.	Wakefield Lake, southwest arm.
7		81.0	....	15	2v	" 6	4:30 P.M.	Wakefield Lake, fork of southwest and northeast arms.
8			1.0	40	2v	" 7	9:00 A.M.	Deer Lake Brook, at road crossing.
9		71.0	1.0	25	2v	" 7	9:30 A.M.	Blanche River, above Wakefield Lake.
10			1.0	50	3v	" 7	9:45 A.M.	Robinson's Lake.
11			1.0	28	2v	" 7	2:00 P.M.	St. Germain Lake, south end, near boat house.
12		81.0	1.0	18	3v	" 7	2:40 P.M.	St. Germain Lake, west fork, opposite club.
13		79.5	2.0	22	3v 1g	" 7	3:00 P.M.	St. Germain Lake, east fork.
13	20	54.0	1.0	18	2v	" 7	3:00 P.M.	St. Germain Lake, east fork.
13	50	47.0	1.0	15	1v	" 7	3:00 P.M.	St. Germain Lake, east fork.
14			1.0	30	2v	" 8	11:15 A.M.	Brook at Blackburn Mine.
15		82.5	0.5	15	1v	" 8	1:45 P.M.	Battle Lake, middle.
15	20	55.0	0.5	12	1v	" 8	1:45 P.M.	Battle Lake, middle.
15	50	46.0	0.5	12	1v	" 8	1:45 P.M.	Battle Lake, middle.
15	100	45.5	0.5	12	1v	" 8	1:45 P.M.	Battle Lake, middle.
16		81.0	1.0	12	3v	" 8	2:20 P.M.	Rheaume Lake, middle.
16	20	54.0	1.0	12	2v	" 8	2:20 P.M.	Rheaume Lake, middle.
16	40	47.5	0.5	12	2v	" 8	2:20 P.M.	Rheaume Lake, middle.
17		83.0	14.0	45	2v	July 9	3:30 P.M.	Mud Bay.

4 B.H.

TABLE 2.—(Continued)

Station.	Depth in feet.	Temperature.	Turbidity.	Color.	Odor.	Date.	Hour.	Location of sample.
18	....	81.0	0.5	15	1v	July 9	4:30 P.M.	McGregor Lake, Martin's Bay.
19	....	83.0	....	15	......	" 10	10:15 A.M.	Green Lake, near outlet.
20	....	83.0	0.5	17	2v	" 10	10:45 A.M.	McArthur Lake, near outlet.
21	....	84.5	....	......	......	" 10	1:50 P.M.	Grand Lake, north-east end.
22	....	84.3	....	21	......	" 10	2:00 P.M.	Grand Lake, below Betsy's house.
22	20	62.0	....	20	......	" 10	2:20 P.M.	Grand Lake.
23	....	82.5	....	......	......	" 10	2:30 P.M.	Grand Lake, below Big Point.
24	....	81.5	....	17	......	" 10	2:50 P.M.	Grand Lake, near outlet to Dam Lake.
25	....	81.0	....	......	......	" 10	3:15 P.M.	Grand Lake, above Narrows.
26	....	83.0	....	......	......	" 10	3:20 P.M.	Grand Lake, below Narrows.
27	....	82.5	....	......	......	" 10	3:35 P.M.	Grand Lake, near Bone Rock.
28	....	83.5	....	18	......	" 10	3:50 P.M.	Grand Lake, near Isle au Pete.
29	....	83.0	....	20	1v	" 11	2:15 P.M.	Double Dam Lake, west of island above dam.
29	25	52.5	....	23	1v	" 11	2:15 P.M.	Double Dam Lake, west of island above dam.
29	45	46.5	....	45	1v	" 11	2:15 P.M.	Double Dam Lake, west of island above dam.
30	....	83.0	....	18	......	" 11	3:00 P.M.	Double Dam Lake, Narrows inlet, from Grand Lake.
31	....	79.0	....	20	......	" 12	9:50 A.M.	McGregor Lake, west of Rabbit Island.
32	....	79.0	....	20	......	" 12	10:10 A.M.	McGregor Lake, near island, and in cove.
33	....	79.0	....	17	......	" 12	10:20 A.M.	McGregor Lake, Gouinville's Bay.
34	....	79.0	0.5	15	1v	" 12	10:30 A.M.	McGregor Lake.
34	20	54.0	....	15	......	" 12	10:30 A.M.	McGregor Lake.
35	....	79.5	0.5	20	......	" 12	12:15 P.M.	McGregor Lake, opposite Marcelais Point.
35	10	77.0	0.5	20	1v	" 12	12:15 P.M.	McGregor Lake, opposite Marcelais Point.
35	15	67.0	0.5	20	1v	" 12	12:15 P.M.	McGregor Lake, opposite Marcelais Point.
35	20	54.0	0.5	20	1v	" 12	12:15 P.M.	McGregor Lake, opposite Marcelais Point.
35	25	50.8	0.5	25	1v + 1a	" 12	12:15 P.M.	McGregor Lake, opposite Marcelais Point.
35	30	49.5	....	20	......	" 12	12:15 P.M.	McGregor Lake, opposite Marcelais Point.
35	50	47.5	....	15	......	" 12	12:15 P.M.	McGregor Lake, opposite Marcelais Point.
35	100	45.0	....	15	......	" 12	12:15 P.M.	McGregor Lake, opposite Marcelais Point.
36	....	79.0	0.5	20	1v	" 13	9:15 A.M.	McGregor Lake, Cove west of Narrows.
37	....	79.0	0.5	20	Iv	" 13	9:20 A.M.	McGregor Lake, Dufresnes Bridge.

TABLE 2.—(Concluded)

Station.	Depth in feet.	Temper-ature.	Tur-bidity.	Color.	Odor.	Date.	Hour.	Location of sample.
38	....	79.5	0.5	20	1v	July 13	9:25 A.M.	McGregor Lake, east of Sheep Island.
39	....	79.0	0.5	18	v1	" 13	9:30 A.M.	McGregor Lake, above Consineau's Bridge.
40	0–15	....	0.5	20	......	" 13	9:35 A.M.	McGregor Lake, below Brick Point (chemical sample).
41	....	80.0	24	......	...... 2v	" 13	10:40 A.M.	McGregor Lake, Mud Bay middle.
42	....	80.0	22	45	2g	" 13	10:45 A.M.	McGregor Lake, Mud Bay upper end.
43	....	80.0	8	......	......	" 13	10:50 A.M.	McGregor Lake, Mud Bay lower end.
44	....	80.0	0.5	18	......	" 13	11:10 A.M.	McGregor Lake, near Bone Point.
44	15	63.5	0.5	16	1v 1a	" 13	11:10 A.M.	McGregor Lake, near Bone Point.
44	20	53.0	0.5	16	1v+1a	" 13	11:10 A.M.	McGregor Lake, near Bone Point.
44	25	50.2	0.5	18	1v+1a	" 13	11:10 A.M.	McGregor Lake, near Bone Point.
44	100	45.0	....	18	......	" 13	11:10 A.M.	McGregor Lake, near Bone Point.

TABLE 3.

CHEMICAL ANALYSIS OF SAMPLES OF WATER FROM MCGREGOR LAKE, JULY 13, 1911.

Laboratory Number	4,405	4,406
	Below	Near
Locality	Birch Point.	Bone Point.
	Parts per Million.	
Turbidity	1	1
Color	19	17
	Very faint	
Odor..	moldy*	Faint moldy*
Nitrogen as alb. ammonia	0.138	0.174
Nitrogen as free ammonia	0.04	0.054
Nitrogen as nitrites	0.002	0.002
Nitrogen as nitrates..................................	0.05	0.07
Nitrogen as total organic—		
Oxygen consumed	4.60	4.90
Total residue	59.00	56.00
Loss on ignition......................................	14.00	21.00
Fixed residue	45.00	35.00
Iron	0.05	0.20
Total hardness..	23.50	23.00
Alkalinity..	23.50	23.00
Incrustants	0.0	0.0
Chlorine	0.80	0.80

*After standing ten days.

TABLE 4.

WATER ANALYSIS, OTTAWA, ONTARIO.

(Supplementary Sheet).

Laboratory No.—Station..	1	2	3	3	3	3	3	17	18	31	32	33	34
Source of sample—Depth, feet	0	0	0	25	50	80	90	0	0	0	0	0	0
McGregor Lake, July, 1911 ..	5	5	6	6	6	6	6	9	9	12	12	12	12
Microscopical Analysis. (Standard Units per c.c.)													
Asterionella					4		6						
Diatoma													
Fragilaria													
Melosira				4	2		10		6				
Navicula													
Stephanodiscus													
Synedra	8	1			1		8		10		4		10
Tabellaria	26	171	54	437	128	110	148		78	150	264	264	236
Cyclotella				5	4	2	6		4				
Protococcus	4	2	2	4				100	4				
Closterium													
Dimorphococcus													
Conferva													
Eudorina													
Pediastrum													
Scenedesmus													
Staurastrum	7				2		1		2		4		4
Raphidium									3				
Anabaena			15		2				49	26	34	31	56
Clathrocystis	7	5										23	
Coelosphaerium													
Microcystis	9	10	13	13	10	7	5	50	15	16	18	10	25
Oscillaria													
Aphanizomenon	51	53	16	29	18	14	2	1,080	12	5		12	24
Cylindrospermum													40
Leptothrix													
Crenothrix													
Molds													
Dinobryon				32	2		5						
Synura											5	15	20
Peridinium											4		
Trachelomonas	1				1								
Ceratrum	5	10				5		20	10	5		10	5
Cryptomonas		2											
Anthophysa													
Monas													
Vorticella			2						20			5	10
Mallomonas	2	1	5						2	2	2		
Tintinnus				3									
Zoothamnium											2		
Euglena												3	
Anuraca	5			5		5			20				
Polyarthra									10				
Rotifer													
Diaptomus	pr												
Nauplius	pr	pr											
Total Organisms	125	255	107	532	174	143	191	1,250	225	224	337	373	430
Amorphous matter	33	25	20	20	20	20	30	300	30	30	25	30	25

REMARKS.

Station 1—Outlet, bridge near dam-site.
     "   2   "   Dufresne bridge.
     "   3   "   near Marcelais Point.
     "   17—Mud bay.
     "   18—Martin's bay.

Station 31—North-west of Rabbit Island.
     "   32—Cove south of Martin's bay.
     "   33—Gouinville's bay.
     "   34—Lafontaine's bay.

TABLE 4—Continued.

WATER ANALYSIS, OTTAWA, ONTARIO.

(Supplementary Sheet.)

Laboratory No.—Station	34	35	35	35	35	35	35	35	35	36	37	38	39
Source of sample—Depth, feet	20	0	10	15	20	30	30	50	100	0	0	0	0
McGregor Lake, July, 1911	12	12	12	12	12	12	12	12	12	13	13	13	13
Microscopical Analysis. (Standard Units per c.c.)													
Asterionella							4						
Diatoma													
Fragilaria													
Melosira													
Navicula													
Stephanodiscus													
Synedra		10		10	5			10					
Tabellaria	210	200	232	132	98	148	120	110	62	160	88	112	108
Cyclotella				7				5					
Protococcus								4					
Closterium													
Dimorphococcus													
Conferva													
Eudorina													
Pediastrum													
Scenedesmus													
Staurastrum	1		2								4	4	8
Raphidium													
Anabaena	10	76	13	9	4	30	4	10	4	48	90	64	90
Clathrocystis				5		15							
Coelosphaerium			2		10	20	10	5	5			10	20
Microcystis	9	12	5	15		12		5					
Oscillaria													
Aphanibomenon	7	18	5	6		12	8				490	310	350
Leptothrix													
Crenothrix													
Molds													
Dinobryon					115	150	10	10	5				
Synura	5		35	85	25	10		20					
Peridinium													
Trachelomonas							1						
Ceratium			15	25	15	5	5						
Cryptomonas													
Anthophysa													
Monas													
Vorticella						5					20		60
Mallomonas					2					2			
Codonella						10							
Uroglena												16	20
Anuraea					10	20				10			10
Polyarthra						10							
Rotifer													
Diaptomus						pr							
Nauplius						pr							
Total Organisms	242	316	309	294	284	447	162	179	76	220	692	516	666
Amorphous Matter	20	30	20	25	20	20	20	20	30	20	30	50	50

REMARKS:

Station 34.   Lafontaine's Bay.
"   35.   Opposite Marcelais Point.
       Near station 3.
"   36.   West of Narrows.

Station 37.   Dufresne Bridge.
"   38.   East of Sheep Island.
"   39.   Above Cousineau Bridge.

TABLE 4—Concluded.

WATER ANALYSIS, OTTAWA, ONTARIO.

(Supplementary Sheet).

Laboratory No.—Station :	42	44	44	44	44	44
Source of Sample..Depth	0	0	15	20	25	100
McGregor Lake, July, 1911	13	13	13	13	13	13
Microscopical Analysis. (Standard Units per c.c.)						
Asterionella					48	4
Diatoma						
Fragilaria						
Melosira						
Navicula						
Stephanodiscus						
Synedra		20		4		4
Tabellaria		164	128	64	112	48
Cyclotella		4				
Protococcus						
Closterium						
Dimorphococcus						
Conferva						
Eudorina						
Pediastrum						
Scenedesmus						
Staurastrum						
Raphidium						
Anabaena		122	38	26	50	4
Clathrocystra						
Coelosphaerium				30		
Microcystis		20		40		20
Oscillaria						
Aphanizomenon	15,000	20				
Leptothrix						
Crenothrix						
Molds						
Dinobryon		20		170	150	50
Synura			220	20		30
Peridinium						
Trachelomonas						
Ceratrum		30	20	20		
Cryptomonas						
Anthophysa						
Monas						
Vorticella					30	
Anuraea						
Polyarthra						
Rotifer						
Total Organisms	15,000	400	406	374	390	160
Amorphous Matter		25	25	25	25	25

REMARKS.

Station 42—Mud Bay.
    ''   44—Bone Point.

TABLE 5.

WATER ANALYSIS, OTTAWA, ONTARIO.

(Supplementary Sheet).

Laboratory No.—Station	6	6	7	11	12	13	13	13	15	15	15	30
Source of sample—Depth	0	20	0	0	0	0	20	50	0	20	100	0
Various Lakes, July, 1911	6	6	6	7	7	7	7	7	8	8	8	11
Microscopical Analysis. (Standard Units per c.c.)												
Asterionella	....	....	....	....	....	....	....	....	....	....	8	6
Diatoma	....	....	....	....	....	....	....	....	....	....	....	....
Fragilaria	....	....	....	....	....	....	....	....	....	....	....	....
Meiosira	12	....	....	....	....	....	....	....	....	....	8	....
Navicula	....	....	....	....	....	....	....	....	....	....	....	....
Stephanodiscus	....	....	....	....	....	....	....	....	....	....	....	....
Synedra	....	12	10	10	....	....	....	....	....	20	20	....
Tabellaria	404	515	428	106	122	104	98	84	260	288	150	166
Cyclotella	....	2	....	....	....	....	....	....	....	2	7	8
Protococcus	4	....	....	....	4	....	....	....	....	....	....	....
Closterium	....	....	....	....	....	....	....	....	....	....	....	....
Dimorphococcus	....	....	....	....	10	....	....	....	....	3	....	....
Conferva	....	....	....	....	....	....	....	....	....	....	....	....
Eudorina	....	....	....	....	....	....	....	....	....	....	....	....
Pediastrum	....	....	....	....	....	....	....	....	....	....	....	....
Scenedesmus	....	....	....	....	....	....	....	....	....	....	....	....
Staurastrum	....	....	1	3	....	5	....	....	....	2	....	....
Raphidium	....	....	....	2	....	....	....	....	....	....	....	....
Anabaena	5	....	2	45	....	28	....	....	9	6	....	23
Clathrocystis	....	....	....	....	5	....	....	....	....	....	....	....
Coelosphaerium	....	39	....	....	....	50	....	....	....	10	....	....
Microcystis	50	....	60	17	42	33	15	11	78	30	16	10
Oscillaria	....	....	....	....	....	....	....	....	....	....	....	....
Aphanizomenon	10	10	2	....	....	....	....	....	....	....	....	6
Cylindrospermum	....	....	....	....	....	50	....	....	....	....	....	....
Gloeocystis	....	....	....	....	....	22	7	....	....	....	....	....
Leptothrix	....	....	....	....	....	....	....	....	....	....	....	....
Crenothrix	....	....	....	....	....	....	....	....	....	....	....	....
Molds	....	....	....	....	....	....	....	....	....	....	....	....
Dinobryon	....	....	....	....	35	30	....	....	....	3	....	....
Synura	....	....	....	....	....	....	....	....	....	....	....	....
Peridinium	4	....	....	....	....	....	....	....	....	....	....	....
Trachelomonas	....	....	2	....	....	....	....	3	....	2	....	....
Ceratium	....	....	....	....	....	5	....	3	....	5	5	....
Cryptomonas	....	....	....	....	....	....	....	....	....	....	....	....
Anthophysa	....	....	....	....	....	....	....	....	....	....	....	....
Monas	....	....	....	....	....	....	....	....	....	....	....	....
Vorticella	....	....	....	....	10	....	....	....	....	....	....	....
Uroglena	5	....	....	....	....	....	....	....	....	....	....	....
Mallomonas	1	....	....	....	....	....	....	....	....	....	....	....
Anuraea	....	....	5	....	....	....	....	....	....	10	10	10
Polyarthra	5	10	....	....	....	....	....	....	....	10	....	....
Rotifer	5	....	....	....	....	....	....	....	....	....	....	....
Total Organisms	505	588	510	183	233	322	123	98	370	390	210	221
Amorphous Matter	40	50	30	20	20	30	30	30	20	30	30	20

REMARKS.

Station 6—Wakefield Lake, southwest arm.
" 7 " " fork of southwest and northeast arms.
" 11—St. Germaine Lake, south end.

Station 12—St. Germaine Lake, west fork
" 13 " " east fork
" 15—Battle Lake.
" 30—Double Dam Lake, inlet.

TABLE 5—Concluded.

WATER ANALYSIS, OTTAWA, ONTARIO.

(Supplementary Sheet.)

Laboratory No.—Station	16	16	16	19	20	22	22	22	24	28	29	29	29
Source of sample—Depth	0	20	40	0	0	0	20	95	0	0	0	25	45
Various Lakes, July, 1911......	8	8	8	10	10	10	10	10	10	10	11	11	11
Microscopical Analysis. (standard Units per c.c.)													
Asterionella	....	4	12	....	....	....	....	....	....	....	....	52	6
Diatoma......................	....	....	....	....	....	....	....	....	....	....	....	....	....
Fragilaria	....	....	....	....	....	....	....	....	....	....	....	....	....
Melosira......................	....	10	12	2	....	....	2	2	....	....	....	3	....
Navicula	....	....	....	....	....	....	....	....	....	....	....	....	....
Stephanodiscus	....	....	....	....	....	....	....	....	....	....	....	....	....
Synedra......................	....	12	....	....	10	....	....	....	....	....	....	10	....
Tabellaria....................	28+	192	92	30	558	152	12	16	202	226	192	36	18
Cyclotella	....	2	3	....	2	....	2	....	....	....	....	2	....
Protococcus..................	4	6	....	4	....	2	....	....	2	2	....	....	....
Closterium	....	....	....	....	....	....	....	....	....	....	....	....	....
Dimorphococcus	....	....	....	....	....	....	....	....	....	....	....	....	....
Conferva	....	....	....	....	....	....	....	....	....	....	....	....	....
Eudorina	....	....	....	....	....	....	....	....	....	....	....	5	....
Pediastrum	....	....	....	....	....	....	....	....	....	....	....	....	....
Scenedesmus	....	....	....	....	....	....	....	....	....	....	....	....	....
Staurastrum	2	2	4	2	2	2	....	....	2	4	2	....	....
Raphidium	2	....	....	....	....	....	....	....	....	....	....	....	....
Anabaena	8	....	....	7	21	57	....	7	7	15	11	10	8
Clathrocystis.................	....	2	....	5	....	....	....	....	....	....	....	....	5
Coelosphaerium..............	....	5	10	....	10	....	....	15	....	....	....	10	....
Microcystis	11	40	5	15	25	....	13	5	15	....	20	5	....
Oscillaria	....	....	....	....	....	....	....	....	....	....	....	....	....
Aphanizomenon	....	....	....	....	....	10	....	6	....	....	....	3	2
Lepothrix	....	....	....	....	....	....	....	....	....	....	....	....	....
Crenothrix	....	....	....	....	....	....	....	....	....	....	....	....	....
Molds	....	....	....	....	....	....	....	....	....	....	....	....	....
Dinobryon	10	10	....	....	5	....	....	....	....	....	....	30	5
Synura.......................	....	25	....	....	....	....	....	....	....	....	....	15	....
Peridinium	7	13	2	....	....	....	....	....	....	....	....	....	....
Trachelomonas................	....	....	....	....	....	....	....	....	....	....	....	....	....
Ceratium	....	15	....	....	5	....	....	....	5	....	5	....	....
Cryptomonas	....	....	....	....	....	....	....	....	....	....	....	....	....
Anthophysa...................	....	....	....	....	....	....	....	....	....	....	....	....	....
Monas........................	....	....	....	....	....	....	....	....	....	....	....	....	....
Vorticella	....	....	....	5	....	....	....	....	....	....	....	....	....
Difflugia	20	....	....	....	....	....	....	....	....	....	....	....	....
Mallomonas	....	....	....	....	....	....	....	....	....	....	....	....	....
Anuraea......................	....	20	....	....	....	....	....	10	....	....	....	10	....
Polyarthra	....	....	....	....	....	....	....	....	....	....	....	....	....
Rotifer	....	....	....	....	....	....	....	....	....	....	....	....	....
Total Organisms........	348	358	140	70	638	223	29	61	233	247	230	193	44
Amorphous Matter	30	40	40	20	20	10	10	30	20	25	30	20	20

REMARKS:

Station 16. Rheaume Lake.
" 19. Green Lake.
" 20. McArthur Lake.
" 22 Grand Lake, north end.
" 24 Grand Lake, near outlet to Double Dam Lake.
" 28. Grand Lake, near south end.
" 29. Double Dam Lake.

TABLE 6.

WATER ANALYSIS, OTTAWA, ONTARIO.

(Supplementary Sheet.)

Laboratory No.—Station	4	5	8	9
Source of Sample—Depth	0	0	0 .	0
Various Streams, July, 1911	6	6.	7	7
Microscopical Analysis. (Standard Units per c.c.)				
Asterionella				
Diatoma				
Fragilaria				
Melosira				
Navicula			2	1
Stephanodiscus				
Synedra	2			
Tabellaria				
Protococcus				
Closterium				
Dimorphococcus				
Conferva				
Eudorina				
Pediastrum				
Scenedesmus				
Staurastrum				
Raphidium				
Anabaena				
Clathrocystis				
Coelosphaerium				
Microcystis				
Oscillaria				
Leptothrix				
Crenothrix				
Molds				
Cinobryon				
Synura				
Peridinium				
Trachelomonas				
Ceratium				
Cryptomonas				
Anthophysa				
Monas				
Vorticella				
Anuraea				
Polyarthra				
Rotifer				
Total Organisms	2	0	2	1
Amorphous Matter	100	60	40	50

REMARKS.

Station 4—Outlet to Lake Bonin.
    " 5— " McGlashan's Lake.
    " 8—Blanche River, above Wakefield Lake.
    " 9—Deer Lake Brook.

TABLE 7.

OTTAWA, CANADA.

PHYSICAL EXAMINATION OF SAMPLES OF WATER FROM LAKE DESCHENES, OTTAWA RIVER, COLLECTED JULY 14, 1911.

Station.	Depth in feet.	Temperature.	Turbidity.	Color.	Odor.	Location.
1	....	76.0	12	92	3v	Britannia, 1,000 feet from right bank.
2	....	76.0	20	88	3v	Above Deschenes Rapids, midstream.
2	30	76.5	30	90	3v	Above Deschenes Rapids, midstream.
3	....	76.5	15	92	3v	Opposite Aylmer, half-mile from right bank.
4	....	76.5	12	92	3v	Opposite Aylmer, midstream.
4	20	76.0	15	94	3v	Opposite Aylmer. midstream.
5	....	76.5	18	95	3v	Opposite Aylmer, 1,000 feet from left bank.
6	....	76.0	15	92	3v	Opposite wharf, 6 miles above Aylmer light.
7	....	76.0	15	92	3v	Opposite Sand Point.
8	....	75.8	12	92	3v	Two miles below Quio, in Narrows.
9	....	76.0	12	95	3v	Two miles below Constan Bay.
10	....	76.0	12	92	3v	Near Aylmer Light.

TABLE 8.

CHEMICAL ANALYSES OF SAMPLES OF WATER FROM LAKE DESCHENES, OTTAWA RIVER,

July 14, 1911.

Laboratory No.	4,404	4,403
Locality	Below Quio.	At C.P.R. Bridge.
	Parts per Million.	
Turbidity	3	5
Color	80	78
Odor	0	Very faint vegetable.
Nitrogen as alb. Ammonia	0.162	0.154
Nitrogen as free ammonia	0.034	0.022
Nitrogen as nitrites	0.002	0.002
Nitrogen as nitrates	0.10	0.12
Oxygen consumed	8.70	9.80
Total residue	65.00	65.00
Loss on ignition	25.00	32.00
Fixed residue	40.00	33.00
Iron	0.40	0.40
Total hardness	18.00	18.00
Alkalinity	16.50	17.50
Incrustants	1.50	0.50
Chlorine	0.40	0.80

TABLE 9.

OTTAWA, CANADA.

ESULTS OF MICROSCOPICAL EXAMINATION OF SAMPLES OF WATER FROM LAKE DESCHENES, OTTAWA RIVER, JULY 14, 1911.

	1	2	2	3'	4	4	5	6	7	8	9	10
tation Number	1	2	2	3'	4	4	5	6	7	8	9	10
epth in feet	0	0	30	0	0	20	0	0	0	0	0	0
abellaria	2	....	....	....	6	10	12	4	2	4	2	....
elosira	22	8	18	30	15	17	12	....	....	14	20	12
sterionella	8	....	....	....	4	7	4	....	....	....	....	3
yclotella	....	....	3	....	....	....	2	....	....	....	....	....
ynedra	....	....	....	....	30	....	10	4	5	2	....	....
rotococcus	....	....	....	....	2	....	....	....	....	2	....	....
losterium	....	....	....	....	....	....	....	....	....	....	3	....
andorina	....	....	....	....	....	....	....	....	....	....	....	5
ictycsphaerium	....	....	....	....	....	....	....	....	....	....	....	5
phanizomenon	....	....	....	....	....	....	....	....	3	....	....	....
odonella	5	....	....	....	....	5	....	....	....	....	....	....
ryptomonas	....	2	....	....	3	1	....	3	....	3	....	2
ctinophrys	....	....	5	....	....	....	....	....	....	....	....	....
orticella	....	....	....	....	10	....	7	....	....	....	....	....
iliata	....	....	....	....	....	....	....	5	....	....	....	....
inobryon	....	....	....	....	....	....	....	....	....	15	....	....
olyarthra	10	10	....	....	....	10	....	25	20	10	5	10
otifer	....	....	....	....	10	....	....	....	....	....	....	....
nuraea	....	....	....	....	....	....	....	....	....	....	10	....
auplius	....	....	....	....	....	10	....	....	....	....	....	....
Total Organisms	47	20	26	50	60	62	45	41	32	48	40	37
Amorphous Matter	250	100	120	150	150	200	150	100	120	100	120	150

TABLE 10.

CHEMICAL ANALYSES OF SAMPLES OF WATER FROM GATINEAU RIVER, ONTARIO.

July 15, 1911.

Laboratory No. 4402.
Locality, below Wright Bridge.

	Parts per million.
Turbidity	5
Color	67
Odor	0
Nitrogen as alb. ammonia	0.126
Nitrogen as free ammonia	0.026
Nitrogen as nitrites	0.002
Nitrogen as nitrates	0.08
Oxygen consumed	7.40
Total residue	76,00
Loss on ignition	26.00
Fixed residue	50.00
Iron	0.30
Total hardness	15.50
Alkalinity	15.50
Incrustants	0.0
Chlorine	0.40

TABLE 11.

OTTAWA, CANADA.

RESULTS OF MICROSCOPICAL EXAMINATION OF SAMPLES OF WATER FROM GATINEAU RIVER, ONTARIO.

Asterionella	16
Melosira	2
Synedra	4
Monas	2

OTTAWA WATER WORKS.

MEMORANDA AS TO DECOLORIZATION OF WATER BY G. C. W., REFLECTING RECENT
EXPERIENCE.

[Abstract of certain literature regarding decolorization and red water toubles, by
L. N. B., October, 1911.]

DECOLORIZATION OF WATER.

Up to the present time no satisfactory method of removing the peaty color
from water, without the application of chemicals, has been found. Many experiments have been made with this end in view, but the results have not been successful. The color may be reduced in amount by sand filtration, but never wholly
removed.

Decolorization not Effected by Sand Filtration.

The color of water is due, in part, to dissolved humus compound derived from
vegetation, peat, etc., and in part from similar substances in the colloidal state or
in suspension. The suspended matter and a portion, if not all, of the colloidal
matter, can be removed by filtering the water through sand. The amount removed
is dependent upon the fineness of the filtering material and the rate of filtration.
According to the best information now available, that portion of the coloring matter
which is dissolved in the water cannot be removed in this way. For example,
some years ago I made the experiment of filtering colored water through a Pasteur
filter, one of the closest straining mediums known. This removed from one quarter
to one third of the total coloring matter, but the water once filtered could not be
further decolorized by passing it through a similar filter several times. In other
words, the dissolved coloring matter could not be strained out.

During the years 1890-1893, experiments on filtration were made at Chestnut
Hill Laboratory for the Boston Water Department. These experiments showed
that sand filteration alone would not completely decolorize the Boston water, which,
as I remember it, then had a color that varied from 35 to 50. There, also, from one
quarter to one third of the coloring matter could be removed by sand filtration,
but that was all.

In 1904 some experiments were made at Springfield, Mass. by E. E.
Lochridge. A dark-colored water from Borden Brook was first filtered through
mechanical filters at a high rate without using coagulant, and the effluent from these
filters was applied to experimental sand filters at varying rates. The mechanical
filter took out only 8 per cent. of the color. The sand filter removed from 20 per
cent. to 40 per cent., according to the rate used. When the rate of filtration was
that commonly used for insuring satisfactory bacterial purification, *i.e.,* 4 to 6
million gallons per acre daily, the decolorization was from 20 per cent to 25 per
cent.

Under certain conditions sand filtration will remove color to a greater extent
than the figures given above, viz., in the case of waters that have been stored in
reservoirs and have taken up a considerable amount of iron. This occurs in the
stagnant bottom water of deep reservoirs and also in shallow reservoirs where the
amount of organic matter is very large and where the breaking down of the coloring matter may be partially brought about through the agency of bacteria and

ther organisms that grow in the water. For example, in Lake Cochituate, one of he sources of the Boston water supply, the bottom water is stagnant during the ummer and becomes charged with iron. In the fall this bottom water is mixed ,ith the water in the upper layers and a natural decolorization of the top water 'esults. This is brought about by a coagulation of the iron compounds taken into ,olution at the bottom. At Springfield it was found that the filtration of the ,udlow reservoir water by mechanical filters and sand filters resulted in a removal ,f 60 per cent. to 72 per cent. of the color. No chemicals were used, but in this ,ase there was, in the same way, a sort of natural coagulation of the water by the ,ron present.

SUMMARY OF RESULTS OF DECOLORIZATION OF WATER BY FILTRATION.

From Reports of Experiments at Springfield, Mass., made by E.E. Lochridge for Samuel M. Gray and George W. Fuller. Report of Special Commission, March 28, 1904.)

LUDLOW RESERVOIR WATER.	Color.	Per cent. of Removal.
,ugust, 1903.		
Raw water	40	
Effluent of mechanical filters, used without coagulant—		
Rate 120 million gallons per acre daily............................	34	15
Rate 60 " " " " "	33	18
Rate 30 " " " " "	31	22
Effluent of sand filters, treating water of color of 33 that had passed through mechanical filters—		
Rate 10 million gallons per acre daily............................	16	60
Rate 6.5 " " " " "	11	72
Rate 3 " " " " "	11	72
September, 1903.		
Raw water	44	
Effluent of mechanical filters, used without coagulant—		
Rate 120 million gallons per acre daily............................	38	14
Rate 60 " " " " "	37	16
Effluent of sand filters, treating water of color of 37 that had passed through mechanical filters—		
Rate 10 million gallons per acre daily............................	18	59
Rate 6.5 " " " " "	12	73
Rate 3 " " " " "	8	82
BROAD BROOK. BELCHERTOWN.		
August and September, 1903.		
Raw water	125	
Effluent of mechanical filters, used without coagulant—		
Rate 60 million gallons per acre daily............................	115	8
Effluent of sand filters, treating effluent of mechanical filter—		
Rate 6 million gallons per acre daily............................	99	20.8
Rate 4 " " " " "	93	25.6
Rate 2 " " " " "	88	39.6

These are exceptions that prove the rule that sand filtration alone will not decolorize water, for in these cases the reaction is really a chemical one.

There are only a few instances on record where sand filters have been used for purifying colored waters. One instance is that of the filter at Albany, N.Y., which treats the water of the Hudson River. This water is badly polluted with sewage, is more or less turbid, and at certain times of the year, especially in the fall, is rather high colored. Filtration makes the water satisfactory from a sanitary standpoint, but fails to remove all the color. The water used in the city still has a noticeable color and is the subject of more or less disapproval on the part of the consumers. Strangers who visit the city, seeing the dark color of the water, get the idea that it is not a safe water for general use.

The following table gives a summary of the color tests that have been published in the Albany reports. The reports for 1903 to 1908 do not state the results of the color determinations. From the figures given it is seen that during the year ending Sept. 30, 1909, the average color of the filtered water was 23 and the maximum 40, the latter being 174 per cent. of the former. The color of the raw water this year was lower than usual. If the average color of the raw water is taken as 32 and that of the filtered water as 26, the maximum color of the filtered water would probably be between 45 and 50.

ALBANY N.Y.
SUMMARY OF COLOR TESTS.

Average for Year ending	Raw Water.	Filtered Water.	Per cent. Removed.
September 30, 1900	34	27	23
September 30, 1901	34	30	12
September 30, 1902	30	24	20
September 30, 1909	29	23	23

Week Ending	Raw Water.	Filtered Water.	Week Ending	Raw Water.	Filtered Water.
Oct. 3, 1908.......	35	25	April 3, 1909......	25	20
" 10, "	35	25	" 10, "	25	20
" 17, "	30	25	" 17, "	30	20
" 24, "	30	25	" 24, "	25	20
" 31, "	35	25			
			May 1, "	25	20
Nov. 7, "	40	30	" 8, "	40	20
" 14, "	40	30	" 15, "	30	20
" 21, "	35	30	" 22, "	35	25
" 28, "	35	30	" 29, "	30	20
Dec. 5, "	40	30	June 5. "	30	15
" 12, "	35	35	" 12, "	25	15
" 19, "	35	30	" 19, "	30	20
" 26, "	30	25	" 26, "	25	20
Jan. 2, 1909.......	30	25	July 3, "	25	20
" 9, "	30	30	" 10, "	30	20
" 16, "	35	30	" 17, "	30	20
" 23, "	35	30	" 24, "	30	25
" 30, "	25	20	" 31, "	30	25
Feb. 6, "	30	25	Aug. 7, "	25	25
" 13, "	30	25	" 14, "	25	20
" 20, "	30	25	" 21, "	25	20
" 27, "	30	25	" 28, "	25	20
Mar. 6, "	25	20	Sept. 4, "	40	35
" 13, "	25	20	" 11, "	55	30
" 20, "	25	20	" 18, "	45	35
" 27, "	25	20	" 25, "	50	40

Springfield, Mass., is another instance where sand filtration is used for purifying a dark-colored water, but here the water is coagulated and allowed to settle in a sedimentation basin before it is applied to the filter. Furthermore, the color is not high at all seasons of the year and it is not expected that alum will be continuously used.

Minneapolis, Minn., is supplied with Mississippi River water, which is rather dark-colored. A few years ago sand filtration with preliminary chemical treatment was recommended. This plan was not adopted. More recently, the city decided to adopt mechanical filtration and a plant of this character is now under construction.

Sand filters have been used almost invariably with relatively light-colored waters. This is true not only of this country, but abroad.

Decolorization through the Use of Chemicals.

Various chemicals have been used for decolorizing water. The most successful results have been obtained by the use of sulphate of alumina, or alum. Potassium permanganate has also been used as well as various compounds of iron. In all cases the decolorization appears to be effected by coagulation. Attempts to destroy the coloring matter by oxidation, using ozone, bleaching powder, etc., have not been successful, as the quantities of chemical required are enormous.

There are many instances where high-colored, peaty waters are used for public water supply, but such water sooner or later is objected to by the consumer and the supply is either abandoned or mechanical filtration adopted. In some cases the attempt has been made to reduce the color of the water by draining swamps, etc. This is a measure that is obviously applicable only to small drainage areas.

Mechanical filters have been long used for decolorizing water, and with marked success. Among these may be mentioned the water supplies of Watertown, N.Y., Wilmington, N.C., Athol, Mass. These places I mentioned because we have data for them in our office files. Others might be listed, and a few others are referred to below.

Filtration of the Ottawa River.

The Ottawa River water cannot be decolorized by sand filtration alone. This water passes through a large lake before it reaches the city, where sedimentation and storage have an important beneficial effect on the sanitary quality of the water. The coloring matter in the water at Ottawa is probably almost entirely in solution and there is no reason to believe that sand filtration would reduce this color by more than 20 per cent. or 25 per cent. With the color of the river water above 80 it is probable that the effluent of a sand filter would have a color above 60. Water of this color is far too high to be generally acceptable and, as the standard of purity is constantly rising in the public mind, a water of this color would certainly not be regarded as clean. Visitors to the city especially would notice this uncleanness. The matter is therefore one that touches civic pride. It seems certain that only by the use of chemicals can the Ottawa River water be decolorized. It would be possible to use chemical coagulation and sedimentation as a process preliminary to sand filtration, but the chemicals would have to be applied at all seasons and in large amounts, it would require artificial settling basins of great size and expense, so that altogether it would appear to be better practice to use the method of mechanical filtration with this water.

QUALITY OF BLACK RIVER WATER AND OTHER DARK-COLORED WATERS.

The following memorandum has been prepared in compliance with Mr. Hazen's request of Oct. 9, 1911.

QUALITY OF BLACK RIVER WATER, WATERTOWN, N.Y.

The water supply of Watertown is taken from the Black River. Above the pumping station the river has a catchment area of 1,600 square miles. The total population on the catchment area, according to the census of 1910, was 35,963, or 21.7 per square mile. Of this 8.3 per square mile may be classed as urban and village and the difference, 13.4, as rural. The settlements on the river, nearest to the waterworks intake, are as follows:

	Distance above Watertown in miles.	Population.
Black River...................	6	916
West Carthage................	19	1,393
Carthage.....................	20	3,563
Copenhagen	32	585
Lowville.....................	38	2,940

The river receives the sewage, directly or indirectly, from these various communities and at Watertown the analysis of the water shows it to be considerably polluted. The river also receives substantial amounts of pollution from the paper mills. This consists of spent sulphite liquors, wood pulp, etc.

Table 1 shows the average character of the water by years since 1905. The average color during this period was 67. The highest monthly mean was 106 in June, 1911. The lowest monthly mean was 42 in March, 1906.

The quality of the river water is subject to rapid fluctuations in color, alkalinity and number of bacteria. The analyses made at different hours during the day often show marked differences in results.

The effect of filtration on the general quality of the water is shown by the figures in the second part of Table No. 1. The effect on the sanitary quality of the water is shown in detail by Table No. 2, which gives the results of bacteriological examinations of raw and filtered water.

TABLE I.

WATERTOWN, N Y.

SUMMARY OF ANALYSES, SHOWING THE CHARACTER OF THE BLACK RIVER WATER BEFORE FILTRATION.

Year.	Turbidity.	Color.	Nitrogen as		Hardness of samples analyzed in full.	Average alkalinity of daily samples.	Iron.	Microscopic organisms per cc.	Bacteria per cc.
			Albuminoid Ammonia.	Free Ammonia.					
905.........	9	69	.160	.020	34.9	39.0	0.8	57	2,453
906.........	11	62	.198	.025	36.4	39.0	0.9	7	8,003
907.........	11	69	.184	.031	32.0	28.0	1.0	73	22,541
908.........	8	65	.153	.018	32.5	31.0	0.6	54	12,082
909.........	9	67	.153	.021	33.6	30.0	0.5	14	7,463
910.........	6	70	.135	.014	36.5	28.0	0.5	125	20,984

BLACK RIVER WATER AFTER FILTRATION.

Year.	Turbidity.	Color.	Albuminoid Ammonia.	Free Ammonia.	Hardness of samples analyzed in full.	Average alkalinity of daily samples.	Iron.	Microscopic organisms per cc.	Bacteria per cc.
905.........	0	10	.069	.016	36.2	19.0	0.08	5	133
906.........	0	9	.081	.014	38.2	22.0	0.14	0	162
907.........	0	6	.087	.018	32.2	12.0	0.25	0	572
908.........	0	7	.063	.015	37.2	14.0	0.07	0	491
909.........	0	8	.080	.013	33.6	12.0	0.08	0	311
910.........	0	12	.056	.009	37.2	10.0	0.05	0	514

TABLE 2.

SUMMARY OF DAILY BACTERIOLOGICAL EXAMINATION OF THE RAW, FILTERED AND DISINFECTED WATER AT WATERTOWN, N.Y.

Month. 1911.	Number of Bacteria per cc.				Per cent. of Bacteria Removed. as shown by			Average quantity of Alum used. lbs. per million gallons.
	Raw Water.	Coagula- ted Water.	Filter Effluent.	Disin- fected Effluent.	Coagula- ted Water.	Filter Effluent.	Disin- fected Effluent.	

Based on Counts on Gelatine.

Month	Raw Water	Coagulated Water	Filter Effluent	Disinfected Effluent	Coagulated Water %	Filter Effluent %	Disinfected Effluent %	Alum
January.....	23,800	1,091	597	....	95.4	97.5	....	361
February....	19,955	1,834	666	....	91.1	96.6	....	360
March	100,930	10,087	1,763	*831	90.2	98.3	99.2	356
April	48,133	4,744	534	61	90.1	98.8	99.9	345
May	5,873	829	93	10	85.9	98.4	99.8	299
June	4,830	514	109	32	89.4	97.8	99.3	361
July	9,008	949	240	46	89.5	97.4	99.5	385
August......	2,380	592	148	19	75.2	93.8	99.2	384
September ..	1.127	159	55	9	85.9	95.2	99.2	354
October								
November ...								
December ...								
Av. Jan.-Sep.	24,004	2,311	473	29	88.1	97.0	99.4	356
Av. Year....								

Month	Raw Water	Coagulated Water	Filter Effluent	Disinfected Effluent	Coagulated Water %	Filter Effluent %	Disinfected Effluent %	Raw Water	Filter Effluent†
	Based on Agar Counts at 37° C.							Per cent. of Positive Tests for B. coli in one cc.	
January.....	119	8	2	....	93.4	98.3	....	60	11
February....	102	9	2	....	91.2	98.2	....	74	11
March	217	30	8	6	86.3	96.4	98.2	87	0
April	129	30	7	3	76.6	94.6	98.4	57	3
May	211	47	7	1	77.8	93.9	99.7	81	0
June	178	40	11	2	77.6	93.9	98.2	66	3
July	167	32	19	2	80.9	88.7	99.0	100	7
August......	334	50	14	2	85.1	94.3	99.4	97	6
September ..	910	87	28	2	91.5	97.0	99.8	88	8
October									
November ...									
December ...									
Av. Jan.-Sep.	263	37	11	2.6	84.5	95.0	98.9	79	5
Av. Year....									

* Omitted from average.
† Effluent disinfected after March 15th.

TABLE 3.

WATERTOWN, NY.

Summary of tests for B. coli in the raw and filtered water.

| | Per cent. of Samples that gave positive tests for B. coli. | | | | | |
| | Raw Water. | | | Filtered Water; | | |
1910	0.1 cc.	1.0 cc.	10 cc.	0.1 cc.	1.0 cc.	10 cc.
rch....................................	18	61	97	0	0	26
ril.....................................	....	74	....	....	0	....
y.......................................	....	74	100	....	0	9
ne	....	93	100	....	0	16
ly......................................	....	90	93	....	9	5/
gust	....	87	97	....	3	13
ptember...............................	....	100	100	....	0	12
tober...................................	....	97	100	....	3	26
vember	....	96	100	....	0	14
cember.................................	....	80	89	....	5	71
Average..........................	18	85.2	97.4	....	2.0	27.1
1911						
nuary	....	60	88	....	11	....
bruary.................................	....	74	....	....	11	....
rch.....................................	....	87	100	....	0	75
ril......................................	28	57	97	....	3	33
y.......................................	....	81	96	....	0	8
ne	45	66	89	0	3	22
ly......................................	74	100	100	....	7	29
gust	48	97	100	....	6	40
ptember................................	61	85	100	....	8	25
tober...................................	....	....	....	....	....	....
vember	....	....	....	....	....	....
cember	....	....	....	....	....	....
Average..........................	51.2	78.5	96.3	0	5.4	33.2

Remark:

Since March, 1911, the effluent has been disinfected with calcium hypochlorite. Before that date, this chemical was applied to the raw water.

From the above figures, it is estimated that in 1910 the raw water contained, on an average, 2.47 B. coli per c.c. and the filtered water, 0.045 per c.c. The filtered water therefore contained 1.8 per cent. of the number of B. coli found in the raw water. Between Jan. and Sept., 1911, the average number of B. coli in the raw water is estimated to be 5.39 and in the filtered water, 0.072. The number of B. coli in the filtered water was therefore 1.34 per cent. of that in the raw water.

Ogdensburg, N.Y.

The city is now supplied with water from the Osweegatchie River. This water resembles in character that of the Black River at Watertown, but is probably somewhat more highly colored. Comparatively few analyses of this water have been made by us. Samples collected on June 1, 1908 give the following analyses:

Turbidity	3	3	3
Color	84	80	80
Odor	1v	1v	1v
Nitrogen as albuminoid ammonia	.230	.244	.246
Nitrogen as free ammonia	.072	.076	.096
Harkness	36.5	36.5	35.0
Alkalinity	35.0	35.0	34.0
Iron	0.6	0.6	0.6

A new supply is being constructed for this city, taken from the St. Lawrence River and filtered. As soon as this is in operation the Osweegatchie water will be abandoned.

Wilmington, N.C.

The city is supplied with water from the Cape Fear River, filtered by mechanical filtration. The water is very dark-colored, as is shown by the following analyses:

—	1905 May 25	1906 Nov. 6
Turbidity	7	14
Color	160	240
Odor	2v	2v
Nitrogen as albuminoid ammonia	.118	.332
Nitrogen as free ammonia	.092	.032
Hardness	95.0	19.5
Alkalinity	105.0	10.5
Iron	2.0	....
Microscopic organisms	156	....

This water is successfully decolorized. Alum is used as the coagulant. A test of this filter is shortly to be made by M. C. Whipple.

Athol, Mass.

The water at Athol, Mass. is obtained largely from the Phillipston Reservoir, filtered by mechanical filtration. This is a very deep-colored water, as is shown by the following analyses, made on July 3 and October 16, 1905.

—	1905 July 3.	1905 Oct. 16.
Turbidity	2	1
Color	90	96
Odor	3v	3v
Nitrogen as albuminoid ammonia	.152	.160
Nitrogen as free ammonia	.060	.030
Hardness	12.5	12.0
Alkalinity	5.5	6.0
Iron	0.25	0.2
Microscopic organisms	132	88

The filter used here is a mechanical filter of the pressure type. This is now old and is too small for the service. The apparatus for applying the alum is very crude. In spite of this, a satisfactory decolorization of the water is obtained most of the time. There is, however, a good deal of trouble from rusty water in the hot water services.

Bangor, Me.

The city of Bangor takes its water from the Penobscot River. It is filtered by mechanical filter. The water is at times very highly colored. On Feb. 27, 1905, an analysis of this water was made in our laboratory, with the following results:

Turbidity	6
Color	65
Hardness	19.5
Alkalinity	17
Chlorine	1

The Engineering Record, Vol. 62, page 740, gives the following average figures for the turbidity, color and alkalinity of the Penobscot River water between March, 1909 and February, 1910. The analyses are made by Mr. Caird. The color varied from 53 to 107 and averaged 71. The alkalinity varied from 6.2 to 11.0 and averaged 8.8. The turbidity averaged 2.4. Bacterial results are not given.

Ottawa Canada.

Ottawa now takes its supply from the Ottawa River, unfiltered. The following analyses show the quality of the water on July 14, 1911.

Turbidity	3	5
Color	80	78
Odor	0	very faint vegetable
Nitrogen as albuminoid ammonia	0.162	0.154
Nitrogen as free ammonia	0.034	0.022
Nitrogen as nitrites	0.002	0.002
Nitrogen as nitrates	0.10	0.12
Oxygen consumed	8.70	9.80
Total residue	65.00	65.00
Loss on ignition	25.00	32.00
Fixed residue	40.00	33.00
Iron	0.40	0.40
Total hardness	18.00	18.00
Alkalinity	16.50	17.50
Incrustants	1.50	0.50
Chlorine	0.40	0.80

East Providence, R.I.

The supply of East Providence, R.I. is taken from a small stream that at times has a high color. In the Engineering News, Vol. XLVI, p. 434, are given the results of analyses made between April 11 and November 4, 1904. During this period the color of the raw water ranged from 29 to 95 and averaged 55. The color of the filtered water ranged from 0 to 23 and averaged 6. During this time the amount of alum used varied from 0.75 to 1.0 grains per gallon.

WATERTOWN, N.Y.

Relation between the Color of Raw Water and the Quantity of Alum Required.

The following figures show the relation between the color of the raw water and the quantity of alum required to obtain satisfactory decolorizations during the years 1905 and 1910. The figures were obtained as follows: The daily records were gone over and classified into those where the decolorization was satisfactory and those where it was not. Decolorization was considered satisfactory whenever the color was less than 10, the raw water being less than 50; less than 12, when the color of the raw water was between 50 and 75; less than 15, when the color of the raw water was between 75 and 100; and less than 20, when the color of the raw water was more than 100. Taking first the days on which decolorization was satisfactory, the observations were plotted with the color of the raw water as abscissae and the number of pounds per million gallons of alum as ordinates. Maximum and minimum lines were then drawn to mark the boundaries of an area which includes most of these points. A similar plot was then made for the days when the color removal was not satisfactory and the limits obtained. The second plot was then superposed on the first and it was found that the two areas overlapped. A line drawn through the overlapping areas was taken to represent the best value for the amount of alum required for decolorization. The figures in the following table were taken from this line.

WATERTOWN, N.Y.

TABLE SHOWING RELATION BETWEEN THE COLOR OF THE RAW WATER AND THE QUANTITY OF ALUM REQUIRED FOR SATISFACTORY DECOLORIZATION.

Color.	Quantity of Alum in Pounds.			
	Per Million Gallons.		Per Million Gallons for each Unit of Color.	
	1905	1910	1905	1910
50	210	285	4.20	5.70
60	250	305	4.17	5.08
70	280	325	4.00	4.64
80	320	340	4.00	4.25
90	350	360	3.89	4.32
100	390	380	3.90	3.80

It is evident, from the figures given, that when the color of the water is relatively low the amount of alum required to bring about decolorization is greater now than it was five years ago. When the color of the water is high no more alum is now required than was formerly used.

October 10, 1911.

MEMORANDA REGARDING THE DECOLORIZATION OF WATER, RED WATER TROUBLES, ETC.

[Abstract of papers on these subjects. L. N. B.]

Paper by G. C. Whipple; Decolorization of Water; Am. Soc, Vol 46, p. 141 and informal discussions:

The coloring matter in surface waters is in solution and is derived from decayed vegetable matter. Iron also increases color, and under certain conditions, particularly in ground water, and also plays an important part in the hue. Discusses the variations in hue and their causes; and also takes up method of measuring color.

Surface waters vary from 0 to 500 and even 1,000, the latter colors being found in swampy and stagnant waters. Color depends upon character of water-shed. In New England many surface waters have a color of 50, and some large rivers often have color of 100. The greatest amount of color is in autumn.

Water in lakes where there is long storage goes through a natural process of decolorization, by dilution, by precipitation, and by the bleaching action of the sunlight, this latter being the most important factor on waters of long storage.

Color is not injurious to health, but is considered from an æsthetic standpoint. A color of 30 is about the permissible limit for a domestic water supply.

Mr. Whipple considers four methods of decolorization;

(1) Removal of organic matter by drainage of swamps.
(2) Reduction in color without chemicals.
(3) Decolorization by chemicals, followed by filtration.
(4) Decolorization by chemicals alone.

Discussing first method, cites cost of work of drainage done by Metropolitan Water Board of Boston, at $44 per acre, or less than $9 per mil. gals storage.

Second method, sand filtration reduces color slight by taking out organic matter in suspension. There is also a slight decolorization due to the fact that the aluminum compounds generally found in the sand unite with the coloring matter. Water filtered through charcoal may be completely decolorized.

Third method; water must be changed chemically before an appreciable amount of color can be removed, and sulphate of alumina is mostly used to accomplish this. There must be enough carbonates in the water to decompose the sulphate of alumina, or the latter will remain in the water. With some waters the hardness must be increased artificially, and that is not always an economical or wise procedure. With a water both colored and turbid the problem is more complicated, as some of the sulphate of alumina is obsorbed by the suspended matter and has little coagulating effect. Temperature has an effect on the amount of sulphate of alumina necessary to decolorize, a cold water being harder to treat.

Other chemicals are used as coagulants, but they have no advantage over sulphate of alumina.

Fourth method; decolorization by chemicals alone. Ozone, hypochlorite, etc. have been tried, but in general results have not been promising.

Mr. Hazen stated that color did not affect the wholesomeness of water nor in general its mechanical uses. He divided the chemical processes of decolorization into two classes, (1) decolorization by precipitation and (2) decolorization by oxidation. The first process is the only successful one so far, the latter process, although experimental, offers reasonable promise.

Dr. Soper stated that the constitution of coloring matter had not been fully followed up and might be with advantage, and also that the oxidation process should be taken up further. He then discusses the Ozone process at length.

G. W. Fuller stated that in years to come preference for colorless waters would be so pronounced that decolorization would be insisted upon. Discussed the amount of sulphate of alumina used. In general from 2.0 to 2.5 grains per gallon for a color of 100. Speaks of highly colored water from deep wells in New Orleans.

Mr. Maignen: This coloring matter is not in solutions. Speaks of sulphate of alumina as expensive and unsatisfactory; then goes into the subject of filtration by charcoal and asbestos.

F. P. Stearns stated of the results accomplished by draining swamps at Boston; believes that long storage and thorough drainage will make Boston waters practically colorless.

Desmond Fitzgerald: Water should be stored two years to lose all its color. No decolorization in winter, but heat alone does not reduce color. Bacteria probably have no effect on reduction of color.

F. H. Dunham thinks that where the process is artificial, bacteria play a part in decolorization; cites spring water.

PURIFICATION OF WATER IN AMERICA: A. H., TRANS. AM. SOC. C. E., 1904, VOL. 54, PART D; P. 131.

Development in design of mechanical filters. These have been made with reference to the time allowed for chemical reaction. In early filters complete coagulation was seldom accomplished. Also the relations between the amount of coagulant which can be used and the alkalinity of the water have been ascertained. Larger settling basins are used and satisfactory results are gotten with smaller amounts of chemicals than were first used. Double coagulation in some cases has proven beneficial, particularly with turbid waters.

Improvements in mechanical filter construction have been made along the lines of masonry beds and mechanical agitation by means of air, and improvements in methods of washing. The control of mechanical filters differs from that of sand, and controllers have been developed to meet the required conditions perfectly. Important improvements have also been made in the method of controlling the coagulant applied to the raw water. Also improvements have been made in construction tending to prevent contamination of water after filtration, and in general the results obtained, as shown by the efficiencies of mechanical filters, have been as good as with sand filters.

The Filtration of Public Water Supplies: A. H., page 117.

Peaty coloring matter is almost perfectly in solution, and only a portion of it is capable of being removed by simple filtration. Ordinary sands have no absorptive power for color, and only 1-4 to 1-3 is removed. For better results coagulant must be used.

Pages 153-154: Experiments indicate that 80 to 90 per cent of color may be removed with the use of about 2 grains per gallon for waters having a color of 1.00 (100). With less than this decolorization is not effected, and with larger quantities of coagulant all the color is not removed.

The amount of coagulant which can be added depends upon the alkalinity. In general, with sulphate of alumina containing 17 per cent. aluminum oxide, the amount which can be applied in grains per gallon is slightly less than the alkalinity expressed in parts per 100,000 of calcium carbonate.

Clean Water and How to Get it: A. H., p. 97.

Color is not ordinarily removed to any considerable extent by simple filtration, through either sand or mechanical filters. Color is destroyed slightly by the bleaching action of sunlight in large reservoirs. Also by Ozone, but the cost of this process is high. Color is capable of being removed by certain coagulants. Mentions Charleston and Watertown as successfully decolorized river water with alum. Also Quincy, by lime, instead of sulphate of alumina, but the results are less satisfactory.

With some river waters with more or less color filtration without coagulant sometimes reduces the color 25 per cent. Speaks of Putrefaction of shallow waters in assisting in the removal of color, also the removal of color by iron. Also on page 27, if there were no other ways of reducing color, bleaching in reservoirs and draining of swamps would be worthy of most careful attention and frequent use. But at the present time other methods of removing color are known which usually accomplish more for a given expenditure than can be reached in these ways.

Removal of Color, Organisms and Odor from Waters: Clark; N.E.W.W. Assn, 1093, p. 1.

Speaks of experiments at Lawrence, where for seven years, 1893-1900, an experimental filter was operated, having a depth of sand of 5 feet, reducing during that time to 2½ feet. The rate of filtration during that time was 2½ to 3 mil. gals. per acre daily, and the raw Merrimac River water was reduced in color approximately 33 per cent., although the percentage of removal varied greatly during different seasons. In 1899 the river was highly colored by the addition of peat, hay, etc. and filtered slowly through a sand filter. The amount of color in the effluent was less than with the water before the color was added. The results indicated that the color was more easily acted upon if the water was in a state of fermentation due to hot weather. The color was more easily removed if the organic matter was low. Also the more nearly the dissolved oxygen was exhausted, the more complete the color removal if the water was aerated just before filtering. The amount of reduction with the low rates was from 80 to 70 per cent.

Later Ludlow water was experimented with for a year. The color varied from 40 to 86. Three filters were operated at rates of 5½, 5 and 10 million gallons per acre daily. The first two rates reduced from 17 per cent. to over 60 per cent. at times, the latter high removals being due to high temperature of the water, scarcity of free oxygen and increased bacterial oxidation. With the 10 million rate a reduction of 75 per cent. was often obtained. And quotes:

"That is to say, sand filtration, unaided by chemicals, both at Lawrence and Springfield, removed approximately 75 per cent. of the coloring matter of highly colored waters when this organic coloring matter was taken from vegetable matter and when it was in a state of unstable equilibrium so to speak. With the organic matter in the water in a more stable condition, however, as is the case with the Merrimac River water when it is most highly colored, only from 20 to 35 per cent. of the coloring matter can be removed by sand filtration."

PAPER BY G. C. WHIPPLE, " HOT WATER TROUBLES," READ BEFORE THE AMERICAN WATER WORKS ASSOCIATION, ROCHESTER, JUNE 8, 1911.

Hot water troubles are not of a hygienic character but are physical. They are largely problems of corrosion, and are sometimes serious. On an average half the water used in the household is heated.

The paper discusses the methods of heating and systems of circulation, which are, the pressure system, the tank system; the dead-end distribution and the circulation distribution. In small houses pressure or tank system and dead end circulation is used; in apartment houses, pressure system and circulation distribution. Also discusses supplies for high buildings.

The materials of construction generally used for heating are generally cast iron. Boilers, etc., are generally steel or wrought iron; generally distribution system is best brass with some waters. Wrought iron or steel pipes are cheaper and generally as satisfactory. Other metals are sometimes used.

Heated water has a decreased oxygen content and with surface water the color and sometimes the turbidity is increased on heating. Red water troubles are almost entirely due to corrosion. Sometimes, with excessive use of alum, there is corrosion, and in this case both hot and cold water pipes are attacked alike.

Mr. Whipple then goes into the theory of corrosion and formation of iron rust. Corrosion is due to the presence of electrically charged atoms of hydrogen and dissolved oxygen. These are always present in acid waters. The iron is dissolved in a ferrous condition and attacked by the oxygen and iron rust is formed, sometimes precipitating and sometimes not, according to whether the iron particles are electrically charged or not. All water is acid, more or less, and the hydrogen irons vary with the acidity. Alkalies decrease the irons and reduce the corroding power.

According to the electrolytic theory of corrosion, when a water contains these electrically charged atoms of hydrogen, the water becomes a conductor. The electricity goes into the metal, which gives up iron in solution. For a time the remaining hydrogen polarises the metal and the action is stopped. The hydrogen finally unites with the oxygen, the electrical action begins again and the corrosion is continued.   Other metals affect corrosion by their galvanic action, some hastening such as zinc and some retarding, namely copper.

With some of the soft ground waters of Long Island, high in both chlorine and dissolved carbonic acid rusty water has been observed.   Many waters along the Atlantic coast are high in chlorine and low in carbonates.   Some of these have red water troubles.   At Oswego the water is very hard and saline and there is considerable red water.

Soft colored waters have been found to be corrosive if high in dissolved carbonic acid.   Cites Croton waters as having some trouble.   In New England soft surface supplies have led to the abandonment of iron pipes.

Soft waters treated with normal amounts of alum.   Cites Springfield and Watertown.   In the latter there is slight increase in corrosive power, but this was further magnified on account of the clean condition of the water.   Before that more or less sediment has protected fixtures.   There has been considerable corrosion at times when the alum used was larger than normal and alkalinity low.   Cites Springfield at length, and lays their trouble to poor quality of galvanizing of pipes and tanks.   Also cites other instances of red water troubles with mechanical filters.

With waters overdosed with alum the corrosive power of the filtered water is greatly increased.   Cites Athol and Durham.   The use of hard water with alum causes no trouble; with soft waters there may be considerable.   With waters naturally charged with iron rusty water is common.

As to seasonal occurrence, fall and winter months seem to be worst, due probably to heating the water hotter.

Rusty water is not general throughout a supply system, but is local.   Generally it may be said that houses of more recent construction have suffered most from these troubles.

Cites his experiments which indicated soft waters more corrosive than hard.

Dissolved carbonic acid in the presence of carbonates of alkaline earth does not seem to have the same corrosive properties.

Organic acids probably play considerable part in corrosion, particularly if extractive matter is fresh.   In decolorization, the old matter is acted upon more rapidly, and with less chemical.   Acids increase the color; alkalies tend to reduce it.

Goes in at length into the action of sulphate of alumina, with hard waters and soft waters and results with normal, overdosed, and too little coagulant; mentions the alum compounds and cites conditions under which alum might get through filters.

The more rapid the circulation of water the greater the rusting, and the growing use of the circulating system may be the reason for increasing rusting water.

Generally with waters that have been softened there has not been rusty water troubles, as they contain normal amounts of carbonates after softening.

The character of the iron and steel pipe has an important influence upon rusty water.   Wrought iron is generally better than steel, but there are better grades of steel more satisfactory than poor wrought iron.   The character of galvanizing is also important, and this is a part of manufacture that is not up to standard.

The remedies for hot water troubles are to reduce the electrolysis, to get rid of the dissolved oxygen, and reduce the pressures, temperatures and circulation in the distribution systems.   With soft waters the solution is to use brass for the piping and some other metal besides iron and steel for boilers is advisable.   Care should be taken in the galvanizing.   The hardness of the water should be kept as high as possible without being objectionable to the consumer.   The use of alum with soft waters should be avoided.

CLARK AND GAGE: CORROSION OF PIPES BEFORE AND AFTER FILTRATION.

Investigation was taken up in 1910 to determine what effect various natural waters had on iron pipes, and also other metals used in plumbing fixtures.

The results showed that river water filtered by mechanical filters absorbed more iron than the same effluent from sand filters, and the raw river water absorbed least. Both pond and driven well water absorbed more than river.

In experiments with Merrimac River water and also a lake water, and made alkaline with lime, were slightly less corrosive than if soda ash were used. With lime treated water there was slight decrease in corrosiveness as the alkalinity increased.

The experiments included also the relative effection of hot and cold water on galvanized iron pipes. Mechanically filtered lake water was used with added lime, and the absorption of iron was very much greater with hot water than with cold. Varying the alkalinity, however, gave the cold water a greater increase in absorptive power than the hot. The protective coating of the galvanized piping prevented for a time at least the red water.

As to the effect on amount of dissolved oxygen, it was found that the corrosion was greater with water containing high oxygen than with low, the galvanized iron pipes being attacked less than plain iron.

Summary: Red water conditions have become common, but such troubles are generally of not long duration. The experiments indicate that " When soft waters are purified with coagulants and mechanical filters they have greater corrosive action upon iron than before such purification, and greater than the same supply when filtered through sand; but that increasing the hardness on the mechanically filtered water to a reasonable degree has little effect on preventing corrosion."

The results vary greatly, but show that hot water is more corrosive than cold. The Merrimac River is less corrosive than ground supplies. Distilled water from which the organic matter and mineral matter had been removed had very little corrosive action.

Reviews the literature on corrosion with reference to its effect on public health. Outside of lead pipes, corrosion is not supposed to be harmful. Also reviews theory of corrosion in the light of the literature, and the various factors that enter into corrosion and the red water problem. Also the prevention. Prevention has been attempted by protective coatings; by reducing the amount of galvanic action by changing the difference in potential between different metals; by changes in the character of the water as an electrolyte. These methods are discussed at length in the light of the present literature on the subjects.

RED WATER PLAGUE: EDITORIAL ENGINEERING RECORD, VOL. 60; P. 534.

In a number of cities where mechanical filters are used red water has been noticed. This has also happened where ground waters have been used, but particularly with alum treated waters. The worst cases are where the raw water is soft and dark colored. Many cases in the south, and some in New York State come under this class. The probable cause, although not exclusive, is the carbonic acid resulting from the reaction of the sulphate of alumina on the bicarbonates of lime and magnesium. The cold water does not seem to give trouble, but when this water is heated the corrosion appears. The carbonic acid does not disappear as the result of corrosion. but apparently it acts as an intermediary to bring about oxidation without itself being used up. The action is greatest in colored waters of low alkalinity and the reason for this has not yet been solved. It is not yet known whether the corrosion is due to carbonic acid wholly or to some other cause in the reaction. The chemical treatment of water is increasing, and there is also a growing tendency in some quarters to discourage its use. It is hoped that means will be found to prevent such nuisances as red water.

Mr. J. W. Ledoux, (page 701) in a letter, citing the Charleston, S.C. water, which is very soft and has a color as high as 150, thinks that this water in its raw state has corrosive action, but with the elimination of the organic matter by sulphate of alumina, the corrosive action largely disappears, unless an overdose of alum is used, when the corrosive effects appear again.

CORROSION OF HOT WATER PIPING IN BATH HOUSES: IRA H. WOOLSEN, ENG. NEWS, VOL. 64; P. 630.

Corrosion occurred in 1908 in hot water systems entirely new. Examined a great many pieces of pipe, both wrought iron and steel, and made experiments on them as to their relative susceptibility to corrosion. There seems to be no difference between steel and wrought iron.

Does not go into the causes of corrosion.

REPORT OF COMMISSION *RE* WATER SUPPLY FOR THE CITY OF OTTAWA.

To the Mayor and Members of the Council of the Corporation of the City of Ottawa.

GENTLEMEN,—The Commission on Water and Sewage beg to report as to the Water Supply of the City of Ottawa, and in doing so would refer to the instructions contained in a letter addressed to the Commission by Mr. Newton J. Ker, City Engineer, dated June 9th, 1911:

" What is required of the Commission is first to determine where the future supply of water for the City of Ottawa is to be obtained. If filtration is necessary, and the method of filtration, the quality of water supplied for consumption being the first consideration."

The following members of the Commission being a majority thereof, viz.. Allen Hazen, Chas. A. Hodgetts and J. W. S. McCullough, are agreed as follows:

We find the water of the Ottawa River, which is the present source of supply, to be polluted and unfit for a public supply either at the present intake or at any other point where the intake could reasonably be placed. We are of the opinion that the pollution will increase and not diminish.

The hypochlorite treatment now in use greatly improves the supply by destroying the bacteria. It does not remove the colour or other organic impurities. In other words, it disinfects but does not clean up the water as must be done in order to make it acceptable as a public water supply. For these reasons its use must be considered a temporary measure and not a permanent solution of the water problem.

No system of sand filtration, either simple or multiple, without chemical treatment, is capable of removing the colour and the excessive amount of organic matter in the Ottawa river water.

Such processes of filtration are successfully applied to many river waters, such as the Thames at London, the Elbe at Hamburg, the Hudson at Albany, and the Delaware at Philadelphia. None of these waters are as highly coloured as the

Ottawa River water, or carry as large amounts of dissolved organic matter.   It should be clearly understood that these processes, although well adapted to conditions in other localities, are not, in our judgment, applicable to the Ottawa River water.

The colour and excessive dissolved organic matter in the Ottawa River water may be removed by suitable chemical treatment followed by filtration. The water so obtained will be in general of good quality. This process is widely and successfully used in various American cities.

Water so treated will dissolve iron from the pipes and the iron will afterwards separate and give rise to complaints. This is known as the red water trouble. It is a serious and objectionable condition, difficult to overcome, when soft waters charged with dissolved organic matter are cleaned by chemical treatment.

The Gatineau River water is of the same general character as the Ottawa River water and offers no advantages over the latter to warrant the removal of the pumping plant to the opposite side of the river, which would necessitate carrying the delivery pipes under the Ottawa River.

The catchment basin of the Blanche River, located in the Province of Quebec, is capable of furnishing an abundant supply of the purest water. The water would be taken from a reservoir formed by a dam at the outlet of McGregor Lake, within fifteen miles of the City Hall.

The low water flow at the outlet of McGregor Lake is not sufficient to supply the present needs of the City, but there are large quantities of water flowing away during the spring floods, and there are excellent opportunities to hold back these flood flows and make them available in other and drier portions of the year.

On present information, over fifty million gallons of water per day can be obtained from this source with full storage of flood flows. This is capable of supplying one hundred gallons of water daily *per capita* to half a million people.

In addition to the catchment basin of the Blanche River, there are other large systems of lakes to the north.   These are higher in elevation.   In the future, when Ottawa becomes a large city, requiring more than fifty million gallons of water daily, the water from these lakes can be brought into the system of suitable tunnels and aqueducts.

The general method of supply that we recommend, consisting essentially of the storage of flood water from upland areas, is one widely used by cities having suitable areas in their neighborhood.   Among such cities may be mentioned Birmingham, Manchester, Edinburgh, Glasgow, Melbourne, Sydney, New York, Boston, Rochester, Syracuse, Denver, San Francisco, Vancouver, St. John (N.B.), Quebec, and Fort William.

It is seldom that conditions have been found so favorable for this system as those of the Blanche River catchment area.   The waters of the beautiful lakes in this district can easily be raised by inexpensive dams in narrow rocky outlets, thereby obtaining ideal storage at a low cost.   The whole supply for a year can thus be stored, and, if it were desired, two years' supply could easily be held.

The catchment area is rough and rocky, with a scattered rural population which is not likely to increase. Summer visitors are to be anticipated. These can be controlled, as is done in similar cases, so as not to impair the quality of the water.

The Blanche River supply, drawn through McGregor Lake, is high enough to serve the city by gravitation without pumping and will mantain a higher pressure than is now carried.

We believe that the advantages of the proposed gravity system are so great that we should prefer it, even if the cost were substantially greater, than that of filtered Ottawa river water. A greater cost, however, is not indicated by the estimates we have considered.

Upon present information, the cost of the Blanche River water will not exceed the cost of properly filtered Ottawa River water when both operating costs and the costs of construction are given due weight.

There will be no red water trouble with the Blanche River water.

The Blanche River water will not require filtration. It will be of better quality than the Ottawa River water, even after the latter is properly filtered.

Ottawa is the capital city of the Dominion of Canada, and should have the best water supply that can be obtained.

Should it be decided in future to make a Federal District of the Cities of Ottawa and Hull with their environs, residents of such Federal District would be assurred, if this plan were adopted, of a pure water supply, ample in quantity and collected and stored under the best and most approved conditions.

In conclusion, we recommend the catchment basin of the Blanche River as the best source of water supply for the City of Ottawa.

Mr. C. H. Keefer, a member of the Commission, dissents from the above, and is of the opinion that—

The most important question where the future supply is to be obtained depends on changes that may take place in future conditions and will be largely influenced, in my opinion, by the prospect of Ottawa becoming a Federal District, and by the construction of the Georgian Bay Canal, which means that Lake Deschene will be extended by the construction of a dam at the Little Chaudiere to within the city limits, creating at the same time an additional and new water power with a working head of 20 feet, and making Lake Deschene at Ottawa a splendid reservoir for the supply of water as well as power.

Mr. Hazen in his report, Part III., " Conclusions and Recommendations," has already stated that " The Ottawa River supply now in use is in many respects a magnificent supply."

The foregoing statements are made to emphasize the well known fact that the Ottawa River, the largest tributary of the St. Lawrence, is naturally a magnificent source of supply, and more particularly to emphasize my opinion that it cannot be abandoned in favour of any gravitation supply, without the fullest possible consideration and for the strongest possible reasons.

We have to choose between an at first sight attractive gravitation supply with a comparatively small catchment area (including areas which would have to be diverted from the catchment area of the Gatineau and Lievre Rivers) and the inexhaustible supply furnished by the Ottawa River.

Assuming the adoption of a gravitation supply, there are two things to do, to adopt the McGregor Lake supply, with the possible risk of a breakage or failure in the miles of conduit between the lakes and the city, as a sole source of supply, or to use both the McGregor Lake and the present Ottawa supply. The lake supply, being used for all purposes and the Ottawa supply maintained and used as at present protected by hypochlorite in case of failure of the lake supply, or as an additional fire service protection. This arrangement at present to me seems prohibitive.

For the above and following reasons I am of the opinion that the Ottawa

River, under present conditions and for many years to come, is the natural and best source of supply.

The quality of water in both the Ottawa River and McGregor Lake is originally the same, the lake water having the advantage of being bleached by sunlight and held longer by storage in the deeper lakes.

The color of the Ottawa River can be removed, as pointed out by Mr. Hazen, by mechanical filtration. Slow sand filtration, while more expensive in first cost of construction, has the advantage with many waters of accomplishing the same results, without chemicals, and at less than half the cost for operation.

The Ottawa water, technically designated colored, will probably not have much of its color removed by slow sand filtration, though it may probably lose 20 per cent., that is, become 20 per cent. clearer.

As far as reduction of bacteria is concerned, the results will probably be the same.

In England, where the longest practical experience has been obtained of filtration under most difficult conditions compared to Canada, slow sand filtration is the standard method. The same remarks apply to European filtration works.

If the Ottawa section of the Georgian Bay Canal should be commenced in the near future, and the dam at the Little Chaudiere constructed, the location for filter beds would be at a point below the dam, and for mechanical filters might be, as suggested by Mr. Hazen, on Lemieux Island, or more than sufficient provision for present requirements for slow sand filtration also be obtained at that point.

If the canal were not to be constructed for many years there is ample room for either slow sand or mechanical filters on the south shore of the river.

To protect the river, without filtration, existing Health Laws should be enforced, co-operation of the Municipalities and Boards of Health secured on both the Ontario and Quebec sides of the river, between Britannia on one side and Aylmer on the other, to stop pollution and enforce sanitary measures for their own as well as Ottawa's protection. This might be accomplished effectually by the construction of separate sewers, for sewage only, extending from these points to a safe outfall in the river below the Ottawa Water Works pure water pipe.

The McGregor Lakes would also have to be protected against pollution, or the cost of filtration works be added to the estimate already made.

I am informed that the pure water pipe now being constructed in connection with the new aqueduct of the Ottawa Water Works is expected to be in operation within three months' time. This should make a radical change in the situation and prevent chances of pollution between the point of intake, which is about the Canadian Pacific Railway Bridge, and the pumping station of the Ottawa Water Works. As I am convinced that the true, and under the circumstances unavoidable, source of pollution lies in the old pipe between these points. This has been foreseen and is to be very soon removed by the operation of the pure water pipe in connection with the new Aqueduct under construction.

With regard to McGregor Lake supply, I am of the opinion, even with the information we have, more time and definite information is required before it can be safely adopted as the sole source of supply, and the inexhaustible supply, both for domestic and fire purposes, we have in the Ottawa River, abandoned.

Too little is known of the capabilities of the lake supply, with its comparatively small drainage or catchment area, which I consider is not sufficient as a sole source of supply.

The calculations for supply are based on an assumed precipitation or fall of rain and snow. Definite information is being obtained by rain gauges established at Perkin's Mills and Lucerne, but as the only records we have are for Perkin's Mills from May to October, and for Lucerne from June to October, no use for value of yearly precipitation can yet be made of them.

The run off of the Blanche River, as far as we know, is not sufficient to furnish a supply, even at present daily rates of consumption.

If McGregor Lakes are likely to become a source of supply it is very advisable to have monthly measurements at least made and gauges established to determine the maximum, minimum and mean run off, or discharge of this river, which is the outlet of the lakes and "basin" holding the water to be relied on for storage and supply. This information would be of the greatest possible value in determining the capacity for supply of the McGregor Lake area, as being if extended over a sufficiently long period, a more definite measurement of capacity of the catchment area than preciptation records, and, even if only obtained for a year or more, of great assistance.

With the foregoing opinion of Mr. Keefer, the remaining members of the Commission are unable to agree.

Your Commission regrets that it cannot make a unanimous report upon the water supply.

Respectfully submitted.

>ALLEN HAZEN.
>CHAS. A. HODGETTS.
>CHARLES H. KEEFER.
>JOHN W. S. MCCULLOUGH.

Nov. 25th, 1911.

LABORATORY OF THE PROVINCIAL BOARD OF HEALTH OF THE PROVINCE OF ONTARIO.

REPORT ON WATER SAMPLES RECEIVED FROM THE OTTAWA WATER COMMISSION FROM JULY 1ST, 1911, TO OCTOBER 6TH, 1911.

Date.	Lab. No.	Source.	Bacterial Count per cc.	Colon Bacilli.	Chlorine.
1911.					
July 8...	6,771	Ottawa River, opposite Berser's Grove.	526	+	2
" 8...	6,772	Pump House Tap......................	9	—	2
" 8...	6,773	Pier No. 1, before treatment	66	—	2
" 8...	6,774	Hintonburg Pumping Station...........	170	—	2
" 8...	6,775	Pier A, Intake of Ottawa's water supply	22	—	2
" 8...	6,776	Tap in Engineer's Othce	2	—	2
" 8...	6,777	Lake, above Aylmer..................	13	—	2
" 14...	6,855	Pump House Tap	12	—	3
" 14...	6,856	Lake:Deschenes, above Aylmer........	32	—	3
" 14...	6,857	Hiawatha Park	60	+	3
" 14...	6,858	Pier No. 4, Intake	28	—	2
" 14...	6,859	Pier No. 1, before treatment	30	—	2
" 20...	6,971	City Tap	6	—	5
" 20...	6,972	Pier No. 1, before treatment	180	—	4
" 20...	6,973	Pier No. 4, Intake...................	120	—	3
" 20...	6,974	Pump House Tap	4	—	3
" 20...	6,975	Lake Deschenes, above Almer	26	—	3
" 22...	7,014	Hiawatha Park	....	—	4
" 27...	7,109	Pier No. 1, before treatment	2	—	10
" 27...	7,110	City Tap	3	—	4
" 27...	7,111	Hiawatha Park	142	—	4
" 27...	7,112	Pump House Tap	2	—	4
" 27...	7,113	Lake Deschenes, above Aylmer........	50	—	2
" 27...	7,114	Pier No. 1, leak.....................	44	+	3
" 27...	7,115	Pier No. 4. Intake...................	....	+	3
Aug. 2...	7,250	Hiawatha Park	300	+	2
" 2...	7,251	Lake Deschenes.....................	150	—	2
" 2...	7,252	Pier No. 1, before treatment	400	+	2
" 2...	7,253	Pump House Tap	190	—	2
" 2...	7,254	City Tap...........................	100	—	2
" 2...	7,255	Pier No. 4, Intake...................	300	+	2
" 9...	7,423	Pier No. 1, before treatment	80	—	2
" 9...	7,324	Pump House Tap....................	30	—	2
" 9...	7,425	Pier No. 4, Intake...................	100	+	2
" 9...	7,426	McGregor Lake	25	—	2
" 9...	7,427	Hiawatha Park	200	+	2
" 9...	7,428	City Tap	31	—	2
" 9...	7,429	Lake Deschenes. above Aylmer........	20	—	2
" 15...	7,566A	Intake	26	—	2
" 15...	7,567	City Tap. Engineer's Office...........	80	—	2
" 15...	7,568	McGregor Lake	28	—	2
" 15...	7,569	Before treatment	76	—	2
" 15...	7,570	Lake Deschenes, above Aylmer........	26	+	2
" 15...	7,571	Intake surface, Pier No. 4.............	20	—	2
" 15...	7,572	Pump House Tap	22	—	2
" 15...	7,573	Hiawatha Park	200	+	2
" 22...	7,716	City Hall Tap.......................	40	—	2
" 22...	7,717	Lake Deschenes, above Aylmer........	90	—	2
" 22...	7,718	McGregor Lake	40	+	2
" 22...	7,718A	Pier No. 4, Intake...................	120	—	2
" 22...	7,720	Hiawatha Park	380	+	2
" 22...	7,721	Pier No. 1, before treatment	60	—	2
" 22...	7,721	Pump House Tap	30	—	2
" 29...	7,832	Pump House Tap	....	—	3
" 29...	7,833	59 Bolton..........................	....	—	2
" 29...	7,834	No mark	....	—	2

REPORT ON WATER SAMPLES RECEIVED FROM THE OTTAWA WATER COMMISSION FROM JULY 1ST, 1911, TO OCTOBER 6TH, 1911.—*Continued.*

Date.	Lab. No.	Source.	Bacterial Count per cc.	Colon Bacilli.	Chlorine.
1911.					
Sept. 2...	7,867	Pier No. 4, Intake....................	40	—	2
" 2...	7,868	Pier No. 1, before treatment	36	—	2
" 2...	7,869	McGregor Lake	24	—	2
" 2...	7,870	Hiawatha Park	400	+	2
" 2...	7,871	Pump House Tap......................	12	—	2
" 2...	7,872	Lake Deschenes, above Aylmer........	8	—	2
' 2...	7,873	City Tap	10	—	2
" 11...	7,972	Pump House Tap	4	—	2
" 11...	7,973	Pier No. 4, Intake....................	280	—	2
" 11...	7,974	McGregor Lake	96	—	2
" 11...	7,975	City Tap	16	—	2
" 11...	7,976	Lake Deschenes, above Aylmer........	100	—	2
" 11...	7,977	Pier No. 1, before treatment	160	—	2
" 11...	7,996	Health Office	....	+	2
" 11...	7,997	Pier No. 1	....	—	2
" 16...	8,105	Pier No. A, before treatment..........	50	+	2
" 16...	8,106	City Hall Tap........................	4	—	2
" 16...	8,107	Lake Deschenes......................	30	—	2
" 16...	8,108	Pier No. 1	400	—	2
" 16...	8,109	McGregor Lake	8	—	2
" 16...	8,110	Pump House Tap (Bottle broken, contents gone)			
" 23...	8,192	Pier No. 1 before treatment..........	50	—	2
" 23...	8,193	McGregor Lake	60	—	3
" 23...	8,194	City Hall............................	10	—	6
" 23...	8,195	Lake Deschenes	20	—	3
" 23...	8,196	Pump House Tap, after treatment.....	24	—	4
" 23...	8,197	Pier No. 4	40	—	2
" 30...	8,346	McGregor Lake	2	+	3
Oct, 5...	8,431	City Hall Tap........................	4	—	2
" 5...	8,432	Lake Deschenes	2	—	3
" 5...	8,433	McGregor Lake	4	—	2
" 5...	8,434	Pier No. 4	24	—	2
" 5...	8,435	Pump House Tap......................	4	—	3
" 5...	8,436	Pier No. 1, before mixing............	20	—	2

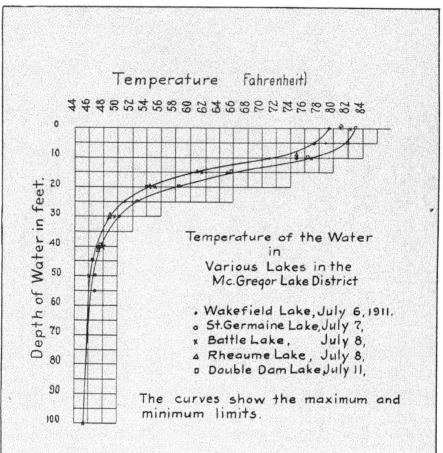

Temperature of the Water
in
Various Lakes in the
Mc. Gregor Lake District

. Wakefield Lake, July 6, 1911.
o St. Germaine Lake, July 7,
x Battle Lake,   July 8,
▲ Rheaume Lake,   July 8,
□ Double Dam Lake, July 11,

The curves show the maximum and
minimum limits.

Hazen & Whipple
Consulting Civil Engineers
103 Park Ave, N.Y.
Aug 4, 1911

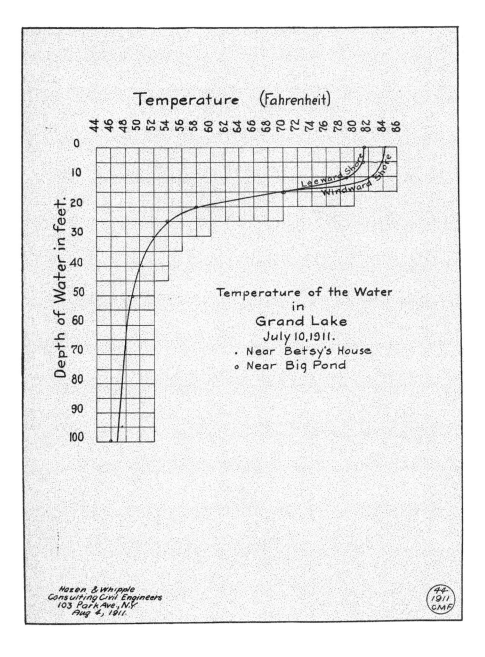

Temperature of the Water
in
Grand Lake
July 10, 1911.
. Near Betsy's House
o Near Big Pond

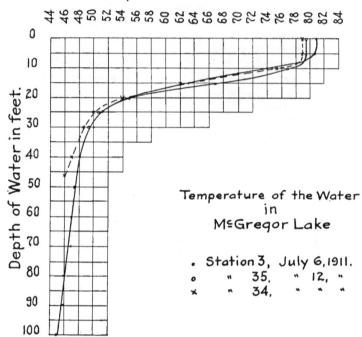

Temperature of the Water
in
McGregor Lake

. Station 3,   July 6, 1911.
o   "   35,   " 12, "
x   "   34,   "   "   "

Hazen & Whipple
Consulting Civil Engineers
103 Park Ave, N.Y.
Aug. 4, 1911.

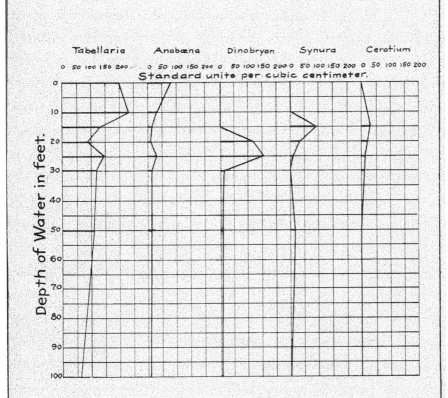

Vertical Distribution
of
Microscopic Organisms
in
McGregor Lake
July 12, 1911.

Hazen & Whipple
Consulting Civil Engineers
103 Park Ave. N.Y
Aug. 4, 1911.

Consta
Bay

ıssıppı Rıⱽ

wha

Graha
Bay   Brittania
              L.H.

Map of
LAKE DESCHENES
Showing Location of
samples of Water
Collected July 14,'11.

Cousineau's Bo
Courville's

22en & Whipple
sulting Civil Engineers
3 Park Ave, N.Y.
Aug 4, 1911.

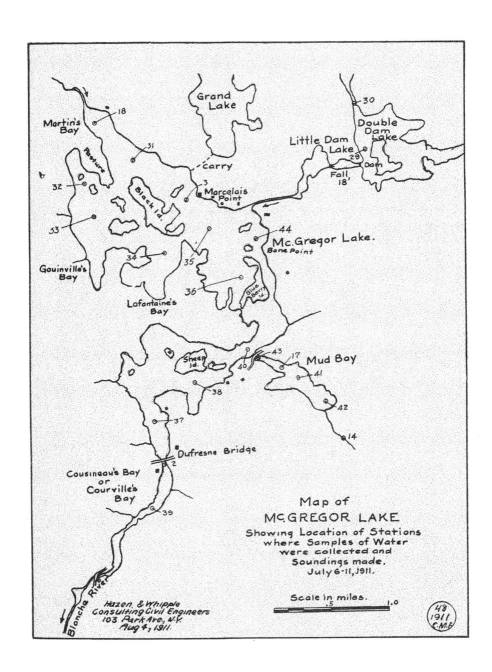

Map of
MC.GREGOR LAKE
Showing Location of Stations
where Samples of Water
were collected and
Soundings made.
July 6-11, 1911.

Scale in miles.

Hazen & Whipple
Consulting Civil Engineers
103 Park Ave, N.Y.
Aug 4, 1911.

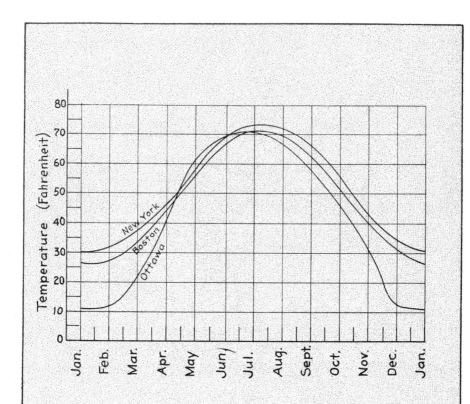

Diagram showing the
Mean Monthly Air Temperatures at
OTTAWA, ONTARIO
from July 1910 to June 1911
and the
Corresponding Average Temperatures
for
NEW YORK AND BOSTON

To the Chairman and Members of the Provincial Board of Health of Ontario.

GENTLEMEN,—I have the honour to present you the following report of the work done in the Toronto Laboratory of the Board.

During the last six months of the year we were occupied much of the time planning, and having fitted out new Laboratories at No. 5 Queens Park and moving from the quarters occupied formerly in the Medical Building of the University of Toronto.

The following is synopsis of the specimens examined during the year.

SYNOPSIS OF SPECIMENS EXAMINED, 1911.

Diphtheria swabs		1,068
Release from isolation	173	
Positive, 91		
Negative, 82		
Diagnosis	895	
Positive, 226		
Negative, 669		
Tuberculous sputa		1,650
Positive	402	
Negative	1,248	
Typhoid blood		749
Positive	70	
Negative	679	
Miscellaneous specimens		565
Rabies	70	
Milks	168	
Liquors for License Branch	241	
Other infectious materials	86	
Water		1,718
Bacteriological	1,668	
Chemical	50	
Totals	5,750	5,750

Over last year the number of specimens examined has fallen off. This is wholly due to the fact that now Toronto has a fully equipped municipal laboratory. During the last four years several Ontario cities have established their own laboratories to do their own work locally. Only such specimens as they have no facilities for examining do they send on here.

Toronto, Hamilton, Ottawa, Kingston, Brantford, St. Thomas, Peterboro and Fort William are now provided with well equipped laboratories.

By arrangement with the Government in connection with the Hygienic Institute a branch of the Provincial Board of Health laboratory will shortly be established in London.

With the exception of the falling off this year, wholly accounted for by Toronto doing its work, the work of this laboratory has gone on increasing in quantity uniformly from year to year.

On Dec. 1st, the laboratory was installed in the new quarters at No. 5 Queens Park. Though the space is not much greater it is so much more advantageously subdivided that all branches of the work can be more efficiently done. With our present equipment we may quite reasonably bid for more routine work. The time has come when outfits for the collection of samples in a more efficient manner could be advantageously introduced for blood, sputa and exudate specimens and when ready to send these out it would be well to have the profession of the Province pointedly circularized as to the facilities at their command.

It might be well also to make some arrangement whereby the results obtained from specimens examined for the physicians be communicated to the Medical Officer of Health of their respective municipalities so that these latter would have some additional hold on the infectious cases in their districts. Each positive finding in Tuberculosis could be used as a means of locating Tuberculous patients probably in a much more accurate way than depending even on confidential reports from physicians. It would at least be entering of the wedge, in getting more complete reports (Typhoid as well as Tuberculosis.)

A great number of the specimens examined showed the absence of the bacilli sought or of the reaction looked for. This has been the experience in many other quarters. The laboratory is being made use of more and more in these doubtful cases that can be decided best by laboratory methods.

Of the miscellaneous specimens examined 70 were the brains of animals suspected of rabies. A portion of my report already in deals with this matter. At the present time 10 patients are taking the Pasteur preventive treatment. We have had cases continuously since September of this kind. So far we have had no slips, all of the cases did invariably well. Beyond some local indurations and some itchiness there were no untoward symptoms.

Through the courtesy of the Board of Health of the City of New York, we have been able to have a continuous supply of vaccine on hand when required. This has been a great saving of expense to the over two hundred people who have found it necessary to take the treatment. They save their railroad journey to New York, their board there and the greater fee they would have to pay for the treatment.

Through the very great courtesy of the Toronto General Hospital, the Hospital for Sick Children and the Western Hospital, who have given us house-surgeon and nurse assistance and kindly provided us with suitable operating rooms, we have been able to carry on this work. Now that we have moved into our own quarters provision is made for the treatment in our own laboratories, where it is proposed in the future to carry on the treatment. Our sincerest thanks are due for the great courtesies we have received from the above hospitals and their good staffs.

We are still continuing the chemical bacteriological examination of milk specimens for the Milk Commission of the Academy of Medicine in their endeavor to procure certified milk. It is proposed shortly in order to prevent clash of authority to hand this work over to the city laboratories. At present about 750-800 quarts of certified milk are being produced daily. It is rarely that any of those examined have shown above the 5,000 in winter and 10,000 bacterial count in summer. The fat content has never been below 3.5 per cent. and often has gone up to 5 per cent. Veterinary inspection monthly is made of the diaries producing this milk, also medical inspection of all the employees and of the sanitary

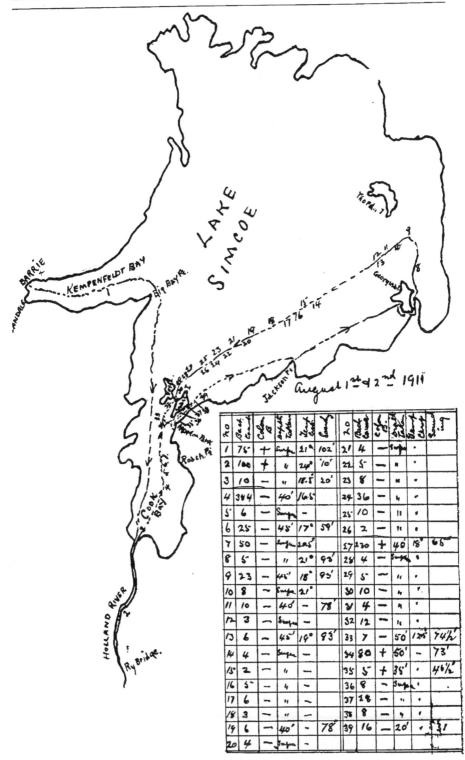

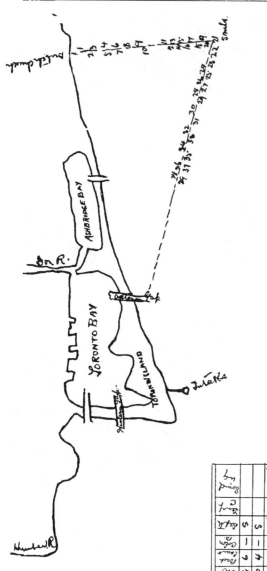

Aug 9th 1911

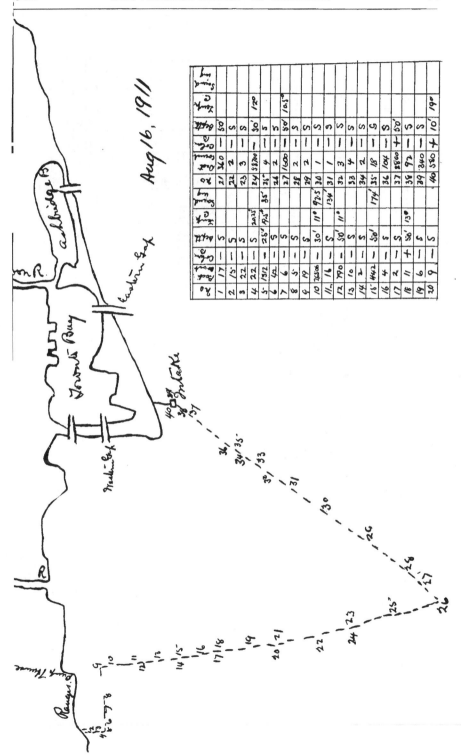

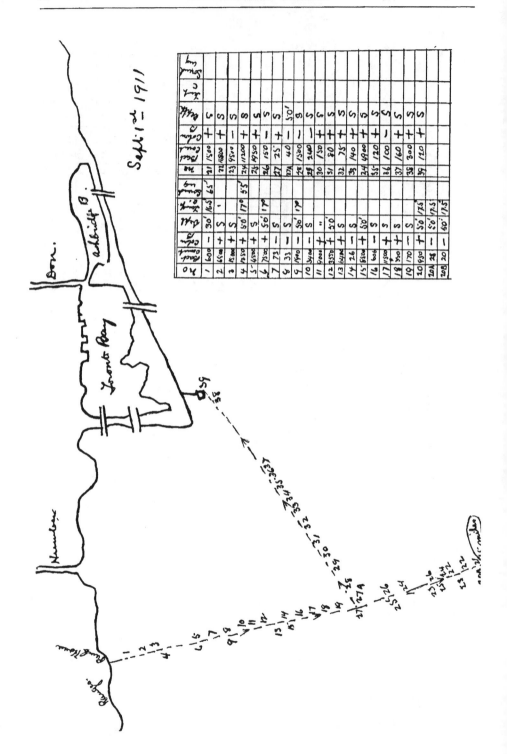

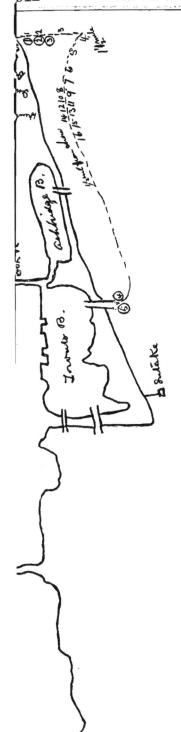

Oct 5th 1911

No.	Bact Count	Chlon R.	Depth Taken	Temp C	Sounding	Remarks
①	16	–	15'	15°	25'	½ min mtrance from Seven Gully
②	30	–	30'	15°	40'	¾ " " " "
③	5·0	1	40'	11.5°	50'	1 " " " "
④	100	+	10'	13°	18'	off Erskine channel
⑤	125	–	10'	13°	20'	¼ min west of Carbrichend
1	10	–	S			¾ " entrance go– Square gulley
2	44	–	S			1
3	14	–	S			½ mile from shore
4	15	–	S			" " "
5	80	+	S			¾
6	40	–	S			¾ " Summeray
7	60	+	S			½ " Buell church
8	125	–	S			½
9	330	+	S			½
10	800	–	S			¼ head g
11	125	+	S		320	¾
12	300	+	S			¾
13	70	+	S			½ Sew 2/
16	160	–	S			Sewer clote

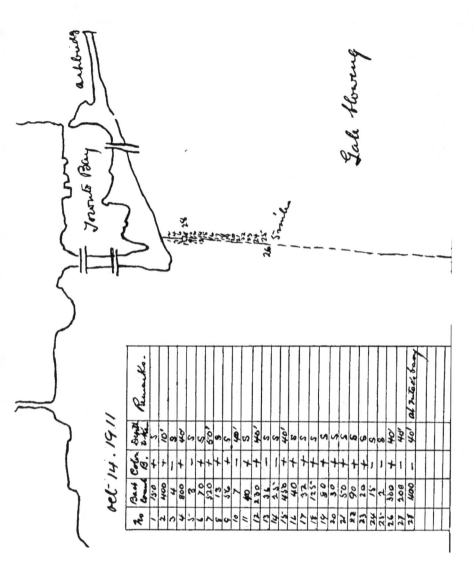

condition is made monthly. The milk is sold at 15 cents per quart. It is produced by three dairies who receive their certificates monthly. The physicians of Toronto can now procure for their patients as nearly pure and safe milk as it is possible to get.

Two hundred and forty-one samples of seized alcohol specimens were examined for the License Department of the Province. Convictions were got on many of these findings. This branch of the work is increasing a good deal of late.

Of the other 86 miscellaneous specimens many were from cases of meningitis, some were tuberculous, some due to staphylococci and pneumococci, we did not find the diplococcus intracellularus in any of the specimens. A number of specimens of pus were examined for the gonococcus, however, we have not encouraged this form of work as so frequently medico-legal complications threatened.

During the last summer some 200 water specimens were examined for the Special Commission appointed by the City of Toronto, to report on the water situation in its broad aspect.

These specimens were collected personally, one set from Lake Simcoe and one from Lake Ontario.

Diagrammatic maps are presented showing where these samples were collected, the dates on which collected and the results tabulated with each map. They make an interesting study.

In view of the very general favor shown the Lake Simcoe water source the results obtained were rather disappointing. This lake has been generally considered very deep. An Indian Chief who has resided practically all his life on this lake, called it a shallow lake. The deepest sounding we were able to get was 125 feet. The average was 40 feet, and when it was proposed to take Toronto's water supply it was only 40 feet at the deepest point.

The water was generally credited with being always free from turbidity; on our visit it was close to ten pails turbid per million almost universally. It is frequently more trubid than this.

The outflow from the lake is said to be 600,000,000 gals. per day. Toronto would need 100,000,000 gals. at least, if it went to this source. With one-fifth of the water removed per day and this increased during the summer months, water powers now established would suffer.

Of course last summer was an exceptionally warm summer. The temperature of the surface water ranged from 69.5° F. to 75.2° F., that of the deep water from 54.5° F. to 66.2° F. Lake Ontario water never gets as warm as this.

Five out of the 39 samples collected showed colon bacilli, not so frequently as on later occasions Lake Ontario showed, but nevertheless infection. With reference to the bacterial content it ranged from 2 to 380, the deep samples especially showing high. This water would have to be purified. Though the population about is still small, it will soon be much larger.

A study of the Lake Ontario samples would lead one to suspect that this lake is becoming more and more infected. The samples collected some years ago would have led one to hope that it was possible to go out into the lake far enough to escape shore infection, but on these trips we found infected samples and those containing high bacterial counts even 15 miles out into the lake. The chemical samples collected at the same time bore out these findings.

Though infection is less frequent far out, still it exists, and comparatively frequently, showing the necessity we have come to of purifying this water.

The following table shows the number by denominations of the specimens examined month by month.

The following tables show in detail the specimens examined, the municipalities from which received, and the number from each.

All of which is respectfully submitted,

JOHN A. AMYOT.

SUMMARY BY MONTHS OF SPECIMENS EXAMINED DURING THE YEAR 1911.

Months.	Diphtheritic Swabs.				Tubercu-lous Sputa.		Typhoid Bloods.		Miscellaneous Specimens.	Waters.		Total Number for Month.
	Release.		Diagnosis.							Chemical.	Bacterial.	
	+	–	+	–	+	–	+	–				
January	5	9	23	49	49	131	13	55	9	5	60	408
February	9	3	14	59	48	126	3	50	35	11	89	447
March	10	6	16	58	44	155	12	76	35	....	92	504
April	.	3	24	58	47	127	6	37	57	1	52	418
May	3	9	17	67	42	110	8	56	47	4	136	499
June	9	14	26	62	28	84	5	37	142	4	124	535
July	9	5	3	46	39	96	1	60	47	2	211	519
August	....	11	6	52	36	95	7	93	35	2	312	649
September	....	....	11	48	13	65	5	84	33	9	255	524
October	6	1	22	35	23	78	8	59	68	3	206	509
November	25	15	33	45	23	80	2	37	29	....	66	355
December	8	6	31	90	10	101	....	35	28	9	65	383
	91	82	226	669	402	1,248	70	679	565	50	1,668	5,750

Report from Laboratory of Provincial Board of Health for Month of January, 1911.

Municipalities.	Diphtheritic Swabs.				Tuberculous Sputa.		Typhoid Bloods.		Miscellaneous Specimens.	Waters.		Total Number for Month.
	Release.		Diagnosis.							Chemical.	Bacterial.	
	+	−	+	−	+	−	+	−				
Algoma				2	1							3
Brant						1					1	2
Bruce		1			2	3		1			1	8
Carleton					1	3	9	9		1	8	31
Dufferin	1			2		2						5
Durham		1	3		1	1					2	8
Elgin			1									1
Essex		2	2	2	2	6	1	2				17
Grey					2	4		3	1			10
Halton			1	2							2	5
Haldimand					3		1				1	5
Hastings						3						3
Huron		2			2	2						6
Kent					3	5			1			9
Lanark						1						1
Lambton				3	1	3		1			2	10
Lincoln				3		2					2	7
Middlesex					1	2						3
Muskoka						3					1	4
Norfolk				1	1	2		1			5	10
Nipissing					1	1		3			3	8
Northumberland						2		1				3
Ontario			1		2	3						6
Oxford			1		1	14					2	18
Parry Sound			1		1	3		1				6
Peel											1	1
Peterboro'					1		1	1				3
Perth					1	3		1			3	8
Prescott									2			2

Report from Laboratory of Provincial Board of Health for month of January, 1911.—*Con.*

Municipalities.	Diphtheritic Swabs. Release. +	Release. −	Diagnosis. +	Diagnosis. −	Tuberculous Sputa. +	−	Typhoid Bloods. +	−	Miscellaneous Specimens.	Waters. Chemical.	Bacterial.	Total Number for Month.
Rainy River				1							2	3
Renfrew					1	2					4	7
Simcoe				2	4	5		1				12
Thunder Bay	3							1				4
Victoria					1	3					2	6
Waterloo			1		2	4					5	12
Wellington			1	2	1	4		1				9
Welland					1	2		1			1	5
Wentworth					1	1		2			1	5
York	1	3	11	29	11	41	1	23	7	4	11	142
Grand total												408

Report from Laboratory of Provincial Board of Health for Month of February, 1911.

Municipalities.	Release. +	Release. −	Diagnosis. +	Diagnosis. −	Tuberculous Sputa. +	−	Typhoid Bloods. +	−	Miscellaneous Specimens.	Chemical.	Bacterial.	Total Number for Month.
Algoma			2	1		1						4
Brant						1						1
Bruce					1	6					1	8
Carleton					2	3	1	10			22	38
Durham						4	1				1	6
Dufferin			1	1		1						3
Essex					3	6		4				13
Grey						2				1		3
Glengarry						1						1
Halton	2				1	2					1	6
Haldimand						2						2
Hastings						4		1		1	3	9
Huron				3	2		1				3	9
Kent					2	9						11
Lambton			1		1			2				4
Lanark						1						1
Lincoln					1	2		2			4	9

Report from Laboratory of Provincial Board of Health for Month of February, 1911.—*Continued*

Municipalities.	Diphtheritic Swabs. Release. +	Release. −	Diagnosis. +	Diagnosis. −	Tuberculous Sputa. +	Sputa. −	Typhoid Bloods. +	Typhoid. −	Miscellaneous Specimens.	Waters. Chemical.	Bacterial.	Total Number for Month.
Middlesex						1						1
Muskoka				1								
Nipissing				2		2		2				6
Norfolk					1	2		1				4
Northumberland					1			1			3	5
Ontario				1		2		1				4
Oxford				1	3	7					6	17
Parry Sound				4		3		1			3	11
Peel				2		1						3
Perth		1				3						4
Peterboro'			1	1		2						4
Prescott						1						1
Rainy River				2	1							3
Renfrew					1			1				2
Russell					1							1
Stormont					1							1
Simcoe			1	3	5	8		1			1	19
Thunder Bay				1				1				2
Victoria				1		1						2
Waterloo				1	2	5						8
Welland			1		1	4	1		3			10
Wellington			3	2	4	3			3	10		25
Wentworth				2								2
York	7	1	5	29	15	34		17	34		41	183
Grand Total												447

Report from Laboratory of Provincial Board of Health for Month of March, 1911.

Municipalities.	Diphtheritic Swabs.				Tuberculous Sputa.		Typhoid Bloods.		Miscellaneous Specimens.	Waters.		Total Number for Month.
	Release.		Diagnosis.							Chemical.	Bacterial.	
	+	–	+	–	+	–	+	–				
Algoma			1		1	5						7
Brant							1					1
Bruce			1	1	3	5					2	12
Carleton					1	1	9					12
Dufferin					1							1
Durham			1	2			2			2		7
Elgin			1									1
Essex					2	5		3			3	13
Grey				1	2	5						8
Glengarry						1						1
Haldimand						3						3
Halton				3	1	5						9
Hastings					2	2		2				6
Huron				1	1	2	1	2				7
Kent	1			1	4	6		3	1		2	18
Lambton						4						4
Lanark					2	1					1	4
Lincoln					1	1				16		18
Middlesex						1						1
Muskoka				2	1	1	1					5
Nipissing					2					1	8	11
Norfolk						3						3
Northumberland				1		7						8
Ontario	1	1		2	1	6					1	12
Oxford					1	14	1				10	26
Parry Sound				1	1	3						5
Peel					1	1					5	7
Perth			2	1		4		1			1	9
Peterboro'			1	2		3		2				8

Report from Laboratory of Provincial Board of Health for month of March, 1911.—*Continued.*

Municipalities.	Diphtheritic Swabs.				Tuberculous Sputa.		Typhoid Bloods.		Miscellaneous Specimens.	Waters.		Total Number for Month.
	Release.		Diagnosis.							Chemical.	Bacterial.	
	+	−	+	−	+	−	+	−				
Prescott							1					1
Rainy River						2						2
Renfrew						3						3
Stormont											2	2
Simcoe				2	3	7	1	3			6	22
Thunder Bay				1				1			1	3
Russell						1						1
Victoria						1		2				3
Waterloo				1	2	3					2	8
Welland	1			1		1	1	2	1			7
Wellington	1	1	1	4	1	10		2	1		1	22
York	6	4	8	30	10	37	6	42	13		47	203
Grand total												504

Report from Laboratory of Provincial Board of Health for Month of April 1911.

Municipalities.	Release +	Release −	Diagnosis +	Diagnosis −	TubSputa +	TubSputa −	Typhoid +	Typhoid −	Misc.	Chemical.	Bacterial.	Total.
Algoma			1		3	2				(1)		7
Brant				1							1	2
Bruce			1		1	1		1			1	5
Carleton					2	1	2	3				8
Dufferin			1			1						2
Essex					1	6					1	8
Grey				2		9		3				14
Haldimand						3		1			2	6
Halton						1				1		2
Hastings					1	1		2				4
Huron					3		2	3				8
Kent				1	2	8	1	1			2	15
Lambton					1	4						5
Lanark					1	1		1			1	4

Report from Laboratory of Provincial Board of Health for Month of April, 1911.—*Continued.*

Municipalities	Diphtheritic Swabs — Release +	Release −	Diagnosis +	Diagnosis −	Tuberculous Sputa +	Tuberculous Sputa −	Typhoid Bloods +	Typhoid Bloods −	Miscellaneous Specimens	Waters Chemical	Waters Bacterial	Total Number for Month
Lincoln				2	1	2						5
Middlesex			1	1			1				3	6
Muskoka					1	3	1					5
Nipissing					1	2					8	11
Norfolk				2			2				1	5
Northumberland				3	5		2					10
Ontario					2	5	1					8
Oxford				2	4	6	1					13
Parry Sound			1		1	2						4
Peel				2		3	1					6
Perth	2	1		2	1	4	1		4			15
Peterboro'							1			1	12	14
Prince Edward					1							1
Prescott and Russell					1						1	2
Rainy River					2						1	3
Renfrew							1					1
Simcoe			1	2	2	11	3				4	23
Stor., Dundas & Glen.					1							1
Thunder Bay	1											1
Victoria						1	5					6
Waterloo		1		5	3	4	1			1	1	16
Welland					1		1					2
Wellington	2	1	3	3		7	1				4	21
Wentworth							2					2
York	2		13	27	9	26	7		42	1	20	147
Grand Total												418

Report from Laboratory of Provincial Board of Health for Month of May, 1911.

Municipalities	Diphtheritic Swabs				Tuberculous Sputa		Typhoid Bloods		Miscellaneous Specimens	Waters		Total Number for Month
	Release		Diagnosis							Chemical	Bacterial	
	+	−	+	−	+	−	+	−				
Algoma				1			2	5			5	13
Brant					1							1
Bruce	1			1	2	6						10
Carleton					1	5						6
Dufferin				1								1
Essex	1	1	2	4	3	6		1			8	26
Grey			1	1	2	5		2			3	14
Haldimand						5		2			1	8
Halton						1		1			4	6
Hastings					2		4				1	7
Huron								3			1	4
Kent				1	4	7		3				15
Lambton				3	2	2						7
Lanark					2							2
Lincoln				2	3	3	1					9
Middlesex					2	1		1	1			5
Muskoka					1							1
Nipissing					1	1	2	1			19	24
Norfolk					3		3		2		4	12
Northumb'd&Durham			1	4	5	5			1		3	19
Ontario					1		3				5	9
Oxford				1	7	10	1	7			13	39
Parry Sound					2	1		2				5
Peel						1						1
Perth				1	1	3		2				12
Peterboro'		2	1	4		1		1	1			10
Prescott and Russell								1	1			2
Prince Edward						2						2
Rainy River								1				1
Renfrew								3				3

Report from Laboratory of Provincial Board of Health for Month of May, 1911—
—*Continued*.

Municipalities.	Diphtheritic Swabs.				Tuberculous Sputa.		Typhoid Bloods.		Miscellaneous Specimens.	Waters.		Total Number for Month.
	Release.		Diagnosis.							Chemical.	Bacterial.	
	+	–	+	–	+	–	+	–				
Simcoe	.....	.....	.....	1	1	6	.....	2	.....	3	2	15
Thunder Bay	.....	.....	.....	.....	.....	.....	1	2	.....	.....	1	4
Victoria	.....	.....	.....	1	1	3	.....	2	.....	.....	3	10
Waterloo	.....	.....	1	2	.....	3	.....	1	.....	.....	3	10
Welland	.....	.....	.....	1	1	1	.....	.....	.....	.....	10	13
Wellington	.....	3	1	2	1	5	.....	1	.....	.....	14	27
Wentworth	.....	.....	.....	.....	.....	1	.....	.....	.....	.....	.....	1
York	1	43	10	27	.....	13	1	9	44	1	36	145
Grand total	.....	.....	.....	.....	.....	.....	.....	.....	.....	.....	.....	499

Report from Laboratory of Provincial Board of Health for Month of June, 1911.

Municipalities.	+	–	+	–	+	–	+	–	Misc.	Chem.	Bact.	Total
Algoma	.....	.....	1	1	1	1	.....	1	1	.....	30	36
Brant	.....	.....	.....	.....	1	2	.....	.....	.....	.....	1	4
Bruce	.....	1	1	2	.....	1	.....	1	.....	.....	1	7
Carleton	.....	.....	.....	1	.....	1	.....	4	.....	.....	.....	6
Dufferin	.....	.....	.....	2	.....	.....	.....	.....	.....	.....	.....	2
Elgin	.....	.....	1	.....	.....	.....	.....	.....	.....	.....	.....	1
Essex	.....	.....	1	2	1	4	.....	3	.....	1	9	21
Grey	.....	.....	.....	1	.....	3	.....	3	.....	.....	.....	7
Haliburton	.....	.....	.....	.....	1	1	.....	.....	.....	.....	.....	2
Halton	.....	1	.....	1	.....	1	.....	.....	1	.....	9	13
Hastings	.....	.....	.....	.....	.....	1	.....	.....	.....	.....	1	2
Huron	.....	.....	1	1	1	2	.....	.....	.....	.....	.....	5
Kent	.....	.....	.....	.....	2	4	.....	.....	.....	.....	.....	6
Lambton	.....	2	1	1	.....	1	.....	.....	1	.....	.....	6
Lanark	.....	.....	.....	.....	1	.....	.....	.....	.....	.....	1	2
Lennox & Addington	.....	.....	.....	.....	.....	.....	.....	.....	.....	.....	1	1
Lincoln	.....	.....	.....	.....	3	.....	1	1	13	.....	4	22
Middlesex	.....	.....	.....	.....	1	2	.....	.....	.....	2	.....	5

Report from Laboratory of Provincial Board of Health for Month of June, 1911.—*Continued.*

Municipalities.	Diphtheritic Swabs.				Tuberculous Sputa.		Typhoid Bloods.		Miscellaneous Specimens	Waters.		Total Number for Month.
	Release.		Diagnosis.							Chemical.	Bacterial.	
	+	−	+	−	+	−	+	−				
Muskoka	.....	.....	.....	4	1	1	.....	1	.....	.....	1	8
Nipissing	.....	.....	.....	.....	1	2	.....	.....	.....	.....	15	18
Norfolk	.....	.....	.....	.....	.....	.....	.....	4	.....	1	.....	5
Northumb'd&Durham	3	1	1	2	3	7	.....	.....	1	.....	2	20
Ontario	.....	.....	.....	1	.....	3	.....	.....	.....	.....	.....	4
Oxford	.....	.....	.....	.....	2	7	.....	3	.....	.....	2	14
Parry Sound	.....	.....	.....	4	.....	4	.....	1	.....	.....	.....	9
Peel	.....	.....	.....	.....	.....	.....	.....	1	.....	.....	.....	1
Perth	.....	.....	.....	1	1	2	.....	.....	2	.....	2	8
Peterboro'	.....	.....	1	1	.....	1	.....	1	12	.....	6	22
Prescott & Russell	.....	.....	.....	.....	.....	.....	1	1	.....	.....	1	3
Renfrew	.....	.....	.....	.....	1	1	.....	.....	.....	.....	.....	2
Simcoe	1	1	2	.....	.....	9	.....	2	9	.....	1	25
Thunder Bay	.....	.....	.....	.....	.....	.....	2	4	.....	.....	2	8
Victoria	.....	.....	.....	1	1	1	.....	.....	1	.....	5	9
Waterloo	.....	1	4	1	.....	3	.....	2	2	.....	4	16
Welland	.....	.....	1	1	1	2	.....	.....	.....	.....	3	8
Wellington	.....	.....	.....	.....	.....	9	.....	3	9	.....	2	23
Wentworth	.....	.....	.....	.....	.....	1	.....	.....	.....	.....	.....	1
York	5	7	11	34	5	7	1	1	91	.....	21	183
Grand Total	.....	.....	.....	.....	.....	.....	.....	.....	.....	.....	.....	535

Report from Laboratory of Provincial Board of Health for Month of July, 1911.

Municipalities.	Diphtheritic Swabs.				Tuberculous Sputa.		Typhoid Bloods.		Miscellaneous Specimens.	Waters.		Total Number for Month.
	Release.		Diagnosis.							Chemical.	Bacterial.	
	+	–	+	–	+	–	+	–				
Algoma				2	1						9	12
Brant		1		2		1					7	11
Bruce						5		2			7	14
Carleton					1			2			26	29
Dufferin								1	3		3	7
Elgin					1						3	4
Essex					3	5		1			8	17
Grey				1	1	2		4	2		6	16
Haldimand				1	1	2					1	5
Haliburton						1						1
Halton	1			4								5
Hastings					3	1		2			4	10
Huron	1			1	1	2					1	6
Kent					3	7					2	12
Lambton						3					2	5
Lanark						1					17	18
Lincoln			1			2		1	1		9	14
Middlesex						3		2			2	7
Muskoka									5			5
Nipissing					1	2					14	17
Norfolk				1	1	3		1			2	8
Northumberland and Durham				1	1	4		2			1	9
Ontario				2		3					2	7
Oxford					3	13		8			12	36
Parry Sound						4		2				6
Peel	1			1				1				3
Perth				1	1			2			5	9
Peterboro'						1		5			6	12
Prince Edward									1			1

Report from Laboratory of Provincial Board of Health for month of July, 1911.—*Concluded.*

Municipalities.	Diphtheritic Swabs. Release. +	−	Diagnosis. +	−	Tuberculous Sputum. +	−	Typhoid Bloods. +	−	Miscellaneous Specimens.	Waters. Chemical.	Bacterial.	Total Number for Month.
Prescott and Russell						1						1
Renfrew											10	10
Simcoe		3	1	7	3	6		5			2	27
Stormont, Dundas & Glengarry					1						15	16
Thunder Bay											2	2
Victoria						2		2			4	8
Waterloo					3	4			1		5	13
Welland					1	2	1	3			11	18
Wellington				4	3	7		7		2	5	28
Wentworth				1							3	4
York	6	1	1	17	6	9		2	39		5	86
Grand total												519

Report from Laboratory of Provincial Board of Health for Month of August, 1911.

Municipalities.	Release. +	−	Diagnosis. +	−	Tub. Sput. +	−	Typhoid. +	−	Misc.	Chemical.	Bacterial.	Total.
Algoma				3		3	1	4			3	14
Brant						1						1
Bruce				2	3	2			1		8	16
Carleton						3	1	5			38	47
Dufferin						1		1				2
Elgin			1	2				1	1		1	6
Essex					3			1			1	5
Grey				1	3	1		6				11
Haldimand				1				1				2
Halton						1		2	2		1	6
Hastings					1	4					9	14
Huron				2							1	3
Kent				1	3	9	1	3	1		1	19
Lambton			1	3		2		3				9
Lanark						1				1	7	9

Report from Laboratory of Provincial Board of Health for Month of August, 1911.—*Continued.*

Municipalities	Diphtheritic Swabs. Release. +	Release. −	Diagnosis. +	Diagnosis. −	Tuberculous Sputa. +	−	Typhoid Bloods. +	−	Miscellaneous Specimens.	Waters. Chemical.	Bacterial.	Total Number for Month.
Lincoln					1	2		4				7
Middlesex						2		2			7	11
Muskoka					2	3		8			4	17
Nipissing				1	1	3					9	14
Norfolk							1	3				4
Northumb'd&Durham					1	6		7			3	17
Ontario			1	2				2				5
Oxford					4	7	1	5				17
Parry Sound			1			3		2			8	14
Peel			1			1	1				3	6
Perth			1			1		3			2	7
Peterboro'					1	6		3			2	12
Prescott & Russell	1		1			2		1				5
Rainy River										1	8	9
Renfrew						2					2	4
Simcoe			3		1	8		6			22	40
Stor. Dundas & Glen.											2	2
Thunder Bay									4		2	6
Victoria					2	1		4			2	9
Waterloo					1	5		6	1	1	2	16
Welland					1	1					16	18
Wallington			1	2	2	5	1	4	1		4	20
Wentworth											1	1
York	11	1	25		6	7		4	27		143	224
Grand Total												669

Report from Laboratory of Provincial Board of Health for Month of September, 1911. —*Continued.*

Municipalities.	Diphtheritic Swabs. Release.		Diagnosis.		Tuberculous Sputa.		Typhoid Bloods.		Miscellaneous Specimens.	Waters. Chemical.	Bacterial.	Total Number for Month.
	+	−	+	−	+	−	+	−				
Algoma	.....	.....	.....	1	.....	4	1	1	.....	.....	.....	7
Bruce	.....	.....	.....	1	.....	.....	.....	1	.....	.....	.....	2
Carleton	.....	.....	.....	.....	.....	.....	.....	3	.....	.....	31	34
Dufferin	.....	.....	.....	.....	.....	.....	.....	2	.....	.....	3	5
Elgin	.....	.....	.....	1	.....	.....	.....	.....	.....	.....	.....	1
Essex	.....	.....	1	2	.....	3	.....	3	.....	.....	1	10
Grey	.....	.....	.....	.....	.....	3	.....	3	.....	.....	.....	6
Haldimand	.....	.....	.....	1	.....	3	.....	1	.....	.....	1	6
Haliburton	.....	.....	.....	.....	.....	1	.....	.....	.....	.....	.....	1
Halton	.....	.....	.....	1	.....	1	.....	1	.....	.....	5	8
Hastings	.....	.....	.....	.....	.....	1	1	.....	.....	.....	14	16
Huron	.....	.....	.....	.2	.....	1	.....	1	1	.....	2	7
Kent	.....	.....	.....	1	2	3	.....	10	.....	.....	2	18
Lambton	.....	.....	.....	1	1	5	.....	1	.....	.....	1	9
Lanark	.....	.....	.....	.....	.....	.....	.....	.....	.....	.....	4	4
Lincoln	.....	.....	.....	.....	3	2	.....	3	.....	.....	24	32
Middlesex	.....	.....	1	.....	.....	1	.....	.....	1	.....	5	8
Muskoka	.....	.....	.....	1	1	1	.....	1	.....	.....	7	11
Nipissing	.....	.....	.....	.....	.....	1	.....	1	.....	.....	43	45
Norfolk	.....	.....	1	.....	.....	.....	.....	1	.....	.....	5	7
Northumberland and Durham	.....	.....	.....	1	1	3	.....	2	.....	.....	5	12
Ontario	.....	.....	.....	.....	.....	1	.....	2	.....	.....	15	18
Oxford	.....	.....	1	.....	2	6	1	4	.....	.....	6	20
Parry Sound	.....	.....	.....	.....	.....	4	.....	1	1	.....	2	8
Peel	.....	.....	.....	2	.....	.....	.....	.....	.....	.....	.....	2
Perth	.....	.....	1	.....	.....	.....	1	.....	.....	.....	3	5
Peterboro'	.....	.....	.....	.....	.....	1	.....	.....	.....	.....	1	2
Prescott and Russell	.....	.....	.....	.....	.....	.....	.....	1	.....	.....	.....	1

Report from Laboratory of Provincial Board of Health for Month of September, 1911.—*Concluded.*

Municipalities.	Diphtheritic Swabs — Release +	Release −	Diagnosis +	Diagnosis −	Tuberculous Sputa +	Tuberculous Sputa −	Typhoid Bloods +	Typhoid Bloods −	Miscellaneous Specimens	Waters — Chemical	Bacterial	Total Number for Month.
Rainy River									3			3
Renfrew				1			1				7	9
Simcoe			3	1	1	9	3				2	19
Thunder Bay				1			1				1	3
Victoria				1		2					3	6
Waterloo				2	1		1		5		4	13
Welland					1				4			5
Wellington			1	4			5		15		3	28
Wentworth					1							1
York	1		2	22			4	9	30	9	55	132
Grand total												524

Report from Laboratory of Provincial Board of Health for Month of October, 1911.

Municipalities.	Release +	Release −	Diagnosis +	Diagnosis −	Tuberculous Sputa +	Tuberculous Sputa −	Typhoid Bloods +	Typhoid Bloods −	Miscellaneous Specimens	Chemical	Bacterial	Total Number for Month.
Algoma					1		3					4
Bruce					2	1	1					4
Carleton					2	2	2				23	29
Dufferin				2			2					4
Elgin			1	1								2
Essex				3			1				1	5
Frontenac											6	6
Grey					1	1	3	1				6
Haldimand					1		1					2
Halton				1	1	1	1	1			9	14
Hastings	1				1	3	1	2				8
Huron				1		1	1				2	5
Kent	1				4		1				8	14
Lambton					3		1			1	3	8
Lanark					1							1
Lincoln					3	1	2		21		5	32

Report from Laboratory of Provincial Board of Health for Month of October, 1911. —*Continued.*

Municipalities.	Diphtheritic Swabs.				Tuberculous Sputa.		Typhoid Bloods.		Miscellaneous Specimens.	Waters.		Total Number for Month.
	Release.		Diagnosis.							Chemical.	Bacterial.	
	÷	–	+	–	+	–	+	–				
Midland	.....	.....	1	1	.....	1	.....	1	.....	.....	25	29
Muskoka	.....	.....	2	.....	.....	3	.....	2	.....	.....	2	9
Nipissing	.....	.....	1	.....	.....	1	.....	2	.....	.....	14	18
Norfolk	.....	.....	.....	.....	.....	1	1	1	.....	.....	.....	3
Northumb'd&Durham	.....	.....	1	3	3	1	1	.....	.....	.....	2	11
Ontario	.....	.....	.....	.....	1	5	.....	.....	.....	.....	1	7
Oxford	.....	.....	.....	.....	2	7	2	4	.....	.....	6	21
Parry Sound	.....	.....	.....	1	.....	2	.....	4	.....	.....	.....	7
Peel	1	.....	1	2	.....	.....	.....	3	.....	.....	1	8
Perth	.....	.....	.....	3	1	.....	.....	2	2	.....	2	10
Peterboro'	.....	.....	.....	.....	.....	.....	.....	.....	.....	.....	4	4
Prince Edward	.....	.....	.....	.....	.....	1	.....	.....	.....	.....	.....	1
Prescott & Russell	.....	.....	.....	.....	.....	.....	.....	1	.....	.....	.....	1
Rainy River	.....	.....	.....	.....	1	1	.....	.....	.....	.....	.....	2
Renfrew	.....	.....	.....	.....	2	2	.....	.....	.....	.....	.....	4
Simcoe	.....	.....	.....	.....	2	11	.....	5	10	.....	7	35
Thunder Bay	.....	.....	.....	.....	.....	1	.....	1	.....	.....	1	3
Victoria	.....	.....	.....	2	1	2	.....	1	.....	.....	3	9
Waterloo	.....	.....	1	.....	.....	2	.....	3	.....	1	4	11
Welland	.....	.....	1	2	.....	2	1	4	.....	.....	8	18
Wellington	1	.....	1	2	.....	5	.....	1	.....	.....	5	15
Wentworth	.....	.....	.....	.....	.....	.....	.....	.....	.....	1	.....	1
York	2	1	8	18	1	2	.....	8	34	.....	64	138
Grand Total	.....	.....	.....	.....	.....	.....	.....	.....	.....	.....	.....	509

Report from Laboratory of Provincial Board of Health for Month of November, 1911

Municipalities	Diphtheritic Swabs. Release +	Release −	Diagnosis +	Diagnosis −	Tuberculous Sputa +	Tuberculous Sputa −	Typhoid Bloods +	Typhoid Bloods −	Miscellaneous Specimens	Waters. Chemical	Bacterial	Total Number for Month.
Algoma							2					2
Brant				1						1		2
Bruce						2	2		1	t	1	6
Carleton						1	4		2		18	25
Dufferin							1		1	2	8	7
Elgin			1	1								2
Essex				1			2		2		1	6
Grey		1	1		3		7				3	15
Halton							3				7	10
Hastings			1				2		1			4
Huron			1	3			1		2	3	1	11
Haldimand							2		1			3
Haliburton							1					1
Kent						1	2		1	2		6
Lanark							1					1
Lambton						2	2				2	6
Leeds and Grenville											1	1
Lincoln						2	1		3			6
Middlesex							2		3			5
Muskoka				2			3		1			6
Nipissing							1					1
Northumberland and Durham	1	3	3	7	1		7		3		8	33
Ontario							3					3
Oxford				2	1	3	3		1			10
Parry Sound	1		1			1	2		1			6
Perth			1				2				1	4
Peel											1	1
Peterboro'							1					1
Prescott and Russell	3	2	5	3								13

Report from Laboratory of Provincial Board of Health for Month of November, 1911 —*Continued.*

Municipalities.	Diphtheritic Swabs. Release.		Diagnosis.		Tuberculous Sputa.		Typhoid Bloods.		Miscellaneous Specimens.	Waters. Chemical.	Bacterial.	Total Number for Month.
	+	−	+	−	+	−	+	−				
Rainy River				1								1
Renfrew					1	2						3
Simcoe				5	1	4			3		2	15
Thunder Bay											1	1
Victoria											3	3
Waterloo					2	2			1	1	5	11
Welland				1	1	2	1		7		1	13
Wellington			1	3		5						9
Wentworth						3						3
York	20	8	14	16	4	6	1	3	20		7	99
Grand total												355

Report from Laboratory of Provincial Board of Health for Month of December, 1911.

Municipalities.	Diphtheritic Swabs. Release.		Diagnosis.		Tuberculous Sputa.		Typhoid Bloods.		Miscellaneous Specimens.	Chemical.	Bacterial.	Total Number for Month.
	+	−	+	−	+	−	+	−				
Algoma					1	3		2	2		1	9
Brant					1			1				2
Bruce					6			5			7	18
Carleton								2				2
Dufferin			1					1			1	3
Elgin			3	1				1		1		6
Essex			1					2	1			4
Grey			1	4	2	5						12
Halton		2		7							8	17
Huron				2		2		4	2		3	13
Hastings			1	2	1	3		1			2	10
Kent				2	2	6		1				11
Lambton						4					9	13
Lanark						2						2
Leeds and Grenville				1								1
Lincoln						1						1

Report from Laboratory of Provincial Board of Health for Month of December, 1911.
—Concluded.

Municipalities.	Diphtheritic Swabs. Release. +	−	Diagnosis. +	−	Tuberculous Sputa. +	−	Typhoid Bloods. +	−	Miscellaneous Specimens.	Waters. Chemical.	Bacterial.	Total Number for Month.
Middlesex				1	1	1		2				5
Muskoka	2		1		1	3		3				10
Nipissing							4				5	9
Northumb'd&Durham			1	13		9				1		24
Norfolk						5		2				7
Ontario				2		2						4
Oxford			1	4	1	4		2	1		1	14
Parry Sound		1		6		2						9
Peel	2			2		4		2			9	19
Perth				2		4		2	1		3	12
Rainy River						1					1	2
Renfrew			1			2			1			4
Stor., Dundas & Glen.											2	2
Simcoe			2	2		5		3			6	18
Thunder Bay								2			1	3
Victoria				1		1						2
Waterloo			1	1		5					2	9
Welland						1			1			2
Wellington			1	1		1		1				4
Wentworth									1			
York	4	3	15	35	1	7		2	16	9	4	96
Prescott and Russell.			1	1		1						3
Grand Total												383

REPORT FROM BRANCH LABORATORY OF PROVINCIAL BOARD OF HEALTH AT KINGSTON, FOR THE YEAR 1911.

Counties.	Release +	Release −	Diagnosis +	Diagnosis −	Tuberculous Sputa +	Tuberculous Sputa −	Typhoid Bloods +	Typhoid Bloods −	Miscellaneous Specimens	Chemical	Bacter a.	Total Number for Year
Algoma								1				1
Bruce				3	2	3	1	1				10
Carleton		2	1	1	8	14	67	33			21	147
Dundas				2	4	17	6	10	2		25	66
Essex						1						1
Frontenac	54	137	55	173	61	270	109	276	64		255	1,454
Glengarry				8	3	19	1		2		21	54
Grenville			2		7	9	10	6	1		15	50
Haldimand						1						1
Haliburton											1	1
Hastings			3	10	12	33	7	7	7		77	156
Lanark		2	1	12	11	14	2	6	5		38	91
Leeds			3	32	20	46	24	45	4		89	263
Lennox and Addington				8	5	47	15	45	1		52	173
Nipissing					1	4					3	8
Northumberland					5	12	7	3	3		8	38
Parry Sound			1	7	2	2						12
Peterborough					2	5	1	1			11	20
Prescott				2		4	3				42	51
Prince Edward					1	4					14	19
Renfrew	1	2	5	3	15	28	4	13	2		25	98
Russell			2	11	2	27	4	15			15	76
Simcoe				7	4	6	10	19				46
Stormont				2	8	11	2	2			27	52
Thunder Bay								1				1
Victoria					2	3		1			11	17
Waterloo					2	4		1				7
Welland					5				1			6
Wentworth					2	3						5
	55	143	73	281	184	587	273	486	92		750	2,924

APPENDIX "A."

The reports appearing in this Appendix were received from the Secretaries f the different Local Boards of Health of the cities and towns of the Province, in onformity with section 60 of the Public Health Act, and have been edited by the ecretary of the Board.

BRANTFORD.

DR. F. G. E. PEARSON, M.O.H.

I herein present to you a brief report of the Health Department for the year ending ctober 31st, 1911.

MORTUARY STATISTICS.

For the period comprising this report there have occurred, exclusive of still births, 02 deaths, which in the population as given by the assessors' returns to be 24,084, gives mortuary rate of 12.5 per thousand.

Among the causes of death we find: Typhoid fever, 12 (2 of which occurred in outide cases at hospital); diphtheria, 4; cholera infantum, 11; tuberculosis, 14; pneuonia, 15; cerebro-spinal meningitis, 3. As to ages we find 87 under 1 year; 16 under years; 73 over 60 years; 20 over 80 years.

CONTAGIOUS DISEASES.

Of this class of disease I am pleased to report that we have had a decided decrease over the preceding year, viz., 140 cases, as compared with 286 cases for the preceding year, were as follows:

Diphtheria.—During the past year there have occurred in all 22 cases of diphtheria, with 4 deaths.

Scarlet Fever.—Of this disease there were reported 34 cases, with no fatalities.

Smallpox.—During the past year we have had but two cases of very mild variety, which were promptly dealt with, and no further outbreak occurred. Both cases were undoubtedly contracted from outside sources, and were not associated either with the other. One occurred in November of last year, and the other in June of this year.

Typhoid Fever.—In this disease as with the others we have had a decided decrease over last year, viz., 55 cases with 10 deaths, as compared with 113 cases for the corresponding year.

This reduction I believe has been largely due to the fact that not only has the city water supply been up to the normal, but people have been generally more careful as regards the house fly and have exercised care in this direction. Yet there is room for improvement, as in many cases where the disease existed there was frequently an uncared for closet near and an abundance of flies to act as carriers.

Again the neglected garbage barrel, which proves a good wrecking place for these pests, I think should receive more attention. The time has arrived I believe when a regulation can with proper cover should be provided both for the above and the facility in handling the same.

Measles.—We have had reported to us 27 cases, with no deaths. It is for this disease that I believe we do not get the full reports; on account of the mildness of the cases they are cared for by the mothers, and we frequently know nothing of them until they require a certificate to return to school.

This, to my mind, is a great mistake, for, although the epidemic may be mild, the complications that so frequently follow this disease are often serious, and especially to children and those not properly quarantined, often lead to dangerous results.

I, therefore, as a matter of warning, wish to state that although a physician may not be called, the householder is equally responsible in the matter of reporting these cases, and according to Act, should, within 24 hours of the occurrence of the disease in his house, report the existence of the same to the office.

Hoping that this intimation will be sufficient notice that all future cases will be promptly reported, and thus we will be able to cope with any mild outbreaks before they become of any magnitude.

Public Abattoir.

As this matter has been so frequently before this Board, I will without going into further details as to the necessity of such an establishment, state that I had hoped before the year elapsed to have seen ways or means devised for such. The proposition was taken up by a committee of the council, and certain arrangements were being dealt with. That, I hope in the forthcoming report to the council, the proposals will be brought to a successful result.

Sewage disposal and river pollution were mentioned in my last report. I wish again to direct your attention to the necessity of protecting our river from pollution, both in the consideration of future water extensins and the ice problem. Our river should be maintained as free from sewage as possible from towns above. At the same time we are face to face with the proper disposal of our own sewage, and I think that the time has passed when we shall further be allowed to trespass upon this matter, and will have to inaugurate a system of tanks and contact. Therefore, from the foregoing, while we will be forced to do this, some representation should be made to have the whole matter of sewage disposal in the river dealt with by the financial board.

Tuberculosis Sanatorium.

In the matter of a tubercular sanatorium, which we have always had a keen desire to see completed, I have been informed by a leading member of the committee in charge that, although some delay has been caused on account of funds to carry out their desire. it will only be a matter of a short time until the difficulties will be overcome, and that we may look forward with expectation of securing in the near future a nicely equipped building for this class of disease.

Sanitary Inspector's Report.

Mr. Glover's report was a very exhaustive one and dealt with a variety of branches of the work that showed that the inspector had been exceedingly active in his duties. The inspector touched on a number of lines, among them being the overcrowding of local boarding houses by foreigners. The inspector stated that he had made numerous visits, but he stated that he had encountered a great deal of opposition from them on account of their not understanding the law. Mr. Glover, however, **sta**ted that the conditions had improved to a great extent, particularly where Armenians were concerned. The objection to garbage disposal was also touched on. Mr. Glover spoke of the complaints that had come in from residents of West Brantford on account of the odors arising from the garbage. The inspector stated that at present the garbage was being dumped at the foot of South Market Street, as the city wished to extend the street in this direction. It was stated that many schemes were advanced for the disposal of the garbage, but the inspector stated that as there was so much low land in the city at the present time the most profitable disposal was at the present dumping ground and at West Brantford. The report also stated that there were at the present time only 34 licensed milk vendors in the city, a decrease in number of six from last year. The inspector also stated that four tests had been conducted during the year, and that with few minor exceptions the tests had been satisfactory.

The report also made clear that the number of earth closets in the city was rapidly decreasing, and that in the near future it would be possible to do away with them entirely. The good work of the board of works in getting such a large number of sewer connections made was also briefly commented upon. The public lavatory on the market square was also referred to, and although a new flush tank had been installed and various other improvements added, it was stated that the place could never be kept in a first-class condition until a man was appointed specially to look after this department.

The junk dealers were referred to as being as a class a more law-abiding community, than the city has been blessed with for some time. A regular system of inspection has been maintained since the first of the year, and every property in the city has been frequently visited, although much of the inspector's time had been taken up with the weed nuisance. The delivery wagons have been examined, the hotels, laundries and bake shops inspected, and all have been found in a creditable state of sanitation.

The inspector concluded his report by thanking the members of the Board for their help and co-operation during the year.

CHATHAM.

Dr. W. R. Hall, M.O.H.

I herewith submit my annual report for the year ending December 1st, 1911.

The Local Board of Health held eleven meetings during the year, nine regular meetings and two special. The Chairman, Dr. Bray, and Mr. W. R. Baxter attended all the meetings; Dr. Charteris, ten; Mr. J. C. Wanless, eight; Rev. Colles, six; Mr. B. Oldershaw, five; the Mayor, three.

Money expended by the Board during the year, $1,315.00; $105.74 of which was for maintenance of isolation hospital.

VITAL STATISTICS.

Births, 202—Females, 107; males, 95.
Marriages, 186.
Deaths, 163; still-born, 15. Death rate, about 1.36 per cent.

AGES AT DEATH.

Under 1 year, 21; between 1 and 5 years, 7; between 5 and 10 years, 0; between 10 and 15 years, 3; between 15 and 20 years, 6; between 20 and 30 years, 10; between 30 and 40 years, 19; between 40 and 50 years, 7; between 50 and 60 years, 13; between 60 and 70 years, 24; between 70 and 80 years, 31; between 80 and 90 years, 19; over 90 years, 3. Total, 163.

Some causes of death: Consumption, 13; pneumonia, 13; apoplexy, 13; cancer, 5.

CONTAGIOUS DISEASES.

Typhoid Fever.—There were 19 cases during the year, with 2 deaths. Three cases contracted the disease outside of the city; three contracted the disease from patients they were nursing—from direct contact. There were no cases traced to the city water supply.

Diphtheria.—As follows: January 1, April 1, June 1, August 2, September 2, October 1. Total, 8; no deaths.

Scarlet Fever.—March 1, April 1, June 5. Total, 7; no deaths.

Smallpox.—June 1. Recovered.

Chicken-pox.—December 2, January 5. Total, 7.

Consumption.—These cases are not yet reported, and we only learn of them after death. There were 13 deaths.

MILK SUPPLY.

There were seven general examinations of the milk supplied by the vendors in the city, and several examinations of samples sent in by purchasers. There were no prosecutions. I have been doing this work under great disadvantages, not having suitable premises or proper apparatus.

The Inspector has made frequent examinations of the city vendors' premises, and once during the year examined all the farm dairies supplying milk to the vendors, and these inspections rated each dairy according to a standard score-card procured from the Provincial Board of Health, leaving a copy with each dairy and a copy in this office. At the same time he suggested to them how they could best improve conditions on their premises, etc. This work involved considerable expense in travelling and time, but should produce good results.

SLAUGHTER-HOUSES

Were reported as in good condition by the Inspector. A new slaughter-house abattoir, with cold storage, has been established near the city, where all animals are inspected before slaughter, and the carcases after, by a competent inspector, appointed by the Government, and the city now has an opportunity to protect its citizens from eating diseased meat, without incurring the expense of employing an inspector of meat, the stamp of the Abattoir Company being sufficient guarantee.

Five lots of pork and one carcase of beef were condemned and ordered off the market, and two lots of fruit were also condemned as unfit for food.

SCAVENGING, ETC.

Three hundred and five householders have availed themselves of the garbage regulations during the year, an increase of fifty during the year.

The Inspector ordered 1,077 closets and 253 yards cleaned during the year, and the city scavenger disposed of 188 dead animals. An incinerator plant for the disposal of garbage and dead animals is very much needed by the city.

FORT WILLIAM.

Dr. R. E. Wodehouse, M.O.H.

The year has been an active one in health matters.

1. The smallpox epidemic in the early part, running from January to June, gave three anxious months.

2. A slight outbreak of scarlet fever in and around Ogden Street showed results from the Department equipment.

3. The active campaign against infant mortality from summer intestinal disorders which met with such excellent success.

4. The launching of a movement against tuberculosis, under the assistance of Dr. Porter.

5. The building and operating of a proper place for slaughtering animals for human food.

6. The aproval of the City Council of the appointment of a qualified veterinary as food inspector.

7. The adoption of an efficient milk by-law.

8. The preparation of a by-law to provide for the construction of a high temperature incinerator of 50 tons capacity.

9. The preparation of a by-law to provide for the construction of a proper conduit or tunnel under the Kaministikwia River, to contain water mains and cables.

10. The opening of lanes in all districts heretofore unprovided.

11. The mandates for construction of sewers.

12. The organizing of the City Hall Health Office, with a permanent stenographer, to take complaints by 'phone or otherwise, at all business hours.

13. The institution of a health visiting nurse.

14. The medical inspection of schools for defects of eyes, ears, nose, throat and teeth.

The epidemic of smallpox, beginning with one case in January, next case 23rd of February, and the third case to come to light from a new focus, being March 16th, was a most discouraging affair, and at once made it evident that there were mild cases existing which were not known to the Health Department. One such unknown case was unearthed by the Health Officer March 23rd, 1911, being a prominent business man, who had been mixing to an unusual extent during three weeks of his infection with all classes of our citizens.

Strict quarantine regulations were enforced upon all people directly exposed, and compulsory vaccination carried out with all parties in the slightest degree exposed and with all children attending schools whose contributory pupils came from possibly affected areas of the city. Fourteen cases and two suspects were taken care of in the Isolation Hospital. Two cases, in fact five cases, never entered the hospital, owing to not being detected until almost recovered. The four final cases of the epidemic were the results of three undetected cases in one home, followed by another case brought to my notice, and a second case next door; the other two being on dredges, whose hands had been associated with a party in original house. This final focus was the most alarming, necessitating the quarantining of a construction camp outside the city, also a school section outside the city, the compulsory vaccination of citizens on one street in the centre of the city; the employees of the Great Lakes Dredging Co., 300 men; the pupils of two schools, and the employees of a steam laundry, as well as quarantining a dredge in the river.

Two points were established during the epidemic:

1. That the cost of handling smallpox is no more excessive than any other infectious disease of similar prevalence.

2. That vaccination is most alarmingly neglected both in our older and younger generations, much to the peril of our community.

The number of people vaccinated were approximately 1,400.

```
4  schools ............................................. 750
1  general hospital ...................................  60
2  lots of workmen ....................................  375
1  hotel ..............................................   50
1  laundry ............................................   30
   General public ..................................... 250
```

Total cost to city was $257.06, being 18 cents each, including cost of vaccine, assistant physician, and all dressings, as well as extra nurses and proportion of second health nurse salary. This cost also provides for $57.00 worth of fresh vaccine, changeable when date expires.

The smallpox and scarlet fever epidemics more than demonstrated the good judgment exercised last year in erecting proper and efficient isolation hospital quarters, which at the present time provides accommodation of 25 beds.

The scarlet fever epidemic developed rapidly, and owing to the following drastic methods was quelled quickly. Two cases, at 308 and 312 Ogden Street, being reported one week apart, we visited 310 Ogden Street, and found a child in the fourth week of scarlet fever which had not been reported or quarantined. The householder was successfully prosecuted. All cases developing afterwards were placed in the hospital at once. The homes of absentees from Ogden School were all visited, and children inspected. All other cases were promptly reported and no further cases developed in homes already affected; the spacious new Isolation Hospital accommodating all the cases, and thus shortening epidemic.

A large freighter entered our harbor, having on board a sick man. The man asked for his pay in full and left ship. He was found in Port Arthur two days later, with smallpox developed. Ship was quarantined and one suspect removed to the hospital. Ship fumigated, hands and officers all vaccinated, and entire cost of bonus to nurse in hospital, hospital daily charge, fumigating ship and vaccination, were paid by ship, being $37.00.

The ship master was pleased with effective methods and exceedingly low cost. A similar case this year in another Ontario town cost captain over $300.00, and necessitated deposit of $1,000.00 by master of ship. This all helps our port.

The number of smallpox patients treated in the hospital during 1911 were 16, with a total number of hospital days of 340.

The number of scarlet fever patients treated in the hospital during 1911 were 10, with a total number of hospital days of 298.

The number of diphtheria patients treated in the hospital during 1911 were 7, with a total number of hospital days of 92.

The amount collected for smallpox at $1 per day, $237.30. The amount uncollected for smallpox at $1 per day, $103.

The amount collected for scarlet fever patients at $1 per day, $135. The amount uncollected for scarlet fever patients at $1 per day, $162.

The amount collected for diphtheria patients at $1 per day, $23.50. The amount uncollected for diphtheria patients at $1 per day, $68.50.

Total collected, $411.80. Total uncollected, $343.20.

The total number of hospital days, including one case of measles and suspects of other cases of diseases, were 755 days.

Antitoxine used was 84,000 units, costing $42.

After properly proportioning cost of nurses, etc., between smallpox term of occupancy of hospital and other diseases, the apparent cost of smallpox epidemic, with outside cost to department, fumigating houses, etc., was $1,071.88. This covers all cost of bonus to nurses, etc., for 16 patients, giving a total of 340 hospital days, spread over the months of January, February, March, April, May and June, with extra heating charges for cold months. This gives an average cost per patient of $67, or a per capita per hospital day cost of $3.15, absolutely entire cost of epidemic.

The cost of maintenance for cases of other diseases, $1,215.55 for entire year, providing for 415 hospital days, and 20 patients. Average cost for patient, $60.78; per capita per hospital day cost, $2.93.

The campaign against infant mortality from summer ailments was most gratifying from the results obtained, and from the interest and co-operation shown by the public in general and mothers. That your honorable Board showed good judgment in providing a second health nurse is certain. Her work was greatly appreciated by the citizens and assisted this department wonderfully in ascertaining the real causes and best measures to be adopted to foster the movement to prevent or reduce our infant mortality from intestinal causes. The visiting health nurse inspected the home of each baby whose birth had been registered during the previous twelve months, and in the foreign districts went from house to house. She reported on condition (sanitary) inside and outside of house, lanes, streets and yards adjoining same. The reports showed as well how many babies had ben born to the mother, how many had died, and how they had been fed; also the method of feeding present baby, and if artificial, whether by doctor's order or not.

(a) 411 babies were inquired into.

(b) 340 babies were breast fed.

(c) 44 babies were fed a few months, but later mixed fed.

(d) 17 cases of Class C were mixed fed without doctor's order.

(e) 27 babies were artificially fed from birth.

(f) 6 babies of Class E were so fed without doctor's order.

The last four classes, C, D, E, F, were all revisited by nurse from time to time to ascertain whether they were sick or not, and to oversee and correct feeding classes D and F.

During August 77 bottle-fed babies were revisited; 13 were ill; 59 sick babies were cared for during August; 246 visits were made during August.

July mortality from intestinal disorders was 75 per cent. less than 1910. August mortality from intestinal disorders was 55 per cent. less than 1910. July and August mortality from inestinal disorders was 65 per cent.

The mortality and conditions surrounding illegitimate babies in our city is appalling, wilfully wrong feeding apparently being a slow form of murder.

The registration of births among the foreigners is about 12 to 18 per cent.

Work to reduce infant mortality must be conducted during twelve months in the year. Each baby registered by physician has a health and feeding circular sent to its mother from the City Hall. Each home is visited at once by the health nurse. During July and August the babies registered were all breast fed but one, showing good results from Publicity Campaign.

The exact cost of this work this year was $194.98, including medicines for poor, nurse's salary, and car tickets.

The banquet given by His Worship the Mayor in the early part of the year, and the facts brought to light in the many good addresses, which were read by the public, thanks to the generosity of our sympathetic press, were features granting unlimited assistance.

The Publicity Campaign, conducted through the kindness of our evening paper, was read with interest, and advice accepted with confidence, for all of which I am very grateful.

That Dr. Porter has been able to visit our city is gratifying. An invitation had been rendered to him nearly twelve months ago, and he has remained true to his promise. The Provincial Government car with tubercular exhibit has been requested, but so far without avail. Our tubercular mortality this year is 21, compared with 22 last year, showing if anything a slight increase in proportion to population.

A fairly sanitary building for slaughtering has been provided and the old resort for such purposes finally condemned.

We are in need of a new city by-law complying with the amended portion of Health Act, which grants cities the power to pass by-laws prohibiting the killing of animals, no matter where, for human consumption within its limits, without the approval of the Local Health Department of the building and methods in use for same.

The sanctioning by the City Council of the appointment of a specially qualified veterinary as Meat, Dairy and Food Inspector is most gratifying, and will be a boon to the class of food supplied in our city. You can surmise what the conditions are in our city, where it is known no adequate inspection of food exists, when in Winnipeg, in the month of September, 1911, where adequate inspection is anticipated by the trade, foodstuffs to the amount of 46,705 pounds were seized and condemned.

Our milk by-law, owing to one misfortune and another, has not become operative until the late date of November 1st, 1911. It is most efficient, and if enforced, as I expect it will be, shall prove a boon to the methods and quality of the supply.

The laboratory has been very active this year, and has reported examinations on milk to the number of 148 samples, with 14 samples containing less than 3 per cent. fats.

The diphtheria swabs examined number 27; the sputum swabs examined number 33; the typhoid widals examined number 3.

The plating of water samples number 11; the plating of milk samples number 7.

The number of water samples found contaminated with fœcal matter being one. It came from a well several miles from the city, and typhoid bacilli were isolated from it.

The number of milk samples found contaminated, or from which typhoid bacilli were isolated, was one, being from the same farm which was the causal factor of seven or nine cases of typhoid, with three fatalities.

Many successful prosecutions have resulted from the laboratory findings, but here it may be permissible to state that this cost and work of obtaining samples, examining same, watching the victuallers' methods, and prosecuting violators of the law, is absolute waste if this Department does not enjoy the sincere co-operation of the Magistrate. The Magistrate is the most effective health officer we can have, and if the public learn that violations of the Health Act or by-laws are awarded convictions and fines, the violations will be fewer, the sworn informations less, and the cost of the two departments just about half, with double the effectiveness. I wish to thank the Magistrate for his moral support in obtaining reports of infectious diseases by the householder and others possessing knowledge of existence of same. It has improved 100 per cent. since two convictions were obtained from his court.

That Fort William is in need of an incinerator is certain, for three good reasons:
1. Sanitary.—The complete destruction of all unsanitary matter.
2. Economy.—The reduced cost of collection and hauling for same.
3. Nuisance.—The abatement of the foulest thing in our district, the nuisance

ground. It is a great source of annoyance from smoke, odors, and contamination of upper part of Neebing River, as well as the certain creation of a hotbed for disease in years to come, when excavation on this property for building is undertaken as it is subdivided for habitation. The by-law should be endorsed by every property-owner for the second reason alone.

The by-law for the construction of a conduit for the conveyance of water mains under the Kaministikwia River is most commendable. We have so far, thanks to Providence, been spared from a break in both pipes at the same time, but owing to their exposed position on the surface of the river bed, and the removal on either side of pipes of the river bed by the Dominion Government dredging operations, it behooves us to move quickly, as a pure water supply cut off, a high pressure fire protection taken from us, at a moment's notice, is too immense a proposition to trifle with long. The cost of repairs for the present two exposed pipes during the past year has been $1,649.22. The estimates of cost of construction of a suitable conduit for all time to convey cables and water mains is $65,000. The present expense is an outlay almost equal to the interest and sinking fund upon the safe system, but even if it were more it would repay the city as an actual insurance or assurance against accidents.

The extension of the lane system to include all the areas of the city previously lacking them is most commendable. It makes sanitation much more effective and reduces cost of conducting same.

The sewer construction in our city continues apace: 1909, 3.32 miles; 1910, 3.48 miles; 1911, 3.81 miles.

Private sewer connections, 413 ordinary applications.

The private sewer connections under the special Legislation, obtained last spring from the Provincial Legislature have promised to assist very much in ridding the city of that menace to Public Health,—the outdoor privy. The number of applications registered by citizens under this Act are nine.

The number of applications registered by this Department owing to non-compliance with Act, are 80.

That the By-law stipulating the form of structure of outside privies is antiquated must be evident. Elsewhere, active Health Departments insist on " Impervious stone, cement or brick, pits under closets, which do not permit of soil contamination. The fœcal matter is in a dark, cool place, does not decompose so rapidly, and is away from flies. The present buildings, with exposed, overflowing cans, are a disgrace. This by-law should be amended.

The proper organization of the City Hall Office with a permanent stenographer attached, who is always there during business hours to record complaints from citizens, assisted materially in the efficiency of this Department and almost doubled available outside working time of your Sanitary Inspector.

The first year of Medical Inspection is nearly completed with marked improvement in condition of pupils along the lines investigated under the system adopted by the Board of Education. Many pupils with deficient vision, have upon notification from Medical Examiner, procured glasses, but some of the glasses procured have proven, upon second semi-annual examination to be improperly provided; which is doubly unfortunate, as the parents resent the suggestion of further expense and are indignant at the result of their efforts to procure proper vision for their children, without success.

The condition of the teeth of the pupils show the most marked improvement. Very few have neglected to take advantage of the suggestion to place themselves under the care of a dentist.

The cases of obstructed breathing have been reported only in grossly evident cases, as public sentiment should not be strained too much, until a grasp of the helpful side of a medical inspection has been appreciated.

The cases of defective hearing have probably been least numerous of all findings.

The examination of heads for vermin was conducted for the entire system of schools during the first two weeks of attendance after vacation, by the health nurse, much to the pleasure of the teachers.

It is impossible to obtain proper conveyance in the City to remove patients from different places to the Isolation hospital. They are all communicable diseases, and according to law must not be removed in a closed rig, or in any public vehicle, without the knowledge and consent of the owner. Many lives are endangered, owing to their low state of exposure to the cold winter.

We should possess in the city an ambulance or conveyance, covered in, absolutely devoid of upholstering and draperies and constructed so that it will be closed air-tight, fumigated, and washed down with disinfectants. Such a rig would be absolutely safe for police work, as we need it so seldom. I would suggest your Honorable Board, communicating with the Police Commissiners, with the hope of sharing the cost equally, and thus providing a great want to both departments.

Steps are under way by this department to secure the reporting of deaths, according to the international classifications of sickness and causes of death.

A set of books will be opened this month to apportion each month's accounts against the department or class of health work, necessitating the expenditure.

I wish to acknowledge with thanks:

1. The co-operation and sympathy of your Honorable Board which I have enjoyed the past year.

2. The outspoken appreciation of the City Council, both by word of mouth of its different members when in session, and by the increased remuneration granted me at my re-appointment.

3. The harmony which exists with other city departments.

4. The untiring efforts and willingness of the staff of your department:

Mr. Stanley, Sanitary Inspector, has been most active. Miss Duncan, 1st Nurse most faithful and competent. Mrs. Williamson, 2nd, was very energetic in visiting work Miss Patch, your stenographer, always courteous and willing.

The financial statement and vital statistics are appended, all of which is respectfully submitted.

Dividing nurses salary in proper proportions to different work conducted, different undertakings this year cost as follows:—

Vaccination	$ 257 06
Smallpox, nursing and fumigating	1,071 88
District health nursing	194 98
Isolation Hospital	1,215 55
Diphtheria antitoxine	84 00
Sanitary Inspector's office, exclusive of stenographer	424 04
Sanitary Inspector's salary	1,000 00
Health othce	43 00
Health Officer's salary	1,000 00
Laboratory	102 79
Isolation Hospital furnishings	1,639 67
Old Isolation building, moving	305 00
Repairing building, fence and plowing	310 00
Collected	$411 80
Uncollected	343 20

BIRTHS.

Births.	Nov.	Dec.	Jan.	Feb.	March.	April.	May.	June.	July.	August.	Sept.	Oct.	Total.
	35	59	34	54	54	49	57	42	61	68	53	25	591

NOVEMBER, 1910—DEATHS—OCTOBER, 1911.

Causes.	Nov.	Dec.	Jan.	Feb.	March.	April.	May.	June.	July.	August.	Sept.	Oct.	Total.
Diphtheria			1	1					1				
Scarlet Fever													
Typhoid	3	1					1				1		6
Measles													
Tuberculosis	5			1	1	2	3	2	2	1	2		19
Ileocolitis	1		1	1	1		3	4	8	11	2		32
Still-born	1	5	2	3		1	4	5	6	5	2	4	38
Old Age			1				1		1		1		4
Alcholitis			1								1		2
Accidental	6		5	2	2	4	7	8	5	4	4	2	49
Pneumonia	3	4			4	3	1	3	1			1	20
Premature Birth	2	5	2	3		1	1	1		2			17
Carbolic Poison						1		1		1		3	6
Other causes	6	2	5	5	13	6	9	5	13	8	6	9	87
	27	17	18	16	21	18	30	29	37	32	19	19	285

NOVEMBER, 1910—INFECTIOUS DISEASES, DEATHS—AS REPORTED OCTOBER, 1911.

—		Nov.	Dec.	Jan.	Feb.	March	April	May	June	July	August	Sept.	Oct.	Total
Tuberculosis	cases....	....	....	....									....	
"	deaths ..	5	....	....	1	1	2	3	2	2	1	2	....	19
Measles	cases....	3	7	1	....	1	....	....	1	2	....	....	2	17
"	deaths ..	....	....	....	....	....	....	....	....	....	....	....	....	....
Scarlet Fever	cases....	....	1	1	2	1	3	1	10	7	....	....	2	28
"	deaths ..	....	....	....	....	....	....	....	....	....	....	....	....	....
Typhoid	cases....	7	....							6	19	25	6	63
"	deaths ..	3	1	....	....	....	....	....	1	....	....	1	....	6
Whooping Cough	cases....	....	....					....	1	....			....	1
"	deaths ..	....	....					1	....	2			1	4
Chickenpox	cases....	....	....			1			1				1	3
"	deaths ..	....	....										....	....
Diphtheria	cases....	1	1	1	....		1	1	....				1	8
"	deaths ..	....	....	1	1	....		1					....	3
Smallpox	cases....	....	....	1	1	4	5	4	....				....	15
"	deaths ..	....	....	....	....	....	....	....	....				....	....

GUELPH CITY.

DR. H. O. HOWITT, M.O.H.

My annual report as your Medical Health Officer, herewith tendered, shows that under the present conditions the state of health during the year has been, if anything, an improvement upon that of the preceding years.

MORTALITY.

There occurred in the City of Guelph during the year ended November 31st, 1911, 211 deaths. Although this number of deaths occurred actually within the city limits, a number were outsiders, who had come to the city for treatment.

Dividing the deaths into decades of years we find that:

There were 46 persons died between the ages of 1 and 10
    "   "   11   "   "   "   "   "   " 10 " 20
    "   "   12   "   "   "   "   "   " 20 " 30
    "   "   8   "   "   "   "   "   " 30 " 40
    "   "   19   "   "   "   "   "   " 40 " 50
    "   "   19   "   "   "   "   "   " 50 " 60
    "   "   25   "   "   "   "   "   " 60 " 70
    "   "   30   "   "   "   "   "   " 70 " 80
    "   "   17   "   "   "   "   "   " 80 " 90
    "   "   3   "   "   "   "   "   " 90 " 100

To be added to the above list, and which probably might be included in the first decade, are 21 still-births, which bring the total up to 211.

It will be seen that the greatest number of deaths occurred in the first decade of life. And of the 46 who died during that period, 41 died at or before the age of two years, emphasizing the fact that it is in the first two years of life that the greatest mortality is found.

During the year there were two deaths directly due to diphtheria and one to scarlet fever. pneumonia claimed 9; bronchitis 2, kidney disease 10, peritonitis 5, blood poisoning 2, pernicious anaemia 1, lockjaw 1, whooping cough 1, 14 were due to cancer, 13 to tuberculosis, acute alcoholism 2, typhoid 2, and suicide and accidental deaths numbered 5. Senile degenerative changes, diseases of infancy, and diseases of the circulatory system carried off the great majority of cases.

The death rate due to malignancy cannot yet well be combatted. The treatment which promises the best results, is early diagnosis and surgery.

The death rate of 13, due to tuberculosis is entirely too large, when one considers that it is almost always a wholly preventable disease.

9 B.H.

INFECTIOUS DISEASES.

There were reported during the year 47 cases of scarlet fever, with one death; 76 cases of diphtheria, with 2 deaths; 14 cases of typhoid fever, with 2 deaths.

In nearly every one of these 14 typhoid cases, well water had been used. Not one case could be traced directly to city water, in spite of the very large number of people in Guelph who use it in comparison with the number who obtain their water from other sources. What an object lesson this should be. The people who use well water are much in the minority, and yet it is from this small minority that the great number of cases of typhoid fever have come. This is true, not only during the year just closed but applies equally to the past three years or so—since the new waterworks system was installed, previous to which the citizens were really consuming questionably filtered river water. From the standpoint of public health, no step taken by the city of Guelph in the past has really equalled or can be favorably compared with the installation of the new water system, whereby the purest of spring water is obtainable through the tap ir the dwelling of every citizen who desires it. It has meant almost the eradication of the disease, known as typhoid fever, and removed the danger which was formerly pending of a large epidemic, which would certainly have occurred had the river water become infected above the old reservoir.

THE HEALTH BY-LAW.

The new Health By-law has so far worked out eminently successfully. Naturally during the first few months certain friction arose, but in the future those precautions which are taken for the benefit of public health should be observed better than they have been in the past. All that is needed now to make everything run most satisfac torily, is the hearty co-operation of every citizen with the officers of the Health De partment.

The garbage area should, and will be, increased.

THE INFECTIOUS HOSPITAL.

The long continued agitations and recommendations of the Board of Health for ar Infectious Hospital are at last about to bear fruit. The Infectious Hospital now nearing completion will surpass in some respects even the hopes of this Board. The hospital is an absolute necessity, and much credit is due to the special committee appointed by the City Council to take this matter up, and to the Council itself for carrying out the recommendations of this Board.

HAMILTON CITY.

DR. JAMES ROBERTS, M.O.H.

SUMMARY OF CONTAGIOUS AND INFECTIOUS DISEASES FROM NOVEMBER 1ST, 1910, TO OCTOBER 31ST, 1911.

—	1910 November.	December.	1911 January.	February.	March.	April.	May.	June.	July.	August.	September.	October.	Total.
Diphtheria	6	7	12	4	5	6	4	5	7	6	9	18	89
Mumps		2	7	4	8	3	17	20	5	2	1	27	96
Smallpox													
Chickenpox	4	22	38	11	2	14	28	21	5	3	4	4	156
Consumption	10	1	3	7	10	4	6	8	8	3	9	9	78
Poliomyelitis													
Whooping Cough	9	3	12	4	5	12	13	11	1	13	36	23	143
Typhoid Fever	3	1	3	4	1	7	6	7	15	15			62
Scarlet Fever	23	20	29	26	27	38	50	44	17	7	24	25	330
Ger. Measles				2	1	30	24	35	2		2	2	98
Measles	1			4	6	4	10		3	2	11	24	65
Erysipelas	3				1	1		1					6
Totals	59	56	104	66	66	119	158	152	64	51	96	132	1,123

Contagious Diseases.

1,123 cases of communicable disease were reported for 1911, as compared with 3,141 in 1910, and 1,146 in 1909. The total deaths from the same group of diseases amounted to 107, while in 1910, 1909 and 1908 respectively, 164, 162, and 127 were recorded from communicable diseases, so that, while, in the general death rate, there was no appreciable decline from the figures of 1910, 1909 and 1908, namely, 13.8, 3.1, and 13.4 per hundred thousand of population, the death rate from this group of diseases was 1.55 per hundred thousand, as compared with 2.25 for 1910 and 2.31 for 1909.

Of the 1,123 cases of communicable disease reported, 89 were diphtheria, 63 cases less than the number reported for 1910, and 93 less than the number recorded in 1909. In 1909, we had 18 deaths, a percentage mortality of 9.9; in 1910, 23 deaths, a percentage mortality of 15.1; while this year our percentage was 11.22 all of which mortality rates are too high, in the light of what has been accomplished in some even very large cities by the scientific administration of antitoxin.

Scarlet Fever.

Three hundred and thirty cases of scarlet fever were reported, as compared with 221 for 1911, and 356 for 1910. The deaths from this disease for the last three years— 8.8 and 13—represent a percentage mortality of 2.42, 3.62, and 3.65, respectively, for 1911, 1910, and 1909. It cannot be too often repeated that the seriousness of scarlet fever is not to be estimated in any adequate degree by the immediate mortality statistics. I overheard, on the street car, the other day, two mothers commenting on the number of children who were suffering from affections of the ears, as a result of having contracted this disease during the past winter. I fear their observations have been only too correct. While some of the misfortunes following scarlet fever are inevitable once the disease has been contracted, we cannot help regretting that the mild and ambulatory cases remain, in many instances, too long undiagnosed, and often altogether overlooked. We take the opportunity of once again emphasizing the urgent need of an up-to-date and adequately sized hospital for the reception of these cases. Hospitalization means the removal of the focus of infection from where it is hardest to control to the place where it can be rendered free from menace, and also the placing of the patient in an environment best suited for the carrying out of proper treatment, should sequelæ supervene.

Tuberculosis.

Caused the lowest number of deaths, namely, 64, for any year during the last fifteen or sixteen of the city's history, notwithstanding the significant strides in our population during the last decade.

In the following table, the deaths from tuberculosis are given as percentages of the total death rate for fifteen years:—

Year		Year	
1897	11.4	1905	7.7
1898	13.5	1906	8.1
1899	12.5	1907	7.3
1900	13.8	1908	8.0
1901	10.3	1909	10.0
1902	13.0	1910	7.1
1903	8.4	1911	5.3
1904	9.9		

The mortality from the white plague will be found, by a simple calculation, to have averaged, during the quinquennial period from 1897 to 1901, 12.3% of the total death rate; during the second period, 9.4, and during the third quinquennial period from 1907 to 1911, inclusive, 8.5% of the total deaths from all causes, so that, notwithstanding any idiosyncrasies presented by the figures for individual years, and which can be explained, in many instances, to some extent, at least, by seasonal variations in meteorological conditions, we are amply justified in making the assertion that the good seed of organized and individual effort against the white plague in this City has brought forth fruit abundantly.

To the Hamilton Health Association, which, through the Local Sanatorium, through the dispensary and the work of the home visiting nurse, has done such splendid work for the city, and to all those who have contributed so generously, either of time or effort or money, to the cause of eradicating this scourge, we offer our sincere congratulations in telling them that the figures above referred to spell to them a lesson of hope and confidence for the future.

TYPHOID FEVER.

Of this disease, 61 cases in all were reported. During the past five or six years, an inspector has been sent to the home from which every case has arisen for the purpose of securing accurate and detailed information with reference to milk supply, water supply, sanitation of premises, possibility of contact with previous cases, etc. By this means, we have been able to ascertain that at least seventeen of our cases were infected at places outside, leaving a total of 44, which originated within the city limits. Considering the character of our population, this small number, the smallest in thirteen years, speaks itself, in no uncertain terms, as to the state of our general sanitation. Our deaths, numbering eight, of actual local typhoid would seem to indicate that some mild or doubtful cases of the disease were unreported, yet we have every reason to believe that, owing to the assistance rendered by the laboratory, we have had during the past year, a fuller report than usual.

LEGISLATION.

BY-LAW FOR THE PROTECTION AND CLEAN HANDLING OF FOOD PRODUCTS.

In September, 1911, the Council passed a By-law, recommended by the Board of Health, for the protection and clean handling of food products, which provides as follows:—

" (1) All meat, poultry, game, fish, fruits, vegetables, confectionery, bread and other bakers' products, intended for sale for human food, shall not be conveyed from place to place, or exposed for sale, unless reasonably protected from dust, flies, animals, and other contaminating influences.

" (2) All persons, while engaged in the handling of articles of food, shall wear clean outer garments, and shall be free from contagious or infectious disease.

" (3) Every pedlar of foodstuffs from wagons, or carts, in addition to the clean covering provided for in the regulations, shall keep his wagon or cart in a sanitary condition."

In October, our By-law governing the production and sale of milk, under proper veterinary inspection, came into force.

This Legislation ensures:—

(1) The protection of milk from infection by typhoid, scarlet fever, diphtheria, and tuberculosis.

(2) The proper cooling of milk.

(3) The keeping of cows, milkers' hands, milkers' clothes, and all utensils, clean.

(4) The keeping of barns and surroundings in a sanitary condition.

The sanitary condition of the city has been thoroughly gone into by a special staff of capable inspectors, and has been much improved by the abolition of over 900 offensive, outside vaults, and the installation of indoor closets.

Next year, we expect to be able to furnish glowing accounts of the good work accomplished by our Woman Sanitary Inspector.

Our work on the Housing Situation during some two or three years has culminated in arousing a very active interest on the part of many of our leading citizens.

REPORT OF FOOD AND DAIRY INSPECTORS.

Below please find report of the work done by the sanitary inspectors from November 1st, 1910, to October 31st, 1911:—

Total number of Inspections 18,238
Inspections re privy vaults and d. e. closets 504
     "   " defective sewer connections 223
     "   " rubbish and refuse 555
     "   " unsanitary houses 59
     "   " overcrowded houses 20
     "   " water on lots 66
     "   " chickens on premises 62
     "   " hogs on premises 3
     "   " nuisance on premises 7
     "   of alleys 19
     "   " stables 32
     "   re accumulations of manure 349

Inspections re houses not being connected with sewer 7
    "   " unsanitary water closets 4
    "   " throwing waste water 40
    "   " typhoid fever 40
    "   " no convenience for workmen 2
    "   " water in cellars 44
    "   " nuisance caused by garbage utensils 27
    "   " throwing refuse 11
    "   of laundries 61
    "   " ice being cut on bay 85
    "   " garbage dumps 6
    "   " lodging houses 4
    "   re blocked drains 2
    "   " offensive odors from sewer 11
    "   " open water courses being blocked 7
    "   " cesspools 7
    "   " nuisance caused by hide horses 3
Miscellaneous inspections 15
Streets inspected for sewers 3
Schools inspected 2
Complaints unfounded 45
Ice Samples collected 6
Privy vaults and d. e. closets located 838
Cesspools located in annex 8
Summonses obtained 20
No. of Re-Inspections 4.728
No. water closets installed during year 900
Notices served re rubbish and refuse 559
    "   "   " defective sewer connections 212
    "   "   " accumulations of manure 301
    "   "   " unsanitary dwellings 23
    "   "   " chickens on premises 52
    "   "   " hogs on premises 3
    "   "   " nuisance 4
    "   "   " offensive privy vaults and d. e. closets 413
    "   "   to provide manure bins 168
    "   "   " provide covers for manure bins 17
    "   "   re unsanitary water closets 3
    "   "   to vacate unsanitary premises 5
    "   "   re blocked drains 3
    "   "   " overcrowded premises 33
    "   "   to put in sewer connections 21
    "   "   " provide convenience for workmen 4
    "   "   re throwing waste water 35
    "   "   to clean alleys 28
    "   "   re water on lots 51
    "   "   re water in cellars 22
    "   "   " garbage utensils 30
    "   "   " stables 16
    "   "   to cut off sink connections 10
    "   "   re throwing refuse and garbage 8
    "   "   to remove rabbits from premises 2
    "   "   " remove pigeons from premises 4
    "   "   " remove horses from premises 2
    "   "   re nuisance caused by hide houses 2
    "   "   to abolish cesspools 5
    "   "   " abolish privy vaults and install water closets 929
Miscellaneous notices served 9
Dead dogs destroyed at crematory 492
Dead cats destroyed at crematory 527
Dead fowl destroyed at crematory 116

WORK IN QUARANTINE AND DISINFECTION.

Schools disinfected for Diphtheria 1
Houses placarded for Scarlet Fever 153
    "   "   " Diphtheria 20
    "   "   " Poliomyelitis 1

Houses disinfected for S. F., patients sent to C. H. 16
    "   "   " Diphtheria, patients sent to C. H. 6
    "   "   " S. F.—cards removed 15
    "   "   " Diphtheria—cards removed 2
    "   "   " Tuberculosis 6
    "   "   " Erysipelas ....
    "   "   " Poliomyelitis ....
    "   "   " Typhoid Fever 2
    "   "   " Measles ....
    "   "   " Whooping Cough ....
    "   "   " Scarlet Fever, patient dead ....
Visits to quarantined houses 82
Clothing disinfected for Scarlet Fever 1

To the Chairmen and Members of the Board of Health.

Gentlemen,—

Below, please find report of the work done by the Food and Dairy Inspector from November 1st, 1910, to October 31st, 1911:

Total number of Inspections 1,94
Inspections of Central market 15
    "   " city dairies 26
    "   " farmers' dairies 18
    "   for milk licenses 3
    "   of butcher shops 36
    "   " bake shops 9
    "   " lunch rooms 11
    "   " fish stores 6
    "   " slaughter houses 2
    "   " fish restaurants ....
    "   " candy kitchens 4
    "   " fruit stores 4
    "   " pickle factories ....
    "   " meat cars ....
    "   " places where ice cream cones are made ....
    "   " bottling works ....
    "   " butter and egg stores 2
    "   " ice cream parlors 8
    "   " hotel kitchens ....
    "   " fertilizing works ....
    "   " milk wagons 5
    "   " cattle sheds ....
    "   " coal oil inlet ....
    "   " grocery stores 1
    "   " canning factories ....
    "   " soap works ....
    "   " cold storage houses ....
    "   *re* offensive trades ....
Sanitary inspections 23
Inspections of overcrowded houses 6
Complaints investigated 3
Number milk samples collected and tested 75
Number temperatures of milk taken 10
Temperatures found too high 2
Number places found selling milk without licenses 2
Bake shops visited and bread weighed 5
Loaves of bread seized 3
Lbs. of beef seized 1 86
Lbs. of pork seized 35
Lbs. of veal seized 18
Number of chickens seized 1
Baskets pears seized 2
Baskets apples seized ....
Bushels potatoes ....
Cream samples tested ....
Maple syrup samples tested ....

Summonses obtained 10
Attendance at police court 25
Butter weighed on Central Market 4
Milk licenses cancelled 9
Water samples collected 32
Ice samples collected 6
Attendance at County Court 2
Dairies closed on account of contagious disease 2
Notices served to renew milk licenses 270
    "   "   on dairymen to provide ice 142
    "   "   on dairymen to whitewash milk-houses 7
    "   "   on dairymen to clean milk wagons 9
    "   "   re offensive odors 2
    "   "   to clean premises 116
    "   "   on meat carriers to provide clean coats 4
    "   "   to provide manure bins 30

(Signed)   DR. CHARLES V. SHAIN,
Food and Dairy Inspector.

REPORT OF BACTERIOLOGIST.

To the Board of Health and M.O.H. of Hamilton. Gentlemen,—

I have the honor to present the following report of public health work done for the year ending October 31st, 1911. As I have only occupied the position of City Bacteriologist and Pathologist since September 1st, 1911, it will be seen that ten months of the work has been done under the regime of my predecessor, Dr. W. H. Tytler, who deserves still further credit for the excellent selection of the equipment of the laboratory and the beginning of the work.

There have been 985 examinations made for Diphtheria bacilli, 328 examinations of sputa for Tubercle bacilli, 200 examinations of blood for the agglutination re-action of Typhoid Fever, and the bacteriological examination of 43 samples of water, making a total of 1,556 specimens examined.

A brief analysis of these and their monthly distribution may be found in the accompanying tables:

EXAMINATIONS FOR DIPHTHERIA BACILLI.

Month.	For Diagnosis.			For Release.			Totals.
	Positive.	Suspicious.	Negative.	Positive.	Negative.	Not Classified.	
1910.							
November	2	1	16	7	12	1	39
December..................	5	2	26	6	0	1	50
1911.							
January	17	6	22	28	25	1	119
February	11	3	33	32	27	1	107
March......................	10	9	40	12	35	9	115
April.......................	5	1	36	3	20	2	67
May........................	10	5	50	....	12	5	82
June	3	1	54	13	15	1	87
July	6	3	39		14	....	62
August.....................	7	1	29	....	13	1	51
September..................	9	6	38	11	12	1	77
October....................	26	6	46	30	16	5	129
	111	44	429	162	211	28	985

EXAMINATIONS OF SPUTA FOR TUBERCLE BACILLI.

Month,	Positive,	Negative.	Totals,
1910			
November	....	29	29
December..................	2	15	17
1911			
January	4	28	32
February	5	15	20
March.....................	9	24	33
April......................	2	28	30
May.......................	7	21	28
June......................	3	13	16
July......................	3	36	39
August	2	13	15
September.................	3	25	28
October...................	6	35	41
	46	282	328

EXAMINATIONS OF BLOOD FOR THE AGGLUTINATION RE-ACTION OF TYPHOID FEVER.

Month,	Positive.	Suspicious.	Negative.	Total.
1910				
November	7	4	20	31
December.......	5	2	6	13
1911				
January	2	1	10	13
February	4	1	10	15
March..........	2	1	5	8
April...........	1	....	2	3
May............	1	3	10	14
June	....	....	4	4
July............	2	2	9	13
August.........	....	4	16	20
September......	7	2	12	21
October	23	4	18	45
	54	24	122	200

BACTERIOLOGICAL EXAMINATIONS OF WATER.

Date.	Number of samples.	Source of samples.	Total.
1911			
January			
12th.....................	6	Bay ice	
13th.....................	2	Reservoir	8
February			
9th.....................	1	Ice	
9th.....................	1	Tap water	2
March			
15th.....................	2	Reservoir	
20th.....................	2	"	
20th.....................	1	Springs	
20th.....................	1	Horse trough	6
April			
27th.....................	4	Barton Reservoir	
May			
11th.....................	2	Well	
13th.....................	2	Creek	
13th.....................	2	Basins	6
October			
2nd	3	Stipes Inlet	
22nd	2	Farm	
20-31st..................	12	Tap water	17
			43

(Signed)   EDWARD FIDLAR, M.D.

KINGSTON CITY.

DR. A. R. B. WILLIAMSON, M.O.H.

I submit herewith my report for the year just closed. A number of important matters have been dealt with during the year, but I just wish to call attention briefly to a few of them.

Last year we suffered from an epidemic of typhoid, due to contamination of our water supply by sewage. Fortunately, under the measures taken to abate the trouble, the epidemic gradually died out. We are still, however, face to face with the question that is agitating a great many other centres of population, namely, pure water supply and proper sewage disposal. These two cannot be considered apart, as the former depends to a large extent on the latter.

Constant testing of the water at Kingston has demonstrated the fact that the water supply is contaminated at the intake, five days out of ten. Previous testing never showed the ratio to be greater than one out of ten, so that conditions are becoming worse in this respect. By the chlorine treatment the water has been disinfected, so that for the past four months it has been uniformly pure at the taps. This, however, is only disinfected water; it is not pure water, and this municipality, as well as every other municipality on our great lakes, will have to in the near future, re-arrange their systems of water supply and sewage disposal. It is quite evident that if we are to be free from the menace of typhoid epidemics, present conditions cannot be allowed to exist. The chlorine treatment for the present is protecting us from this evil, but there is a possibility that with continued contamination of water supply, even this safeguard will be broken down. I am happy to be able to state, however, that during the past eight months our typhoid rate has been low.

In September last, a scarlet fever epidemic broke out among the children attending Victoria School. The number of cases increased rapidly and it was found necessary to close and fumigate the school. It was quite evident from the outset that the epidemic was due to the presence of some mild desquamating case that had either been concealed or not recognized by the parents. A careful and diligent search by the school nurse proved this to be the fact and this in only one evidence of the wisdom of the School Board in the appointment they have made, as the School Nurse is able, without creating suspicion or resentment, to visit homes and get information that it might be impossible for anyone else to obtain. At the present time the epidemic appears to have died out. There are only two placarded cases in the city, outside of the hospital, and by the end of this week there will only be three cases left in the hospital, and these are not all Kingston cases.

During the past year a system of garbage collection was inaugurated, the City Council contracting with certain parties to remove garbage at regular intervals. I think that under such adverse circumstances as the Collectors had to deal with, the collection was fairly good, although no doubt there are many cases where the collection was not attended to. It must be remembered, however, that the fault is not always with the contractors. Unless the city can either guarantee to the contractors that they or he shall get all garbage within the city limits, or unless the city goes into the business of garbage disposal itself, the arrangement will not be entirely satisfactory. The contractor estimates the amount of garbage to be collected and depends on receiving the amount for the purpose of raising swine. If he finds that some weeks he only receives a small fraction of the amount, owing to other collectors going around at irregular intervals, then he is going to be under a financial loss, and the complaint is frequently heard, that the contractors' wagons are forced to call at hundreds of places where they get nothing; whereas other collectors, not under contract, can go where they please. Again, it has been found in other cities that it is absolutely necessary to have household garbage placed in properly covered pails, and set out on the street at certain times during the week. Then, there is no possibility of its not being collected regularly.

A number of other conditions have come before your notice, but these, I think, are the more important ones, and all the more so since they are not at all settled, but will demand the attention of future Boards of Health in this Municipality.

LONDON CITY.

Dr. T. V. Hutchinson, M.O.H.

I beg to submit the following report upon the sanitary condition of the city, and other matters relating to the public health, for the year ending November 15th, 1911. 696 deaths occurred, 68 less than the previous year. The health of the city has been unusually good.

Pneumonia again has the largest number to its credit, viz., 53, one less than in 1910. In 1909 there were forty deaths due to consumption; in 1910, 42; and this year, 45. These numbers relate solely to consumption of the lungs, and do not include deaths from such diseases as consumption of the bowels, or tubercular meningitis, etc. Thus these two diseases of the lungs were the cause of 98 deaths, or over one-seventh of the total number of deaths from all other causes.

Nevertheless, it is encouraging to know that whilst the population of the city continually increases, the mortality from consumption remains about the same, and is therefore decreasing. 17 cases of diphtheria, with 2 deaths, were reported, compared with 99 cases last year, 7 deaths.

166 cases of scarlet fever were reported to the Department, with only one death. The disease was of a mild type. This is the lowest death-rate for many years. Mild cases of scarlet fever give the most trouble to the attending physician and the Health Department, and undoubtedly spread the infection more than the severe cases. In many instances there is no doctor in attendance; the children attend school and play in the street. If the child is seriously ill, there is little trouble in getting the parents to agree with the attending physician's diagnosis, but in mild attacks there is trouble immediately; the doctor is charged with undue haste, if not ignorance in reporting the case as scarlet fever. In probably one-third of the mild cases a physician is not called; the children continue at school, until the teacher notices desquamation, and sends them home.

There were entered at Victoria Hospital, and reported to the Department, 34 cases of typhoid fever, with 7 deaths. It is evident that all the cases were not reported, partly due to the difficulty in making an early diagnosis. Dwellings in which there is typhoid fever are not placarded, but all cases, no matter how mild, should be reported, in order that the source of the typhoid bacilli may be traced, and the spread of the disease restricted. So far, no case has been traced to milk.

Smallpox, which has been an annual visitor, forgot us this year. However, as the Board of Education of London, has annulled the regulations providing for the compulsory vaccination of school children, an invasion of smallpox may be looked for before many years.

There were 20 deaths by violence, 3 less than in 1910.

33 deaths were due to cancer, 2 less than in 1910, and 16 less than in 1909.

Samples of water from the city wells, Springbank ponds, and city taps were sent to Dr. Amyot, Provincial Bacteriologist, in Toronto, for analysis. On two occasions, Colon Bacilli were found, showing that organic matter was contaminating the water. Samples were then taken from fourteen wells and all the Springbank ponds, including the well over the river. All were found pure, except the Colville Pond, which showed the presence of Colon Bacilli. Water from this pond was then immediately cut off. With this exception, London water has always been pure, and is now. Samples of ice sold in the city have also been sent to the Provincial Analyst, and have been found free from impurities.

It is to be regretted that the proposed by-law for the protection of foods exposed for sale from contamination by dust, and dogs, etc., failed to pass the City Council. A similar by-law is in force in Buffalo and some other cities. Foods may be polluted in a variety of ways; the common source is dust, which is more or less rich in bacteria, according to the soil from which it arises.

The readiness with which raw foods, such as meats, milk, fruit, etc., can be contamiated thus, teaches but one lesson, that the greatest cleanliness should prevail, not only for the sake of the dealer, whose goods may be destroyed, but the consumer who may be injured by the food. Cleanliness of the merchant, and the protection from contamination that he bestows upon his goods, should be taken into consideration by his customers. It is encouraging to note that many of our grocers are now protecting foods exposed for sale, from dust, and the filthy disease-carrying housefly.

For years I have endeavored to show the people the necessity in the interests of public health and cleanliness, of adopting a regular system for the collection and destruction of garbage. Plans for an incinerator have been prepared by the city architect, and it now remains for the electors in January, to say by their votes, whether they will have a proper system of garbage collection and destruction, and remove this continual menace to the public health, or go on in the same old way.

Inspection of restaurants, butcher shops, and baker shops, were made. The butcher shops and baker shops were invariably clean; some of them were not sufficiently protected from the disease-carrying housefly. A few restaurants were not as clean as they should be, but better than formerly. The Chinese laundries,—their name is legion—are as sanitary as they ever will be, while they occupy cheap, miserable shacks, which are almost impossible to be kept clean. Sleeping, eating, washing and drying clothes in two or three small rooms, sometimes with only board partitions, are not conducive to health or cleanliness. The steam laundries in the city are all that could be desired. There is no foul air, and they do not use the human mouth as a clothes spraying apparatus.

Seventy-eight complaints of nuisances were received and attended to.

Eighty-nine samples of milk were examined. No formaldehyde or other preservatives were found. The milk was inferior to that of other years. The average percentage of butterfat for the eighty-nine samples was 3.68, and ranged from 3.25 the lowest, to 5.00 of butterfat.

The work of the dairy and herd Inspector, Dr. Tamlin, has been thoroughly and efficiently performed. Three hundred and fifty visits were made to dairy farms. Two thousand four hundred cows were inspected. One hundred and twenty-four cows were tested for tuberculosis; of these there were reactions in thirty-three, proving them to be affected with the disease. These thirty-three were condemned, and one hundred and fifty-six were condemned for other causes, such as uncleanliness of the animals or dairies, thus making one hundred and eighty-nine animals condemned, and unfit for dairy purposes. The dairy quantity of milk sold in the city amounts to fourteen thousand quarts. It is pleasing to note that under Dr. Tamlin's careful inspection, there is a steady improvement from year to year in the condition of the herds and dairies.

OTTAWA.

Dr. W. T. Shirreff, M.O.H.

I have the honor to present to you my first annual report as Medical Officer of Health for the year November 1st, 1910, to October 31st, 1911, along with the reports of the various officers of the department. This has been the most eventful year, and the most unfortunate one for a long time, in the history of the city in health matters.

In April, 1911, Dr. Robert Law, who had been Medical Health Officer for a number of years, decided, owing to stress of work, to resign, and I have the honour to have been appointed in his stead.

During the several months of April, May, June and July the Local Board was fortunate in obtaining the temporary aid and advice of Dr. P. H. Bryce in assisting in the work of checking the smallpox epidemic and of re-organizing the work of the Department.

In the domain of communicable diseases, the unlooked for epidemic of typhoid fever, which afflicted the city in the earlier part of the year, merits the most attention from the fact that it is, above all others, a preventable disease, especially in the epidemic form. You are no doubt quite familiar with the facts by now, as a very fair and comprehensive report was presented to the Board on the cause of the epidemic, by a special Commission and under the direction of the Conservation Commission of Canada.

For the information furnished and data collected we are much indebted to the efforts of the gentlemen who formed that Commission, and under the heading of typhoid fever I give a short synopsis of their findings.

Unfortunately soon after the typhoid epidemic was under control, it was found that we had in our midst a number of very unwelcome guests in the nature of smallpox patients, and although every means was taken in the way of quarantining, isolating and disinfecting to check the spread of the disease, we have had a considerable number of cases more or less persistently since. The difficulty in checking its spread has been mostly due to the large number of people unprotected by vaccination and to the mis-guided idea of some against availing themselves of the protection of vaccination. It is also part due to concealment of cases by some of the more careless, ignorant people, and owing partly to the mildness of the epidemic, and partly to the belief that persons would not receive proper accommodation at the Island. There is not the least possible doubt that if the council had, on the advice of your Board, passed a measure of compulsory vaccination, this disease, which can undoubtedly be prevented by persistent vaccination and re-vaccination, would have been readily checked and eradicated.

Statistics.

Total number of deaths in Ottawa for the year ending October
     31st, 1911, was 1,591
Previous year 1,395

     Increase over last year 196

Total number of births in Ottawa for the year ending October
     31st, 1911, was 2,067
Previous year 1,998

     Increase over last year   69

Of the deaths, 146 occurred among non-residents of Ottawa who came here for treatment in the different hospitals. Ninety-eight (98) children were stillborn.

Estimated population of Ottawa was 90,520
Total mortality per thousand population, exclusive of
     stillbirths was . ... 14.88 per 1,000
Including stillbirths . ... 15.96 per 1,000
Birth rate was .... 22.83 per 1,000
Death rate was . ... 16.22 per 1,000

Thus, notwithstanding the epidemic of typhoid in the first quarter of the year the death rate has decreased by .26 per 1,000.

DEATHS ACCORDING TO AGE WERE AS FOLLOWS:

Under 1 year	656	25 to 29 years	53
1 to 2 years	69	30 to 39 years	72
2 to 4 years	56	40 to 49 years	89
5 to 9 years	54	50 to 59 years	108
10 to 14 years	46	60 to 69 years	117
15 to 19 years	50	70 to 79 years	118
20 to 24 years	47	80 years and up	58

Of the deaths under one year of age there were ninety-eight stillbirths, and of the remainder, ninety-one deaths occurred in children under one year of age in the House of Bethlehem, seventy of which were from outside the city. Hence the deaths of children under one year of age in the city, exclusive of stillbirths, was four hundred and eighty-eight (488), or two hundred and thirty-six (236) per thousand births, or 5.39 per thousand of population. If stillbirths were included the mortality would be 250 per thousand births.

DEATHS ACCORDING TO NATIONALITY.

Irish	202	French	653
Scotch	120	English	530
	Others	96	

CLASSIFICATION OF DEATHS ACCORDING TO WARDS IN THE CITY.

Ward.	Area.	Total Population.	Population per Acre.
Rideau	322 acres	2,991	9.29
Ottawa	228 "	9,876	43.31
By	262 "	7,739	29.5
St. George's	572 "	11,891	20.78
Central	424 "	12,531	27.19
Wellington	325 "	13,206	40.63
Dalhousie	1,096 "	15,657	14.28
Capital	1,164 "	9,279	7.97
Victoria	650 "	7,350	11.3

Ward.	Total Mortality.	Mortality per M.	Births.
Rideau	47	15.68	87
Ottawa	238	24.09	107
By	123	15.76	99
St. George's	199	16.73	229
Central	195	15.56	238
Wellington	189	14.31	251
Dalhousie	203	12.97	299
Capital	91	9.8	164
Victoria	131	17.82	97

Ward.	Births per M.	Infant Mortality Total.	Infant Mortality per M. Births.
Rideau	29.08	27	9.02
Ottawa	10.83	61	6.17
By	12.79	59	7.62
St. George's	19.25	67	5.63
Central	18.99	50	3.909
Wellington	19.006	78	5.905
Dalhousie	19.09	98	6.25
Capital	17.67	38	4.09
Victoria	13.19	29	3.94

House of Bethlehem	96
Maternity Hospital	19
Misericordia Hospital	34
Total	656

This table furnishes some rather interesting comparisons, as it will be noted that Ottawa Ward, with a population of practically the same as Capital Ward, has a mortality of 2.5 times as great. This may be accounted for to some extent by some of the deaths in the Water Street Hospital being credited to Ottawa Ward; but at the same time there is no doubt that the death rate is at least twice as high in that ward as in Capital, owing in part to the crowded population and to the less sanitary conditions. Comparison can be made between other wards by the same ratio.

Deaths Occurring in Institutions.

House of Bethlehem	96	St. Joseph's Orphanage	2
Protestant Hospital	116	Perley Home	6
Water Street Hospital	112	Home for Friendless	2
St. Luke's Hospital	49		
Isolation Hospital	20	Total	403

Total Number of Acute Contagious Diseases Reported.

Disease.	No. of Cases.	Deaths.	Percentage.	Mortality per Thousand.
Typhoid Fever	987	83	8.40	.91
Diphtheria	461	32	6.94	.35
Smallpox	126	1	.79	.001
Scarlet Fever	94	3	3.19	.003
Whooping Cough	42	16	3.80	.017
Tuberculosis	148	116	78.39	1.28

Note.—Of the deaths from Typhoid Fever seventy-three occurred in the first six months of the year.

Deaths According to Sex.

Male 900   Female 651

Illegitimate Births and Deaths.

Number of illegitimate births registered was	77
Number of illegitimate deaths registered was	62
Under six months of age	42
Over six months and under two years	17
Over two years and under five years	3

Diphtheria and Scarlet Fever.

These two reports will be taken together, as a report on these practically means a report of the work at the Civic Isolation Hospital.

Table Showing Cases of Diphtheria and Scarlet Fever.

Disease.	Total.	No. Treated in Hospital	Deaths in Hospital.	Percentage.
Diphtheria	461	432	20	4.6
Scarlet Fever	94	78	1	1.28

Disease.	No. Treated at Home.	Deaths.	Percentage.
Diphtheria	29	12	41.3
Scarlet Fever	16	1	6.25

Of the deaths from Diphtheria twenty occurred in the Hospital, which gives a mortality of 4.6 per cent. Of the Diphtheria patients treated outside the Hospital the mortality was twelve, or 41.3 per cent. for the twenty-nine cases treated outside the Hospital. The Scarlet Fever mortality was one, or 1.28 per cent. in the Hospital, and 6.25 outside the Hospital.

Diphtheria and Scarlet Fever.

Number of cases treated in the Hospital:	
Males	215
Females	299
Total day stay of Diphtheria patients at the Hospital	4,478

Total day stay of Scarlet Fever patients at the Hospital   3,880
Average day stay of Diphtheria patients at the Hospital 10.37
Average day stay of Scarlet Fever patients at the Hospital ..   46.75
Cost of maintenance per year $15,271 40
Fees collected 4,665 53
Total outlay 10,605 87
Average cost of patient per day 1 82

Ages of Patients.

	Diphtheria.	Scarlet Fever.		Diphtheria.	Scarlet Fever.
Under 1 year	3	2	15 to 19 years	36	4
1 to 2 years	6	5	20 to 24 years	45	2
2 to 4 years	115	16	25 to 29 years	19	1
5 to 9 years	130	35	30 years and over ...	32	1
10 to 14 years......	47	8			

DIPHTHERIA AND SCARLET FEVER.

Many of these cases of Diphtheria could have been prevented and undoubtedly some lives saved if the parents or those responsible had fully appreciated the importance of reporting the cases early, either to their family physician or to the Medical Health Office, or Officer.

This should always be kept in mind by parents, "That a sore throat in a child is a *dangerous malady, and should always be seen by a physician at once.* No delay should take place; do not wait till this afternoon or to-morrow, but have him see the child at once. It is fatal to delay. It will be found the most expedient in the end. Also, no child suffering from a sore throat should be allowed to attend school. No child which has suffered from a sore throat should be allowed to resume school without first obtaining a certificate from a physician. Antitoxin should be more generally given to the other members of the family by the attending physician.

COMMUNICABLE DISEASES (OTHER THAN ACUTE).

Tuberculosis.—This disease still ranks first as the cause of death among the communicable diseases, having claimed 116 victims in the past year, or a mortality of 1.28 per thousand, which is a considerable reduction from the previous year, which, with a mortality of 122 and a population of 86,000, gives a mortality of 1.41 (a reduction of 0.15 per thousand).

Too much praise cannot be given to the public-spirited band of citizens, who, at great personal expenditure of both time and money have been coping with this dread disease, and that with notable success. They have succeeded in having a thoroughly equipped hospital erected for the treatment of advanced cases, and are about to have another one constructed for the treatment of incipient cases.

For the care and treatment of those cases either incipient or advanced, which for one reason or another cannot be sent to the hospital at Gravenhurst or Weston, instruction, advice, help and care are given by a visiting nurse of the Association. They have also opened a dispensary where patients can come for diagnosis or medical treatment, at stated hours, and from which help, either material or nursing, is sent out with instructions as to treatment and mode of life.

To this band of citizens "The Anti-Tuberculosis Association," headed by Mr. James Manuel, President, to the May Court Club Dispensary and the visiting nurse, the heartfelt thanks of the city are due.

The work would be much facilitated and no harm could possibly come to anyone if it was made a compulsory notifiable disease, for it will be noticed that there are almost as many deaths as cases reported, whereas there must be at least six times as many cases as there are deaths in any one year.

Typhoid Fever.—The number of cases reported officially during the year was 978; all but 55 were reported before May 1st, 1911.

The Commission which reported on the epidemic reported the total number of cases as 1,196, but there must have been some duplication of cases brought about by their having had cases reported from the different hospitals, which had already been reported to this office, and added to the report from this office. Nevertheless, there is no doubt that a number of cases were either not reported or missed. The total number of cases, therefore, for the year was approximately 1,100, with 83 deaths, or a percentage of 7.54, being a fairly high death rate as typhoid fever averages.

The epidemic mark began early in January, 1911, and continued up to March 1st, 1911, when the cases decreased rapidly.

The hypochlorite plant for the treatment of the water was started January 31st, 1911, with the addition of 18 lbs. per million gallons to the water. This amount was gradually increased till the maximum of 58 lbs. was reached on March 18th. At that time the epidemic was practically under control.

The cause of the epidemic was due to several circumstances, which combined to contaminate the water supply. The report of the Commission gives the cause as follows:

The direct cause was the infection of the water supply by polluted matter coming from the south shore of the river, from the vicinity of Lazy and Nepean Bays. The infection further found entrance through the emergency valve at Pier No. 1 when opened, and also through possible leaks in the joints of the intake pipe. The pollution of the water supply began about the middle of December, and was undoubtedly due to the unusual lowness of the water in the river and the freezing of the shallow places to the bottom, thus diverting the currents of the shallow water through to the main south current which passes Pier No. 1."

To understand this more thoroughly it must be understood that on the south shore, above where our intake pipe passes through the water of what is known as Nepean Bay, there is a considerable unsewered portion, which was formerly a suburb of Ottawa, and which now belongs to Ottawa itself.

Through a portion of this section a small creek runs, near which the excreta from a case of typhoid fever, which occurred earlier in the fall of 1910, was deposited and undoubtedly discharged into this creek, which in turn discharged into the Ottawa River. The currents carried this polluted matter over a part of the intake pipe in which there was a valve, and which was, in times of fire, opened for emergency purposes, and also where it was afterwards known that part of the pipe was broken. This was the immediate cause of the epidemic.

As soon as it was seen that the number of cases were increasing so rapidly that the hospital accommodation of the city would be overtaxed, it was decided to open an emergency hospital under the supervision of the Health Department, and the building known as the "Old Museum" was kindly loaned by the Government for that purpose. It was opened with an efficient staff of nurses and a doctor in charge. A large number of patients were treated there, and when the hospital was closed a convalescent home was kindly opened for those that needed recuperation before returning to their homes.

The epidemic was practically over by April 15th. As a result of this outbreak it was shown conclusively that our water supply under these conditions was very unsatisfactory, and it was decided to continue the hypochlorite treatment till such time as some radical change was made either in the source or method of obtaining our water supply.

Smallpox.—The first case of smallpox was reported on October 1st, 1910, and there were two or three cases every month until in March, 1911, the number of cases increased. In March there were eleven cases. As the cases occurred they were removed to Porter's Island, and at the end of March a nurse was engaged for their care. During April the number of cases increased rapidly, 36 being reported in that month. It was then seen that it was necessary to secure extra accommodation, and to this end a number of tents were procured and erected on the Island, where ample accommodation was provided for all.

After May the cases gradually decreased, but in October they started to increase rapidly, and there is every prospect of having a considerable number during the coming winter.

As this is a disease that can easily be eradicated by systematic vaccination and re-vaccination, and as a person that takes it has only himself to blame, it seems incredible that there should be so many suffering from the disease, when there is a sure protection from it in vaccination.

In this respect I may only repeat the words of the Medical Health Officer of New York, who says: "Successful vaccination will always protect against smallpox for at least five years after the performance of the operation," and I have no hesitancy in saying that vaccination is the best and only scientific prevention against smallpox, and there is no fact in the history of medical literature more incontestable than that the vaccination for smallpox has in all cases, when properly performed, eradicated the disease with an infinitesmal amount of inconvenience to those on whom it was practised."

By this time next year it is hoped to have a well-equipped and properly constructed hospital for the care and treatment of smallpox cases. There is no doubt that the persistence of the disease is primarily owing to cases being concealed, partly because of the mildness of the type, partly because of the fear of financial loss through being quarantined, and partly from lack of confidence in the accommodation provided for the sick at the hospital.

INFANT MORTALITY.

As will be noticed in the report of deaths by ages there occurred in Ottawa during the year 656 deaths of children under 1 year of age. Ninety-eight of these were stillborn, leaving 558 deaths occurring after birth. Of these 558 deaths, 94 occurred in one institution, of whom some 70 were non-residents of the city, leaving 488 deaths under 1 year in actual residents of the city, or 236 per thousand of births, or 5.39 per thousand of population.

This is an unnecessarily high infant mortality, and in fact is more than twice that of London, England, and of some of the larger cities in the United States, and almost three times that of some. This means that almost one out of every four died before it was one year of age, and three-fourths of these died before they were six months old.

Infant mortality is the most sensitive index we possess in social welfare, but the popular realization of the fact grows slowly. The excessive death rate among babies has been accepted as inevitable for so long a time that the possibility of reducing it is equally slow.

The chief causes of infant mortality may be summarized as follows: (a) Improper feedin; (b) Disregard of the essentials of baby hygiene; (c) Overcrowding; (d) Bad housing; (e) Impure milk; (f) Ignorant, indifferent and irresponsible mothers; (g) Questionable industrial methods; (h) Inadequate obstetrical care.

Some of the means of prevention are these: Pre-natal care of mothers; Proper registration of births; Systematic home instruction by trained nurses under the direction of the Department of Health; Education of mothers in baby hygiene; Breast feeding; Milk stations to secure medical and nursing supervision of mother and child during the first year of baby's life, or longer if necessary; Adequate and sanitary housing facilities; A living wage; Supervision of the milk supply from the cow to the consumer; Distribution of pure milk properly prepared, for babies for whom artificial feeding is a necessity; Public control of the sources of infection.

If the infant mortality in Ottawa could be lessened by one-half, "and at that it would certainly be high," which in my estimation could be done, we would have one of the lowest total death rates of any city on the continent. If the different causes of death as given further on are observed, it will be noticed that the chief causes of death among infants are:

Cholera	51	Indigestion	24
Diarrhœa	23	Dyspepsia	20
Dysentery	3	Convulsions	20
Infantile Debility (which by the way is a very unsatisfactory cause of death, as it explains nothing)	63	Asthenia	44

These deaths mean that practically that number of children died of diarrhœal diseases which were chiefly brought about by improper feeding or care.

Both my predecessor and myself, realizing that it was imperative that something be done, adopted the principle in June of distributing modified milk for infants from a central depot.

As only $1,000 was appropriated for the work, we were unable to do all we might have done had more funds been available. The milk was actually delivered to the houses, prepared previously for the child. The formulas which we used are those in use in the Sick Children's Hospital in Toronto, and are graded to a certain extent according to the age of the child, but more especially as to its apparent powers of assimilation. We had 175 applicants for the milk, with an average of 86 cases delivered daily. Twenty-six of these applicants remained for two days or less, 19 for less than two weeks, and the remaining 120 for two weeks or over, and a considerable number of them were for the whole period.

For the whole 175 there were 8 deaths, 4 of which occurred amongst children who were under our care for less than two days, showing conclusively that they were very ill when we got them. We had only three deaths in those we had for over two weeks from diarrhœal causes. One of these was a twin and the mother neglected it shamefully, and the other was a child whose parents were addicted to drink, and who gave the child soothing syrup. Of the 5 who died within a very short time after coming to the station, 1 died of pneumonia, 1 of tuberculosis, and the other 3 were too sick when they came to us. You will see by this that of the 120 cases treated by us in this manner it gives a mortality of 2.5 per cent. This I consider a very good showing, especially in such hot weather as we had during the past summer, after taking into consideration the following report on the mortality in Ottawa of all children under one year of age who died from diarrhœal causes from the 10th of June to September 1st.

There were 157 deaths in Ottawa of children under one year of age from this cause during the two months. I had an investigation made as to the cause of these deaths, and as to the conditions under which they took place. Of these 134 deaths the families of 18 had either moved or gone away from town, and no information could be got.

Out of 116 deaths, 21 babies were breast fed, 23 had barley preparations, 16 had Allenbury's food, 6 had certified milk modified at home, 5 had Nestle's food, 3 had condensed milk, 2 had malted milk, 1 had Berger's food, 1 had everything, 10 had other various preparations, 2 had modified milk, 2 had milk and water, 23 in the House of

Bethlehem were mostly fed on milk and water and albumen water. The babies in this institution were well cared for, but the sisters had very little knowledge as to how to feed them.

It will be noticed by this that 136 children died who were artificially fed and 21 who were breast fed. Of these who were artificially fed some 17 or 18 were breast fed for three months or less, and when this means was discontinued it was invariably from one to five months till death took place.

The total birth rate in Ottawa for the year 1910 was 1,998. Of these I would estimate that two-thirds were breast fed, leaving the number who were artificially fed at 666. This is an approximate estimate which I think will be found to be nearly correct.

Now of these 666 who were artificially fed the death rate was 136, or 20 per cent., for these two months, against a death rate of 2.5 per cent. when feeding by modified milk, and 1.6 per cent. breast fed children.

This estimate as to the number of children that are breast fed and artificially fed can only be made approximately, and as the result of my own observations it will be noticed that the mortality of artificially fed children is fifteen times as great as those breast fed, and eight times as great as those fed upon modified milk.

As to the cost, I might say that the introduction of this scheme cost the city an actual outlay of some $900, of which $300 was capital expenditure in materials which we have on hand. Besides this a considerable amount was paid by the Ottawa Dairy Company for the supplies which they furnished ($300), making in all some $900 which it actually cost to deliver some 6,500 cases of milk, each case containing the number of bottles corresponding to the feeding for the day.

In regard to the locality in which the mortality is the greatest, taking it all in all, this is in the most congested and poorer parts of the city. In Lower Town, that is between Rideau Street and Rideau River, some 42 deaths occurred in that locality; in St. George's Ward only 2; Rideau Ward, 6; Hintonburgh and Mechanicsville, 24; Rochesterville, 24; Wellington and Central Ward, 12; Ottawa South, 3. It will be apparent that these correspond with the districts which were the most unsanitary localities.

As a result of the experience here and that in other cities in coping with the infant mortality, we have concluded that it would be better to have infant milk depots, say three in different parts of the city, from which milk could be distributed, instruction given to mothers in the care and feeding of their infants, and also from which visits could be made to their homes for the same purpose. If this method was systematically and adequately carried on we could undoubtedly reduce the infant mortality by 50 per cent. We should have at least three properly equipped milk depots.

Classes should be opened for the instruction of mothers in the care and feeding of their infants. If the mother does not know how, or through financial disability is unable to provide and care for her child properly, she should be taught and helped. Instructions should be given in our schools to the prospective mothers in household economy and in the care and feeding of infants and to the elder sisters.

A municipal ice supply should be established for supplying the poor of the city with ice to maintain their food supplies in a good condition.

A physician should visit the depots every day and give free advice and instruction in the treatment of sick babies, and also should visit babies that are sick in their homes, where they are too poor to have a physician.

This is a very important matter, and is one of Ottawa's most pressing needs, and no financial consideration should be allowed to stand in the way of proper steps being taken to lower this very high mortality.

It has been pithily said that the measure of civilization of any country or place is well indicated from the average infant mortality. When in its final analysis it is the mother, and the mother alone, who is to save the child, and if she does not know how to care for it, or from any disability as overwork, poverty, feeble health, overcrowding, care, the stress of individual needs, she cannot do so, then she should be either taught or helped, and that by the municipality.

"Plenty of children are born, but too few are alive."

SANITARY CONDITIONS.

During the typhoid epidemic, before, and since, various persons have made criticisms as to the sanitary conditions of the city. Many assertions have been made, some authentic and some otherwise. In order to ascertain the exact facts of the case it was decided to make a complete sanitary survey of the city and ascertain the actual conditions, where possible. With that end in view a number of men were engaged and given a list of questions to which they were to obtain answers as to the condition of the premises and surroundings. The preliminary report of the same appears farther on, and the detailed report will be completed shortly.

The general facts ascertained by this report may be summed up as follows:

(1) That in Ottawa we had our share of unsanitary housing conditions, both as

regards single dwellings, tenements and apartments. We have not a great number of foreigners, but what we have are inclined, like in every other city, to overcrowding. We found we had buildings being occupied as dwelling places that were not fit for habitation and never could be made so, and therefore they were closed. There were still others which if the strict letter of the law were followed, would also be closed as unfit for habitation, but it was found that autumn was coming on and if all places were closed that should be closed, it would create considerable distress and certain overcrowding in other places. During the coming summer a determined campaign will be made to eradicate these places. Of course we understand that these are conditions that will take some time and a determined campaign to remedy, as they have been allowed to exist for some time.

(2) Besides these houses we have in Ottawa, and especially in the newly annexed districts a large number of streets on which there is no sanitary sewer, nor can there be until extensive large sewer systems are completed. A considerable number of dwellings are built practically on the solid rock, and it would be very expensive and in some cases practically impossible to construct sewers to serve the existing dwellings.

It will be noticed that some 14,700 places were inspected, and of these some 357 were found unfit for habitation; some 2,038 had outside privies; some 6,234 had no proper garbage cans; some 1,107 yards were unclean and untidy; some 748 stables were improperly constructed or kept, out of 1,190; and some 900 had no proper manure boxes.

A further report will shortly be made as to the average number of rooms in each house, number of people living in each house, and in one, two, three, or four-roomed houses and more, and the number of people per acre in certain districts, etc.

The causes that brought about these conditions may be summarized as follows:

(1) Lack of sanitary supervision by the Health Department, owing to the ridiculously small staff employed.

(2) The naturally dirty habits of some of the inhabitants.

(3) The lack of an education in health of those who may not be naturally dirty but at the same time are not alive to the seriousness of the lack of proper sanitary care.

(4) The desire of the landlord or the owner to construct something which with the least outlay he can call a dwelling to protect the occupants more or less from the elements, but irrespective of any unsanitary conditions that he knows will result from the lack of proper construction.

(5) Unsuitable building sites, as low marsh ground, and also where there is no sewer provision, and where none can be provided for some time.

(6) No intelligent supervision of buildings being erected, in so far as the builder is allowed to build something, that if built, is entirely unsuitable for the installation of modern improvements, or which cannot be properly drained, or where no adequate yard space is provided; no proper light is available; some of the rooms are made ridiculously small; no adequate provision for ventilation, or for disposal of garbage, rubbish, waste, etc.

(7) Lack of sanitary supervision of some sections of the city before being annexed.

(8) After the disastrous fire of eleven years ago, as so many were rendered homeless, shacks were allowed to be constructed, owing to the urgency of the cases, that would otherwise not have been tolerated, and these shacks have been allowed to continue as dwellings in some cases till the present time. In endeavoring to remedy some of the conditions found it was seen that some new legislation was necessary in order that some of the conditions be more readily abated.

New Legislation Needed.

I would recommend:

(1) That Tuberculosis be made a notifiable disease.

(2) That Infantile Diarrhœa be made a notifiable disease.

(3) That it be compulsory for municipal councils in cities where the infant mortality is over 120 per thousand births to set aside an adequate sum to provide for the care and feeding of infants and instruction of mothers, when they are unable to supply the same.

(4) That a fine be imposed upon anyone who knows or suspects that a case of contagious disease exists in a house and does not notify the Health Department within twelve hours, or meanwhile changes his place of residence.

(5) That it be compulsory that a physician who discovers a case of diphtheria in a house give an immunizing dose of diphtheretic antitoxin to the other members of the family within 24 hours; to be paid for where necessary by the municipality, like vaccination.

(6) That when smallpox exists in a municipality the Medical Officer of Health, in conjunction with the Board of Health, may require a certificate of vaccination from all children or persons attending any school, private or public, high or collegiate, and colleges.

(7) That landlords be held responsible for any unsanitary condition arising from frozen plumbing or water service, when it is obviously due to defective construction

of the building, by which each separate dwelling or tenant have a separate water service from the main.

(8) That garbage be removed from certain places or sections of the city more frequently than once a week.

(9) That all unsanitary dwellings be placarded as such.

(10) That a by-law be passed authorizing the city to install improvements where the people are unable to pay the total cost of such improvements at the time and they be allowed to repay the city in seven equal annual instalments, the same to be levied against the property till such is paid in full.

CONCLUSION.

In conclusion, I may say that the additions that have been made to the staff have been very welcome to your Medical Health Officer, and if we could have a first-class bacteriologist appointed in the near future, as is absolutely necessary, it would certainly facilitate the work and keep a proper check over our water and milk supply.

Finally, I wish to thank the employees of my staff for the faithful work done by them during the trying year just passed, and the chairman and members of the Board of Health for their kind co-operation and assistance.

PETERBOROUGH CITY.

DR. A. W. McPHERSON, M.O.H.

I beg leave to present the health report for the year 1911. It is with pleasure that we can look back and note some progress that has been made. At the same time we see many things have been left undone, but which should receive attention in the near future, if we wish to live under conditions most conducive to health.

One of the most important steps in the health work was the establishment of an Isolation Hospital, and it is encouraging to note that the citizens appreciate the advantages to be had from it. This is evidenced by the fact that nearly all the cases reported since the hospital was opened were sent in for treatment. The part the hospital plays in checking the spread of the disease is plain. Since its opening no subsequent case occurred after the removal of the patient and the number of cases reported has diminished.

I am glad to be able to report the absence of any epidemic of a severe nature. Early in the year German measles, chicken pox, and whooping cough were prevalent. These have to a great extent disappeared. Below is found a record of the cases reported, showing where treated and the number of deaths. It will be noted that there were but few cases of typhoid during the year. These were all investigated and the source of the infection was found to be either from outside of the city or from a contaminated well.

	Treated.			Deaths.
	Number Reported.	At Home.	In Hospital.	
Scarlet Fever	46	16	33	....
Diphtheria	10	6	4	....
Smallpox	5	1	4	....
Typhoid	10	2	8	....
Tuberculosis	?	?		23

It may not be out of place to mention here, that the Council are to put up a small building that will be used for smallpox. It will be sufficiently large to accommodate one or two patients, and to store the supplies that have been used in this connection. This will make it more comfortable for the patient, more economical for the ratepayers and less difficult in the handling of suspects and infected persons.

Another feature of the year's work that is worthy of special notice, is the formation of a health society for Peterborough. Of its aims you are well aware, and I know that you will give it the active support that its importance demands.

The sanitary work has made some progress, but there is still opportunity for a great deal of improvement. Our responsibility does not end, when we make a hasty examination of the lanes and back yards, and see that the winter's refuse has been disposed of. The sanitary conditions inside and outside the house, public or private, the water supply, the disinfection of infected houses, the inspection of all food supplies and of the premises where they are prepared, or offered for sale, all come under the duties of the Sanitary Officer.

In the city there are a great many wells, some of which are so situated or so constructed that surface water continually contaminates them and in the majority of cases they are not cleaned out yearly as required by law. The privy pits, manure heaps, pigpens, etc., within the more thickly settled parts of the town are a source of much annoyance to the neighbors and a menace to health. If these are to be permitted to remain, there should be a much more rigid inspection than at the present time. During the year a number of complaints were made about the condition of fowl offered for sale on the market. This brings up the question of inspection of any and all kinds of meat offered for sale within the city, and further, the inspection of hotels, restaurants, confectionery stores, bake shops, butcher shops, fruit stores, and all stores where food is prepared or offered for sale.

During the past two years, the sanitary work has been done by the police. Experience has shown that this is very unsatisfactory. This year the whole city was covered in 6 weeks, and about 800 notices to clean up were left where unsanitary conditions were found. Then, through the absence of members from the force, it was impossible to follow up the work. Thus our inspection loses its efficiency.

During the year, two communications were sent to the Council, recommending two by-laws, one to regulate the production and sale of milk, and the other to provide for the regular collection of garbage within certain areas of the city. Both were considered, but it was so late in the summer when sufficient information was obtained about the garbage systems in other places, that it was thought advisable to leave it over until the next year. However, a milk by-law was framed and passed and now awaits the assent of the provincial authorities before going in force.

In conclusion, I would like to make some suggestions for your consideration:

1. To provide for the inspection of all meats offered for sale in the city.
2. The inspection of butcher shops, bakeries, confectionery stores, restaurants, hotels, fruit stores, and all places where food is prepared or offered for sale.
3. The prohibiting the exposure of foods to the dust and flies.
4. The disinfecting of all houses vacated by one suffering from tuberculosis.
5. The extension of the area of compulsory sewer connection.
6. The prevention of building of privy pits without the consent of the M. O. H.

PORT ARTHUR CITY.

Dr. C. N. Laurie, M.O.H.

I have the honor to present my report for the year 1911. We started the year with a serious outbreak of diphtheria and scarlet fever, most of the cases being treated in the Isolation Hospital. In this connection I might point out how important it is that all contagious cases should be removed from their homes to the hospital for the better protection of the public. Last summer the Health Authorities at Ottawa caught a number of flies in the Isolation Hospital and treated them to a spray of a solution of rosalic acid and alcohol, then letting the flies go. Afterwards a number of these flies were caught by tanglefoot fly paper in different parts of the city, showing the danger of disease being carried by these filthy pests, and the necessity of keeping the yards, lanes, and the city generally, as clean as possible. I am satisfied that different outbreaks of sickness which have taken place and have been blamed on the water and milk supplies, have been due entirely to flies. We have treated in the Isolation Hospital during the year, nine cases of diphtheria, thirteen cases of scarlet fever, two of chickenpox, two of smallpox, and three cases of erysipelas. There was a very gratifying decrease in the number of cases of typhoid during the year, although we had a number of cases in the hospitals from outside places as early as July. These cases were from widely separated places, some coming from places on the C. P. R., east of here, some from the G. T. P., others from the C. N. R. and P. D. Extension. As these cases coming into our city for treatment are always a danger to our citizens, I again draw your attention to a recommendation I made in my past reports: That the

Provincial authorities be urged to appoint a medical Inspector for the unorganized parts of our district, to keep a supervision of the men working in the camps, mines, on railway construction, and also in the small villages, where no attempts are made, or even thought of, to take proper sanitary precautions against disease. There were 10 deaths from typhoid reported in our city office during the year, 16 from consumption, 2 from measles, 1 from whooping cough, and 3 from cerebro-spinal meningitis. It is a matter for serious consideration that we had so many deaths from that dread disease, consumption. The hospitals do not care to take these cases, and, indeed, they should not, unless they have separate accommodation for them. We cannot take them in the Isolation Hospital, as we have not got the room to keep them away from other patients. I think a sanatorium for the treatment of consumption should be established in this district, and if possible, check the spread of the disease now, before our homes become infected. The Government should be asked to give assistance towards this end. We have watched the milk supply very carefully, and there has been a decided improvement in the quality of the milk supplied the public. The water is good and free from all infection at present, still I think, the question of extending the intake pipe from the other side of Bare Point should now be seriously considered. There is going to be a lot of work done in the harbor near the dry dock in the near future, such as dredging, building the break-water, etc., this will always be a danger to our present intake pipe. We all remember the trouble and danger caused by the dredge breaking our pipe last fall, and there is always a possibility of its occurring again.

I would again draw your attention to the unsanitary condition of the swamp section, lying between our city and Fort William, until some system of drainage is devised for that part, we cannot hope to free our city from disease. I would earnestly advise that the Council take up this question as soon as possible and have something done.

There was a very serious outbreak of hog cholera in this district last summer and some hundreds of animals were killed and burnt by order of the meat Inspector.

In closing this report I want to notice the faithful and good work done by the Sanitary Inspector, and also by the Matron of the Isolation Hospital.

SANITARY INSPECTOR, A. G. SEAMAN.

I herewith beg to submit my annual report on behalf of the Board of Health

We have found it necessary to spend more money this year than usual, on account of improvements to the Isolation Hospital, which cost about $1,600.00. These improvements consisted of heating plant and putting foundations under the Hospital, and doing some minor improvements. I am pleased to say that these improvements are about completed. We keep a permanent staff of three—a matron, cook and caretaker—at a cost of $150.00 per month, and we pay twenty-five cents per meal for the patients. We have treated twenty-nine patients in the hospital this year. A number of these cases were brought in from outside points. We have no city water supply for this hospital. We have a wind-mill, which is not satisfactory, and I hope when you are putting the water and sewer on Balsam Street, you will continue on to the hospital.

I am pleased to notice the number of sewer and water connections that were made last year, and hope you will continue this work until all the dwellings are supplied with water and sewer connections.

I do not think our public school children are getting the necessary medical attention for a city of this size. I think the schools should be visited by a medical man or trained nurse once each week. This would prevent the spread of measles and other children's diseases to a large extent. This may be a matter for the School Board to deal with, but I would like someone to attend to it.

ST. CATHARINES, CITY.

JAS. A. McMAHON, CHAIRMAN L. B. OF H.

In accordance with Paragraph 3, Schedule " B," Section 122, ' Public Health Act, Ontario." I have the honor to submit my annual report.

I am pleased to be able to state that the standard of health and sanitary conditions of our City are in a very good condition.

The total deaths from all causes was 212, deducting 18 still-born, there remains 194 deaths, a mortality of about 14.5 per thousand.

There were 8 deaths from typhoid. Every case of typhoid I saw was traced to sources outside of the City. There was one death from diphtheria. No deaths from scarlet fever, whooping cough or measles. There were reported 15 cases of scarlet fever, 7 cases of whooping cough, 13 cases of diphtheria and 51 cases of measles, in all 86 cases of contagious diseases, with one death.

The many tests of the city water made during the year have shown it to be free from any pathogenic germs.

There were 60 sewer connections established during the year, 3 more than the previous year.

It is gratifying to see that the number of deaths from tuberculosis, 15; is less than in previous years, although our population has increased a couple of thousand.

J. A. PAY, SECRETARY L. B. OF H.

I beg leave to submit this, my report, for the year ending November 15th, 1911.

Attached to this report is a list of all deaths during the year and the causes, also a summary of the age at time of death.

There has been no epidemic of any contagious diseases, 9 deaths in all, resulted from diseases classed as contagious, 8 from typhoid, and 1 diphtheria. In the typhoid cases nearly all were traced to outside the city where the disease was contracted.

The population of the city, taken from the last revised Assessment Roll is 13,413, and the number of deaths from all causes, which included 23 who died in the hospital and were from outside the city, and 18 still-births, make a total of 212, which is 15.81 per 1,000, which shows a death rate which will compare favorably with any other city of our population.

During the year 289 births have been registered, being 13 more than in 1910, and no doubt a number are not registered as required by the Statutes.

156 marriages were registered, being 2 more than the previous year.

The deaths number 16 more than last year, pneumonia being the highest, 29 cases.

The Sanitary Inspector placarded all houses where contagious diseases existed. In some cases the patient was removed to the Isolation Hospital, after recovery all houses were fumigated.

3,600 feet of 15-inch, 12-inch and 10-inch sewers were laid, and 60 sewer connections made, and several more are now under construction.

The contagious diseases reported are as follows:—

Typhoid Fever	38 cases	8 Deaths.
Scarlet Fever	15 "	Recovered.
Diphtheria	13 "	1 Death,
Whooping Cough	7 '	Recovered.
Measles	51 "	Recovered.

AGES AT THE TIME OF DEATH.

Premature and Still-births	18
Deaths under 1 year	31
" from 1 to 5 years	12
" " 5 to 10 "	2
" " 10 to 20 "	12
" " 20 to 30 "	14
" " 30 to 40 "	19
" " 40 to 50 "	14
" " 50 to 60 "	15
" " 60 to 70 "	32
" " 70 to 80 "	31
" " 80 to 90 "	10
" " 90 to 100 "	2
Total	212

STRATFORD CITY.

DR. J. A. ROBERTSON, M.O.H.

In presenting my annual report I am pleased to state that the health of the city during the past year has been up to the standard of previous years.

There were in all 107 deaths, a decrease from the previous years. Of the preventable diseases we had 41 cases of typhoid fever, with 3 deaths; 32 cases diphtheria, with one death; 20 cases of scarlet fever, with no death. Three cases are reported as dying from tuberculosis, quite a decrease from previous years. This is undoubtedly due to the fact that the public are becoming aware of its communication from one to the other, and the care which is being taken has prevented its spread.

Your Board deserves credit for the interest manifested by them in sanitation work, their regular attendance at meetings and activity in having every means possible carried out to aid in prevention of preventable diseases. The diphtheria hospital is a credit to their efforts, considerable time having been spent in seeing it properly completed.

The Hospital Aid should not be overlooked for their generosity and good taste in furnishing the same.

I congratulate the Board for framing the milk by-law, properly drafting it in accordance with the milk Act passed by the last Legislature, and endorsed by the City Council. This is an important measure, for the lives of hundreds of infants are being endangered by having an improper milk supply.

The Board is also to be congratulated on recommending to the Council and passing of a by-law to do away with all pit and outside closets within certain limits, and at a stated time throughout the entire city. The closing of all wells within the city limits will before long be accomplished, and typhoid fever will accordingly disappear.

For years I have urged upon your Board the necessity of having some system of garbage collection and disposal adopted. At the beginning of the year the City Council took this matter up, appointed a special committee to look into all details, so that we may have the assurance that at no distant date we will have a proper system working under municipal control.

Time and time again I have urged on the Board and City Council to take into consideration the desirability of having a public abattoir, and am pleased to know that a special committee of the Council has now that matter in hand, and will doubtless report at no distant date. The Sanitary Inspector's report is hereby attached and worthy of your consideration, shewing the work done during the year and giving certain important recommendations.

SANITARY INSPECTOR, THOS. DUNSEITH.

In presenting my Annual Report I may state there has been considerable improvement made in the sanitary condition of the city during the year. I inspected practically all the yards, vaults, cellars, alleys, and lanes and found some improvement over past years. But in some instances I found people very remiss in the care of their premises and this always gives me a lot of trouble, for I find it very difficult to make some people understand that they must do their part in keeping the city clean.

Now this state of affairs would be greatly helped if we had a proper system of garbage and night soil removal, for I find that most people would be glad to clean up their yards if they could get the stuff removed, but under present conditions that is often impossible. Then their neighbors complain to me of odors, etc., and I am often at my wits' end to know what to do in the matter. Therefore, gentlemen, I would again petition you to give this matter your most careful attention, for I am convinced that if we were abreast of the times in his particular, we would have the cleanest, healthiest and most beautiful city in the Province.

During the hot summer weather the odors from Romeo Creek became so offensive that complaints were both loud and numerous in regard to it, so at the suggestion of the Medical Health Officer, the Board of Works had it cleaned out. This was a step in the right direction and was greatly appreciated by those living near it, but it ought to be covered throughout its length as it is unsightly and is still to some extent an open sewer.

Erie Creek is still worse and will always be a nuisance until covered.

I have tested water from wells in all parts of the city and found that over fifty per cent. of it was unfit for drinking. I also tested the city water weekly and found always that it stood the test. I therefore consider it safe for all purposes.

On making official tests of our milk supply we found it all above the standard. Last year in making my report I made reference to the fact that we ought to have some way provided whereby we might lawfully inspect the dairies from which we derive our milk supply. I am pleased to say that the City Council has this year passed a by-law governing the sanitary conditions in which the dairies are to be kept. Mr. J. Trow, Chairman of the Board of Health, Dr. J. A. Robertson, Medical Health Officer, and myself, made an inspection of the various dairy barns and found some of them in good condition, others were not quite up to the standard required by the by-law, but all are making strenuous efforts to improve their premises and we expect all will be able to have their licenses at an early date.

On inspection of the slaughter houses, we found they were not all such as we desired, showing the imperative need of a public abattoir where all meat offered for sale in the city butcher shops and on the public market would be butchered under the eyes of qualified inspectors.

As to contagious diseases, we had 32 cases of diphtheria and 20 cases of scarlet fever. I quarantined and disinfected all houses where the diseased persons were and also disinfected 50 other places which were exposed to infection, either from the patient himself or from some other person who had been in contact with him. There were over 100 places disinfected. I also disinfected quite a number of places that were exposed to tubercular infection.

I had a good deal of trouble with the dumping ground on Erie Street. The odors arising from it were so complained of by the people living near it that I think it would be advisable to discontinue its use in the future.

<hr>

WINDSOR CITY.

Dr. J. A. Ashbaugh, M.O.H.

I have the honor to report to you as Medical Health Officer as follows:

The Secretary of the Board has in his report enumerated the number of cases of diseases reported, with the mortalities, so that I do not think it necessary to refer to these, except in a few instances.

My report will refer more to some recommendations which I earnestly request you to consider. Some time ago I asked for the passing of a by-law which would require merchants selling foods to keep them properly protected, as against dust, dirt, dogs and flies. Nothing, I am sorry to say, has been done in this matter, and the Sanitary Inspector and myself, with the aid of the police at times, have used our persuasive powers to remedy conditions, with some effect.

The refuse barrels are all too few, and the number should be largely increased, and signs posted warning persons not to throw refuse on the streets under a penalty. In this I have more particularly in mind newspapers and other paper. Other refuse, as much as is possible, should be burned.

The regulations as to spitting on sidewalks are not being enforced, and a few examples should be made.

We have not had many contagious diseases in the city during the past year. Mr. Lusted's report gives five deaths from typhoid fever, a very low rate, notwithstanding the reports of the Provincial Board. Some people blame the typhoid cases to our water supply. We have repeatedly had samples tested by the Provincial Board analyst, also by an expert in Detroit, and did not get one unfavorable report. The water at certain times is cloudy, and sometimes even muddy, but this does not indicate that it is necessarily contaminated and dangerous.

The precaution should be for our water supply to boil before using. This will positively destroy any possible danger.

Typhoid is not always carried by water; there are other sources, such as milk and certain foods. Many persons go away on their vacations to summer resorts and farms, many on boats, etc., return and develop the fever, so that with all these adjuncts we can make a reduction in the percentage of deaths directly attributable to Windsor's water supply.

We have had four cases of smallpox this year, the only ones for the past four years. Three of these were directly traced to Detroit, where they had been exposed; the other acquired it from one of these, so that we were in this case indirectly responsible.

The milk dairies have improved very much, both in their premises and method of handling. There is, however, more room for improvement, and we are endeavouring to bring them up to the highest standard.

If it is possible to arrange for a proper place or places for bathing facilities, I think it advisable. Under proper supervision it would be the means of teaching many a lad to swim, and care for himself in the water, as well as the cleanliness and exercise he would receive.

S. Lusted, Secretary L. B. of H.

In pursuance of my duty, I herein make my annual report upon the work of the department during the year just closed.

Contagious Diseases.

While it seems probable that few cases of either diphtheria or scarlet fever are kept from the knowledge of your Secretary, it is manifest that occurrences of typhoid fever are only occasionally reported for registration, as witness the fact that five deaths from that disease have occurred and sickness from that cause have been made known in only two instances. The Medical Health Officer affirms that he has persistently asked practitioners to comply with the law in that respect.

According to our register the number of families visited by contagious diseases during the year is as follows:

Diphtheria	23.	Deaths from that cause,				2
Scarlet Fever	38.	"	"	"	"	2
Typhoid Fever	2.	"	"	"	"	5
Tonsilitis	1.	"	"	"	"	1
Measles	1.	"	"	"	"	1
Totals	65					11

This shews an increase over the year 1910 of four families visited by diphtheria and of two deaths, and an increase of three families afflicted with scarlet fever and two deaths; while the fatal cases of typhoid fever have been reduced one-half. It is to be noted that the single case of tonsilitis and of measles resulted fatally.

SANITARY WORK.

Under the systematic operation of the City Engineer's plan of gathering up and disposal of house garbage and rubbish, ashes, etc., the thoroughfares have been well cleaned throughout the year. There is still room for improvement, however, on the part of the householders, who still betray indifference or parsimony in the matter of providing necessary and convenient utensils for handling the materials, and frequently do not place receptacles in a position to be conveniently handled by the men employed for that purpose, while in some instances garbage is wilfully scattered in alleys or vacant lots. A few prosecutions may have to be employed to cure these evils. The actual expenditure of the Public Works Department in this service during the year was a trifle over $1,091, to which sum there should be added interest upon the value of the horses employed and their food and the value of the vehicles, which will bring up the full cost of scavenger work to $1,450 or $1,500.

The inspection of premises reported to be in an unsanitary condition has been thoroughly done by Inspector Hillier; 85 of such cases having been carefully enquired into, and where practicable the trouble has been abated. When ordinary means have been ineffectually tried and failed, resort has been had to the police court and eight convictions obtained. The effect of this proof that the Board means "business" in the endeavor to enforce the law against offenders, it is believed will prove a material gain to the health and comfort of the inhabitants.

As shewing the advance of public recognition of the danger of contagion from other than the heretofore recognized dangerous diseases, it is interesting to note that the Inspector has been called upon to disinfect eight houses from which consumptive patients had been removed.

The direction of the Board is respectfully directed to the provisions of chapters 67 and 68 of the Ontario Assembly, passed last year, which not only increase the power of local boards of health in preventing and suppressing nuisances, but imposes on municipal bodies certain duties and obligations respecting the pollution of sources of water supply which at any rate in some municipalities are being rigidly enforced at the present time according to newspaper reports and may at any time be brought into effect in Windsor. In this connection, however, I might refer to a prevailing rumor that during the present session of the Legislature the whole law in respect to the powers of local boards is to be consolidated and materially changed; and the measure for that purpose will be awaited with much interest.

DEATHS AND THEIR CAUSES.

In accordance with the provisions of the Health By-law, I have prepared a statement showing the number of deaths and their causes occurring during the year 1911 for your consideration, as follows:

Arterio Sclerosis	7	Accidental	3
Accidental poisoning	1	Asthena	2
Anaemia	1	Bronchitis	3
Apoplexy	9	Bright's Disease	3
Abortion	1	Blue Baby	1
Alcoholism	3	Burns	3
Asphyxiation	1	Cancer	8
Appendicitis	1	Colitis	2

Carcinoma	8	Meningitis	7
Cardiac Disease	2	Malnutrition	4
Cerebral Convulsions	1	Marasmus	6
Colporrhaphy	1	Myocarditis	1
Concussion of Brain	1	Measles	1
Cardiac Insufficiency	1	Natural Causes	5
Cholera Infantum	7	Nephritis	3
Cholera	1	Natural Decline	2
Cerebral Disease	1	Obstruction of Bowels	2
Convulsions	1	Old Age	1
Congenital Hydrecephales	1	Obscure Disease of the Chest	1
Cirrhosis of Liver	2	Premature Birth	16
Delirium Tremens	1	Pneumonia	30
Diphtheria	2	Pericarditis	1
Dropsy	3	Paralytic Stroke	1
Diarrhoea	2	Pyaemia	1
Dysentery	2	Pernicious Anæmia	1
Diabetes	1	Rheumatism	4
Drowned	4	Still-born	10
Difficult Labor	1	Senile Decay	5
Enteritis	1	Suppurative Choleeystitis	1
Eclampsia	1	Stone in Urethra	1
Fistula of Rectum	1	Senile Dementia	1
Gastritis	1	Septicaemia	1
Gunshot Wound	1	Scarlet Fever	2
Heart Disease	5	St. Vitus Dance	1
Hepatic Cirrhosis	1	Skull Crushed	1
Head smashed	1	Spina Bifida	1
Hemorrhage on Brain	1	Tuberculosis	15
Influenza	1	Typhoid Fever	5
Inflammatory Rheumatism	3	Tumor	3
Inanition	5	Tonsilitis	1
Ileocolitis	2	Uraemia	7
Infantile Paralysis	1	Uraemic Poisoning	5
Indigestion	2	Uterine Tumor	1
Injuries	2	Valvular Disease of the Heart	2
Jaundice	1	Whooping Cough	1
La Grippe	1	Weak Heart and Stomach	1
Miscarriage	1	Weakness	1

WOODSTOCK CITY.

Dr. F. S. Ruttan, M.O.H.

I herewith present the annual report of the Health Department for the year ending November 15th, 1911.

The number of deaths for the year was 123, or a decrease of 15 of the number of deaths for 1910, which gives the mortality rate per thousand population of 12.18.

Deaths were due to the following causes:—

Artero Selerosis	16
Cancer	11
Heart Disease (Organic)	8
Cerebral Hemorrhage	8
Consumption	6
Pneumonia	6
Pleuro-Pneumonia	5
Ileocolitis	5
Appendicitis	4
Bright's Disease	4
Septicaemia	4
Intestinal Obstruction	3
Influenza	3
Marasmus	3
Uraemia	2
Tuberculosis (other forms)	2
Typhoid Fever	2
Meningitis	2
Alcoholism	2

One death from each of the following causes:—
Pernicious Anaemia, Measles, Diabetes, Hodgkin's Disease, Anaemia, Sarcoma of Kidney, Locomotor Ataxia, Status Lymphaticus, Cirrhosis of Liver, Cystitis, Puerperal Fever, Cerebro-Spinal Meningitis, Miscarriage, Chronic Rheumatism, Railway Accident. The deaths occurred between the following ages:—

	Male.	Female.
Still-born	0	1
Premature	4	0
Under one week	1	0
Under one year	3	9
From 1 to 5 years	2	1
5 " 10 "	2	0
10 " 20 "	0	4
20 " 30 "	5	4
30 " 40 "	6	6
40 " 50 "	7	1
50 " 60 "	6	5
60 " 70 "	7	10
70 " 80 "	13	10
80 " 90 "	8	8
90 " 100 "	1	0
	65	59

This high infant mortality is lamentable and in my opinion could be materially reduced by having a children's ward at our hospital where infants could receive the necessary care and treatment so essential to infantile diseases.

On investigation, I find a high mortality among bottle-fed infants. In many cases parents have no idea how to prepare food for infants and others have not the proper facilities. Undoubtedly scientific methods would be a means to lessen this high percentage of mortality among the young.

REPORTABLE DISEASES FOR 1911.

Disease.	Dec.	Jan.	Feb.	Mar	Apl.	May	June	July	Aug	Sep.	Oct.	Nov.	Total.
Scarlet Fever	9	....	....	1	....	2	....	1	....	....	1	....	14
Smallpox	2	2	....	....	....	....	....	....	....	....	....	....	4
Mumps	....	1	....	....	....	....	....	....	....	....	....	....	1
Measles	....	1	6	48	65	45	3	....	....	....	....	....	168
Chickenpox	....	....	....	9	1	....	....	....	....	....	....	4	14
German Measles	....	....	....	....	1	....	....	....	....	....	....	....	1
Typhoid Fever	....	....	....	....	....	....	....	5	2	5	2	....	14
Diphtheria	....	....	....	....	....	....	....	....	....	....	....	2	2
Totals	11	4	6	58	67	47	3	6	2	5	3	6	218

INFECTIOUS AND CONTAGIOUS DISEASES.

218 cases of infectious diseases were reported during the year, and of this number 168 were measles, an epidemic of which prevailed from February until May. Measles is the most communicable malady with which we have to deal, and having once become prevalent is difficult to eradicate. Quite frequently infectious and contagious diseases are of so mild a nature that parents do not consult a physician and do not consider it their duty (as required by the Public Health Act) to report the disease, hence an epidemic is almost inevitable under existing conditions.

The occurrence of smallpox should remind us to enforce vaccination. I am quite confident that the majority of our school population are not vaccinated. It is a mistake to neglect vaccination until we are visited by an epidemic of smallpox.

14 cases of typhoid fever were reported during the year.

4 of these cases were residents of outlying districts, 3 cases were contracted elsewhere, while 7 cases were apparently contracted in the city, 3 of which originated at one house and were probably due to the existence of a cesspool. The other city cases originated where sanitation was quite unknown, and which calls for thorough sanitary inspection and the placing of sewers.

SANITATION.

The suggestions made in last year's report for improved sanitation have received little attention.

We should insist on a proper standard of cleanliness of the lanes, backyards, vacant lots and outhouses. This may be accomplished by a regular and systematic inspection.

Several of the alleys in the congested parts of the city, require paving and drainage. The care and disposal of garbage is criminally neglected. Our by-laws pertaining thereto are not enforced and I therefore ask you to determine who shall enforce said garbage by-laws.

MILK SUPPLY.

Dairies were inspected twice during the year by our Veterinary Inspector, and his report would indicate that existing conditions could be materially improved, so that milk may be produced and conveyed to the consumer in as pure a condition as it is possible.

During the year, milk has been quite up to the standard required—only one case of preservatives being detected.

PLUMBING.

I would again direct your attention to the necessity of some inspection of this important work. All plumbing should be thoroughly inspected as a guarantee to sanitation. The chief function of "Boards of Health" is to prevent disease. I, therefore, desire to impress on this board to seriously consider the various reforms I have presented during the year and endeavor to elevate Public Health standards.

ANNUAL REPORTS OF LOCAL BOARDS OF HEALTH OF TOWNS HAVING A POPULATION OF 5,000 OR OVER.

BARRIE.

Dr. A. T. Little, M.O.H.

I beg to present to you my annual report for the year 1911.

The municipality must be congratulated upon its good health and sanitary condition during the year.

Diseases reported are as follows: Scarlet fever, 6 cases; diphtheria, 1.

Deaths: Measles, 1; whooping cough, 1; typhoid fever, 2; tuberculosis, 4.

The number of cases of measles, whooping cough and typhoid were not reported fully to the Board.

The total number of deaths was 101; births, 157.

Garbage Disposal.

We are still suffering from the want of a proper system for disposal of garbage, and it is to be hoped that some method can be devised so that our citizens may not be obliged to break our health by-laws in order to get rid of their kitchen garbage.

Meat Supply.

Our Sanitary Inspector keeps a watchful eye on our slaughter-houses, and endeavors to see that they are kept in a cleanly condition. Most of the butchers try to assist him in his work; an improvement is looked for in some of them, however.

Milk.

The milk reaches the consumer in a better condition than formerly. The cow byers and premises are kept in a more sanitary condition, and on the whole a great improvement has taken place. Milk utensils are washed with town water or artesian well water in most cases. If the water so used is suspected of being impure, samples are submitted to the Provincial Analyst, and if found contaminated the vendor is at once notified.

Water And Ice.

Our town water continues to be pure, as shown from reports received of analysis from time to time.

We are compelling our icemen from year to year to go farther out in the bay for their supplies, to insure purity.

I would strongly urge upon the Board the advisability of enforcing sewer connections in any places admitting of the same, and where impossible the substitution of the dry earth closet for the old filthy vault, and under all circumstances the doing away with cesspools, unless properly constructed.

BERLIN.

Dr. J. McGillawee, M.O.H.

I beg to submit the report of the Medical Health Officer for the year ending November 24th, 1911.

There have been 44 houses placarded for scarlet fever; 2 deaths.

Twenty-six houses placarded for diphtheria; 12 deaths.

For the last six months the town has been almost free from scarlet fever and diphtheria, there being only two cases of each during that time. No cases of either scarlet fever or diphtheria at present.

There were 10 cases of typhoid fever during the year. The great majority of the cases were mild. No deaths from typhoid.

Twelve cases of infantile paralysis, mostly mild; 2 deaths.

Eight deaths from tuberculosis during the year.

W. Cairnes, Chairman L. B. of H.

Pursuant to the regulations set out in The Public Health Act, I beg to submit herewith my annual report of the work of the local Board of Health during the past year, and the sanitary condition of the municipality, as rendered to the Board by the Medical Health Officer.

Early in the year the question of the milk supply was taken into consideration and it was deemed necessary, after an exhaustive investigation, to notify all milk vendors to give the Board each month a list of the persons from whom they obtained their supply. This has been followed out, and the premises of the farmers from whom the several supplies have been obtained have been closely watched and kept in a sanitary condition.

Following an epidemic of diphtheria at the Berlin Orphanage, it was considered in the interest of the public health to notify the agent of the Waterloo County Children's Aid Society to use every precaution when bringing children into the municipality from outside points. This was done, and subsequently no contagious diseases have been found among the orphans at the institution.

In January of this year both the questions of a public abattoir and an isolation hospital were taken into consideration, and after much discussion and investigation, and with the assistance of a committee of your honorable body, the question of isolation hospitals has been finally disposed of by the erection of three buildings—one for smallpox, one for scarlet fever, and one for diphtheria. The public abattoir question, however, is still in abeyance.

The storing of manure was also considered, and on the recommendation of this Board your honorable body passed a by-law regulating such storage. The plumbing area has also been enlarged, thereby doing away with a large number of privy vaults, which in the centre of a growing community are a menace to the public health. The pollution of the Victoria Park lake has been gone into extensively and several remedies advanced. Although we have had the assistance of your honorable body our efforts seem to have been in vain. The by-law diverting the Wilmot Street storm drain, if carried by the ratepayers at New Year's will, we are confident, abate this nuisance.

The erection of a tuberculosis sanitarium is still under consideration by the Council, and your Board of Health has always tried to lend its every effort to a solution of the difficulties to be met with in such an undertaking, and hope in the coming year to see the matter finally disposed of.

The slaughter-houses throughout the town have been periodically inspected, and orders have been issued that all such houses shall be whitewashed and cleansed, and the present condition is much better than previously, although there is still much to be wished for. The abattoir question we hope, will, when finally settled, ensure a sanitary and healthy meat supply to the town.

Upon analysis it was found that the ice supplied to the town from the Park lake was unfit for human consumption, and the Park Board was immediately ordered not to allow any more ice to be cut there, and your honorable body was recommended to have the ice in Shoemaker's Dam harvested for use in the town. This matter, I believe, is now under your consideration.

I submit herewith the Medical Health Officer's annual report to the Board as to the sanitary condition of the town.

Thanking the Council for its co-operation and assistance in the undertakings of this Board.

BROCKVILLE TOWN.

Dr. A. J. Macauley, M. O. H.

In my annual report for the year 1911 I beg to state that the reports of contagious and infectious diseases are somewhat smaller than last year, and the fatalities following these are considerably less.

There is still great negligence on the part of the medical profession in reporting contagious and infectious diseases, particularly typhoid, and hence the great difficulty in furnishing correct data.

Tuberculosis, with such a large death rate and its well-known contagious character, I believe should be reported to this Board, when an investigation could be made as to the sanitary condition of infected homes, and the condition of such be improved by the aid of this Board.

The new grounds for the disposal of garbage, etc., is an improvement on the former grounds, but my suggestion that a quantity of lime be applied daily to the deposited refuse has not been carried out.

The collection of garbage is not improved, either in methods or time of collection, but improvements are promised by collectors for next year.

The keeping of pigs inside the corporation, I believe, should be stopped, as many just complaints are made of the nuisance.

Our streets have been kept only fairly clean during the past year, their deplorable condition making it difficult for the sweeper to do good work. The method of watering our streets during the dry and dusty season is bad from a sanitary standpoint, and there seems no good reason why the watering of a part of any street should be left optional with tenant or landlord, but for the safety of the public all streets which are much travelled by vehicles should be watered or treated.

Tunnel bay is now pretty thoroughly dredged. Our waterfront is being improved, but greater vigilance should be observed that citizens be prevented from polluting the bay by dumping garbage and ashes into it.

GEO. K. DEWEY, SECRETARY L. B. OF H.

I beg to submit the following report as Secretary of the Board, for the year ending October 31st, 1911.

There have been registered during the year 216 births, 114 males and 102 females; 196 deaths, 101 males and 95 females; 38 of the deaths were of persons non-resident, brought to our hospitals for treatment, leaving the deaths of residents of the town at 158, about 16.65 per thousand of population.

INFECTIOUS DISEASES.

Typhoid Fever.—4 cases and 1 death.
Diphtheria.—47 cases and 3 deaths.
Scarlet Fever.—11 cases and no deaths.
Tuberculosis.—19 deaths.
Samples of our water supply are sent monthly to the Provincial Analyst at Kingston for examination, the result showing the water to be generally free from infection.

The returns required by the Provincial Board have been regularly made to the Department.

SANITARY INSPECTOR, N. GORDON.

I beg to submit my annual report for the year ending October 31st, 1911, as follows:
During the year the following cases of infectious diseases have been reported: Diphtheria, 47 cases; scarlet fever, 11 cases; measles, 5 cases; typhoid fever, 4 cases; chicken-pox, 5 cases. Ninety-one fumigations were made of houses and schools. The Children's Shelter on Charles Street was quarantined for a period of six weeks through exposure to smallpox; fortunately, there were no developments.

The published notice, requiring the cleaning up of yards, etc., was generally complied with, about one hundred cases requiring written notice. Frequent and systematic inspection is made, and there is found a general disposition on the part of the residents to clean up.

Butcher shops and bakeries have been visited and found to be kept clean. Samples of milk have been taken from the several vendors three times during the year, and tested as to the quantity of butter fat, the percentage being over the requirement.

I found that in five instances pigs were being kept in limits contrary to the provisions of the by-law, and had them removed.

The dump formerly in use on Brock Street has been closed and a new one opened at the north end of William Street, which is more convenient and suitable for the purpose. The man in charge keeps it in good shape.

Pursuant to the request of the Board, a by-law was passed by the Council, requiring that all outside closets within the limits served by the town sewerage system should be removed by May 1st next. I find that over one hundred closets have been connected with the sewers during the year, and that there are about four hundred and fifty outside closets within the area.

One well was closed by order of the Medical Officer of Health.

Many and frequent complaints are made by persons unable to have garbage removed which is the cause of much inconvenience and annoyance, and as there is no municipal control we are unable to deal with the matter.

The Isolation Hospital has been regularly visited, and is in shape for occupancy when required.

M. M. BROWN, CHAIRMAN L. B. OF H.

I herewith transmit to you the annual report of the Secretary of the Board, and also those of the Medical Officer of Health, Sanitary Inspector and Veterinary Inspector.

You will notice that the contagious and infectious diseases have been kept well in check during the year, the deaths being only *23*, of which *19 were due to tuberculosis*. This large number of deaths from tuberculosis shows the necessity of taking special measures to combat this disease, and the suggestion of the Medical Officer of Health that all cases of tuberculosis should be reported is particularly timely.

The vital statistics of the town show that the births of the town during the year have exceeded the deaths by 58.

The regular bacteriological analysis of the water during the year has shown the same to be comparatively pure, a fact which is also indicated by the small number of typhoid cases, namely, four only, during the whole year.

The milk has been uniformly good in quality. I am glad to note the recommendation of the Veterinary Inspector to have printed instructions issued by the Board of Health regarding the care of milch cows and the handling of the milk before it reaches the consumers. This suggestion will no doubt be acted upon.

I very much regret that, owing to our inability to get contractors to carry on the work, we were unable to put in force the garbage by-law passed during the year. If it were once in operation, I am satisfied that it would by its own merits disarm all criticism. The present state of affairs as to the disposal of garbage is highly unsatisfactory and prejudicial to the public health. It might be well for your body to consider the feasibility of the town acquiring its own plant and carrying out the proposed system through its own employees.

D. McALPINE, VETERINARY INSPECTOR.

In this my annual report of the work done for your department for the year 1911, I beg to point out the very excellent condition of live stock in this district, the absence of anything of a contagious or infectious nature, and in my inspection of the dairies I found fewer cattle showing signs of constitutional trouble than in former years.

I have had some difficulty keeping track of the farms where milk is procured, as the milk vendors, to keep up their supply, are forced to change farms or buy in small quantities from others not on the regular inspection list, and in a great many cases forget to notify the proper authorities of the change.

As to the slaughter-houses, they are about in the same condition, only not so much in use, as a large part of our meat supply is coming through the packing-houses, the slaughter in the private slaughter-houses being principally of sheep and hogs. I find the condition of the surroundings of these places about the same as in former years and the provisions of the by-law requiring the cooking of offal, etc., being complied with.

I have investigated a few complaints of the offering of immature veal for sale on the market.

Attached hereto are some regulations as to the handling of the milk supply, and the care of the cows from which it is procured, which I would suggest might be printed on suitable cards and supplied to the dairymen, with a view to improving the conditions.

CORNWALL.

DR. C. J. HAMILTON, M.O.H.

In compliance with the requirements of the Public Health Act, I hereby submit my annual report for the year 1911.

To begin with, I have to congratulate the town on the freedom which it has enjoyed from any serious disease or epidemics during the season which has now closed.

We have had during the year 1911 a few mild cases of typhoid fever, but in no instance has there been a death therefrom.

There was also a very widespread but mild form of scarlet fever during the latter months of the summer. In many instances it was so light that it was thought little of by the members of some families, and consequently escaped the attention of the Medical Officer of Health. Those cases that were reported were duly placarded and quarantined as far as it was possible, and in no instance was the epidemic followed by fatal results.

As in former years, the corporation has continued to extend its sewerage system, and also has increased its water service, which has naturally added to the sanitary improvements of our town. We now have, in my opinion, a town well supplied with sewerage and water. A test of our water has shown it to be perfect and wholesome, and in no instance has typhoid fever taken place amongst people who are using the town water.

An inspection of the yards and other premises was carefully carried out during the year. In the middle of the summer we had one case of smallpox, which came from New York, such being a medical man. He gained admittance to one of our hospitals on the assumption that he was suffering from typhoid fever, but a medical man was called in to attend him, and he at once identified the disease, and it was handed over to the Medical Officer of Health, for his transfer at once to the Isolation Hospital. The patient was from the Hotel Dieu, Cornwall, and the Mother Superior at once arranged to furnish the hospital with two well-trained nurses, and took absolute care and control of him during his whole sickness.

11 B.H.

The town contributed a caretaker, in the person of a man who waited on the Sisters, and supplied them with water and other necessaries.

Too much credit cannot be given to the management of the Hotel Dieu Hospital for tne great care and attention they gave, through their Sisters, to the patient during the five weeks of his retention in the Isolation Hospital.

The patient returned home in perfect health, after all precautions as to disinfection had been observed.

As in former years, I now draw the attention of the Board to the fact that we have no proper place for the care of contagious diseases, and I would recommend that this Board use its influence with the Municipal Council to procure, at as early a date as possible, some proper place where contagious diseases can be easily and cheaply cared for.

J. H. RAMSAY, CHAIRMAN BOARD OF HEALTH.

In accordance with Section No. 3 of the Public Health By-law of tne town of Cornwall, I now report that during the year the Board of Health has been active in the discharge of its duties.

A single case of smallpox—imported from the United States into one of our hospitals, in ignorance of what the disease really was—was immediately recognized by the Medical Health Officer, was at once removed to the contagious diseases' hospital, and successfully treated.

Several cases of scarlet fever were also successfully treated without the disease gaining a foothold.

The Medical Health Officer's Report deals more fully with the infectious diseases treated.

The Board has interfered and prevented the construction of cesspools which, in their opinion, would be detrimental to the public health.

It has also recommended that certain parts of the town be drained, and that some existing systems of drainage be improved, and, although some of these recommendations have not yet been carried into effect, it is hoped and confidently believed that with the coming spring existing difficulties will have disappeared, and that the improvements will be made.

GALT.

DR. T. W. VARDON, M.O.H.

In making this my annual report for the year ending October 31st, 1911, I am pleased to say that the health of our people has been as satisfactory as could be expected. You will see by the appended report from the Division Registrar that the total number of deaths from all causes during the year was one hundred and thirty-nine. Deducting from that the still-born, and those who died in our hospital from outside places, makes the average death rate a little less than thirteen per thousand of our population. The total number of deaths from tuberculosis was ten, a little less than one per thousand.

The total number of births was 217, making the birth rate over 20 per cent.

About nine weeks ago we had an outbreak of scarlet fever. As there had been no case of that disease reported for some months prior to this it was difficult to trace its origin.

I had a number of the patients removed to the Swiss Cottage, where they are being carefully looked after by a professional nurse, and I am in hopes that we will soon be free from this epidemnc. With this complaint, as with mild cases of diphtheria, a doctor is often not called in, and the health officers do not receive any notification of their existence. These form a nucleus from which diseases spread before proper measures can be taken to prevent serious trouble. I have requested the principals of all our schools not to allow any child to return, who has been absent from school through illness, unless they have a certificate from a physician, certifying to the nature of illness they have been suffering from.

Our schools are well heated and ventilated and are in good sanitary condition, and are being disinfected from time to time. The other public buildings of the town are in a satisfactory condition. The lock-up, I think, can be improved upon, and I believe our city fathers would do well to enquire into this matter, with a view of bettering the same. I would advise the town to acquire the water right of the dam on Main Street and do away with said dam, leaving only a sufficient space for a canal or channel to convey the waters of the Mill creek to the river and to reclaim the land on either side of the canal. This could easily be filled in without great expense. The dam is now a nuisance and a menace to the public health. Unsanitary deposits from the surrounding lands on Mill creek have been washed into it for years, and many of them still remain there; in hot weather, when the water is low, evaporation takes place, and those living in the vicinity suffer much. At any time it is no beauty spot. To clean it out would entail endless expense and would often have to be repeated.

I would recommend all householders to be very careful in the handling of milk. As soon as milk is received from the dealers it should be placed in the refrigerator, ice-box or cellar, and kept at a temperature not exceeding 45 degrees. It should never be kept in the kitchen or be left uncovered. Milk should not be placed in a room where there is any person ill. If you are in any way suspicious of the milk you are using, sterilize the same for 20 minutes, at a temperature of 140. Never leave fresh meat or milk exposed in the kitchen, for they both absorb floating germs very rapidly and, if exposed to moderate heat, the germs multiply fast and often transmit disease or ptomaine poisoning to the users.

I would strongly recommend the Council to appoint a health inspector. Our town is now of that size that we require the constant services of that officer. There is sufficient work to keep a man busy for ten hours daily. The said officer should be under the control of the Board of Health and report to the Medical Health Officer at least three times daily. I would recommend our school boards to take the necessary steps to have our schools placed under medical inspection. While the state is under obligation to see that all our children receive a good common school education, it is of equal or greater importance to see that any defects the child may have should receive immediate attention. Also that every effort should be made by personal examination of the children, either by a physician or nurse, to detect and discover in its earliest stages any infectious diseases that they may be exposed to, so that prompt measures may be taken to afford the child relief and to prevent other children being contaminated. Diseases from the nose, throat, ears, eyes and teeth are very common amongst children, and they are often allowed to suffer much from neglect. I hope that our worthy School Board will carefully look into this matter, and make the necessary arrangements for said inspection.

I would recommend the Town Council to pass a by-law closing up all outside closets, cesspools on the lines of sewers, giving these residents who have not made connection with the sewers a reasonable time to do so. We have a sewer system costing in the vicinity of a quarter of a million dollars, and I am very sorry to say that the connections so far made are very small in proportion to the population.

It takes about 200,000 gallons of water to flush our sewers every day. If the premises on the lines of sewers were connected, possibly very few flush tanks would be required. Again, the disposal of nightsoil is becoming a serious question, and it will be only a short time before we will have to make use of our sewers, whether we wish to or not. It is not reasonable that we should be allowed to continue to dump this offensive material on a neighboring municipality for all time to come.

I am very thankful to the Board of Health for the help and assistance they have so ably given me during the past year.

CONTAGIOUS DISEASES REPORTED.

Disease.	Cases.	Deaths.
Diphtheria	17	1
Typhoid Fever	18	5
Scarlet Fever	17	1
Tuberculosis	10	10
Measles	25	5
	87	22

Population, 10,333.

INGERSOLL.

Dr. J. A. Neff, M.O.H.

I herewith beg to present my annual report for the past year.

The number of births registered was 109, of which 51 were males and 58 females. The number of deaths during the same time was 79, thus showing a gain of 30 in the population of the town during the year from natural causes. Only 10 of the deaths were due to communicable diseases, viz., 1 of measles, 1 of typhoid fever, and 8 of tuberculosis.

There were only 3 cases of contagious and infectious diseases reported during the year, 2 of scarlet fever and 1 of diphtheria. The patients were isolated and so well taken care of by the attending physicians that no epidemic occurred.

The Local Board of Health accompanied and aided me in making a thorough inspection of the premises and dairies of the various milk vendors of the town, the slaughter houses, the water works system, the St. Charles Condensing Co.'s premises, the Public Schools and the Collegiate.

All the dairies and slaughter houses are kept fairly sanitary. We found some conditions which we considered should be changed in the interest of the health of the town. The proprietors in every case willingly acceded to our request and the changes have been made. The water works system was found in good condition, some needed repairs having been made during the past year.

The St. Charles Condensing Establishment is kept thoroughly sanitary and is a great credit to the management.

We thoroughly inspected the general school building and found many defects in its construction, its heating, its lighting, its ventilation and its fire escapes. The lavatory system especially in connection with this school is very primitive, and was condemned as being inadequate, etc. This should receive the immediate attention of the Board of Education of the town. The best results would be obtained by pulling down the whole structure and building a modern, up-to-date building on its site.

The Ward School was found in excellent sanitary conditions, with the exception of the lavatories, which should be flushed oftener.

The Collegiate is well kept, the lighting and heating being good. One objectionable feature exists here, however, viz., the residence of the janitor in the basement. This should likewise receive the immediate attention of the Board of Education.

The Separate School is well kept, and is in a sanitary condition, with the exception of the lavatories, which should receive the attention of the Trustee Board of that school.

In all the schools pupils with defective eyesight were found, which goes to demonstrate that medical inspection of the pupils would be of great benefit to the community.

I wish again to direct the attention of the citizens of Ingersoll to the very great need of a proper sewerage system; and, in connection with the dairy inspection, I strongly urge on the Town Council the necessity of appointing a competent veterinary surgeon to inspect all dairies and cows belonging to the various milk vendors supplying milk to the citizens of our town and to report his findings to the Local Board of Health. This inspection should be made at least three times a year. Also all meats marked for consumption by the citizens should be thoroughly inspected by a competent veterinary surgeon.

I wish also to report that in this section of Ontario there is a large volume of business done in dealing in slink veals. I am strongly of the opinion that this business should be thoroughly inspected and controlled by inspectors appointed by the Provincial Board of Health.

At the proper season due attention was directed to the fly nuisance , and the citizens urged to destroy all flies found in their homes and their breeding places by keeping their premises clean and sanitary.

SAULT STE. MARIE.

Dr. A. S. McCaig, M.O.H.

As required by the Public Health Act, I beg to submit for your consideration my report of the sanitary condition of the Town of Sault Ste. Marie for the year 1911.

Vital Statistics.

During the year there were 216 births, 220 deaths, and 172 marriages.

Infectious Diseases.

(1) *Typhoid Fever.*—During the year there have been 125 cases of this disease treated in town. Of this number probably 40 cases originated in town. There were 22 deaths from this disease. Last year there were 135 cases with 13 deaths.

The chief agents in the spread of Typhoid Fever are impure water, contaminated milk, and house flies. Our water supply must be maintained free from pollution, the milk supply requires constant watching, and the efforts for the extermination of the dangerous house fly must be vigorously continued.

(2) *Diphtheria.*—There have been 69 cases of this disease during the year, with 7 deaths. This disease has been prevalent during the whole year. The need of an isolation hospital for the treatment of this and other infectious diseases is becoming more urgent every year. Where the patient has to be kept and treated in a boarding house, it inflicts an unjustifiable hardship upon the boarding house keeper and also makes it almost impossible for the health authorities to maintain a satisfactory quarantine.

(3) *Tuberculosis.*—There were 11 deaths from Consumption during the year.

(4) *Scarlet Fever.*—2 cases, no deaths.

(5) *Cerebro-spinal Meningitis.*—2 deaths.

(6) *Measles.*—No deaths.

(7) *Smallpox.*—2 cases occurred among the prisoners in the gaol, but owing to the prompt measures taken by the gaol authorities no further cases developed.

Dairies and Milk Supply.—The dairies have been inspected several times during the year by the Sanitary Inspector and members of the Board of Health. The Board of Health is going to take vigorous measures against the dirty dairy. A license will not be given to any one selling milk whose stables are not kept clean, whose cows are not healthy, and who does not handle the milk as required by the regulations of the Board of Health. Bi-monthly milk tests were made.

Slaughter Houses, Butcher Shops and Meat Supply.—A public abattoir to replace the unsanitary slaughter houses at present in use is a pressing necessity. The butcher shops, with one exception, have been conducted in a clean and sanitary manner. The meat supply has been good.

Water.—Samples of water were frequently examined and no contamination was found.

Stables.—A by-law governing the erection of stables would be in the interests of the public health.

The Board of Health.—This has been an active organization during the year, and is doing good work in the interests of the public health. The Board held fourteen meetings during the year, which were attended by the different members as follows:

W. R. Cunningham, Chairman ...... 13 meetings.
His Worship the Mayor ...... 7 "
R. Brydges ...... 13 "
J. H. Huston 13
C. A. Leaney 11
W. J. Detweiler 10
M. C. McCuaig 9
Medical Health Officer 13

The Board of Health is waging a vigorous war against the dirty dairymen. Inspection and publicity are the means used. If the dairyman has clean stables, clean and healthy cows, clean milkmen and adequate facilities for handling the milk properly he will be commended as readily through the papers as the one with dirty stables, dirty cows and dirty milkmen will be condemned. The Board is preparing for publication a report of the different dairies and the public will be able to judge as to the best sources to obtain clean and wholesome milk. No license will be given to any vendor whose premises do not conform absolutely to the requirements of the Board, and anyone who, after receiving a license, allows his premises to become unsanitary, will have his license cancelled and will be prosecuted.

By an amendment to the Public Health Act the Board of Health has now the power to take steps for the abatement of any nuisance, and the costs incurred can be returned to the clerk of the municipality, who shall place the same against the property on the collector's roll to be collected along with the ordinary taxes.

I think that the municipal system of garbage collection should be adopted, and I would suggest that before any money is spent in the purchase of a dumping ground that steps be taken to ascertain the cost of construction of a modern incinerator.

The contract of Allen Cameron with the Board of Health for the removal of garbage was carried out in a satisfactory manner, and the duties of sanitary inspector were diligently performed.

The three matters to which I would call your attention as most urgent from the public health point of view are:

1. The providing of an isolation hospital at once.
2. The necessity of a public abattoir.
3. A municipal system of garbage collection and the construction of a modern incinerator.